Jacques Demy

Manchester University Press

FRENCH FILM DIRECTORS

Jacques Demy

DARREN WALDRON

Manchester University Press

Published by Manchester University Press
Altrincham Street, Manchester M1 7JA, UK
www.manchesteruniversitypress.co.uk

British Library Cataloguing-in-Publication Data is available

ISBN 978 1 5261 0699 5 *paperback*

First published by Manchester University Press in hardback 2014

This edition first published 2017

The publisher has no responsibility for the persistence or accuracy of URLs for any external or third-party internet websites referred to in this book, and does not guarantee that any content on such websites is, or will remain, accurate or appropriate.

Printed by Lightning Source

In memory of my mum, Patricia Ann Waldron
(31 July 1940–17 May 2012); my Lola

Contents

List of plates

Series editors' foreword

To an anglophone audience, the combination of the words 'French' and 'cinema' evokes a particular kind of film: elegant and wordy, sexy but serious – an image as dependent upon national stereotypes as is that of the crudely commercial Hollywood blockbuster, which is not to say that either image is without foundation. Over the past two decades, this generalised sense of a significant relationship between French identity and film has been explored in scholarly books and articles, and has entered the curriculum at university level and, in Britain, at A-level. The study of film as art-form and (to a lesser extent) as industry, has become a popular and widespread element of French Studies, and French cinema has acquired an important place within Film Studies. Meanwhile, the growth in multi-screen and 'art-house' cinemas, together with the development of the video industry, has led to the greater availability of foreign-language films to an English-speaking audience. Responding to these developments, this series is designed for students and teachers seeking information and accessible but rigorous critical study of French cinema, and for the enthusiastic filmgoer who wants to know more.

The adoption of a director-based approach raises questions about auteurism. A series that categorises films not according to period or to genre (for example), but to the person who directed them, runs the risk of espousing a romantic view of film as the product of solitary inspiration. On this model, the critic's role might seem to be that of discovering continuities, revealing a necessarily coherent set of themes and motifs which correspond to the particular genius of the individual. This is not our aim: the auteur perspective on film, itself most clearly articulated in France in the early 1950s, will be interrogated in certain volumes of the series, and, throughout, the director will be treated as one highly significant element in a complex process of film production and reception which includes socio-economic and political determinants, the work of a large and highly skilled team of artists and technicians, the mechanisms of production and distribution, and the complex and multiply determined responses of spectators.

The work of some of the directors in the series is already well known outside France, that of others is less so – the aim is both to provide informative and original English-language studies of established figures, and to extend the range of French directors known to anglophone students of cinema. We intend the series to contribute to the promotion of the formal and informal study of French films, and to the pleasure of those who watch them.

DIANA HOLMES
ROBERT INGRAM

Acknowledgements

I would firstly like to thank the respondents to my doctoral audience study, whose enthusiastic evocations of Jacques Demy were the trigger for me to embark on this project. I am very grateful to Ursula Tidd, whose help and guidance, both professional and personal, have been invaluable. I thank Ros Murray for having read a first draft of the manuscript so carefully, Chris Perriam for his patience and support, and Fabrice Menaphron for the many enriching conversations we had about Demy. My gratitude also goes to Florian Grandena for putting me in touch with Olivier Ducastel and Jacques Martineau, to whom I also express my appreciation for allowing me to interview them. Elsewhere, my thanks to Claire Humphrey, whose thesis on contemporary representations of women in Paris helped me refine my knowledge of phenomenology and Beauvoir, and all my students, undergraduate and postgraduate, for our stimulating conversations about French cinema in general. Finally, I would like to express my gratitude to the staff at Ciné-Tamaris and at Manchester University Press for their invaluable kindness, understanding and support, and to Diana Holmes and Robert Ingram for having read and commented on an early draft of the manuscript.

Introduction – 'Un demi, Jacques, bien frais, avec de la mousse': background and early filmmaking

Few directors are as ambiguously placed in the French popular imaginary as Jacques Demy. Saccharine for some, poignant for others, his *cinéma enchanté* is familiar to generations of French audiences accustomed to watching Christmas repeats of *Peau d'âne* (1970) or seeing Catherine Deneuve and Françoise Dorléac prance and pirouette in *Les Demoiselles de Rochefort* (1966). With nine shorts and thirteen full-length features, Demy's filmography is solid, if not prolific. Though varied, his work is unified by recurring themes. Abandoned lovers await the return of errant partners, and passionate affairs are abruptly curtailed by external events or stifled by social pressures.

Demy's cinema is lyrical, at times melancholy, at others uplifting. He re-mastered the opera and the melodrama in *Les Parapluies de Cherbourg* (1963) and *Une chambre en ville* (1982) and adapted the spectacle of the Hollywood musical to French cinema in *Les Demoiselles de Rochefort* and *Trois places pour le 26* (1988). When his films lack big numbers or dialogues performed through song, their melodic tone and romantic plots transmit a sense of musicality, their appeal ensured by their bright colours and/or transformation of everyday places into enticing locations. Regularly set in coastal towns, his films combine a longing for an elsewhere, particular the United States, with affection for French provinciality, with Demy's devotion to his home city of Nantes arising in unexpected locations. If his films seek to teach us anything, it is that joy is sustained once melancholy has been endured, and that pleasure can exist in anticipation. By bucking the trends of his time through his passion for the musical and fairytale, Demy is one of French cinema's most unique filmmakers.

Although he died in October 1990, Demy's legacy as an iconic director for generations of admirers and filmmakers endures. His films attracted renewed interest from the mid-1990s, evoked by directors including François Ozon, Olivier Ducastel and Jacques Martineau, and Christophe Honoré. If these filmmakers are associated with a wave of queer cinema, the link is not fortuitous. With their palette of incandescent colours, affecting scores, energetic choreography, camp iconography, defiant heroines and vulnerable heroes, settings in cabarets, casinos or hairdresser salons, Demy's films have been read as the products of a filmmaker with a queer eye (Colomb, 1998: 39–47; Duggan, 2013). However, his cinema resists simplistic categorisation based on the logic of the binary. It chimes with both straight and queer-identifying viewing groups, concerns men and women, appeals to children and adults, and elicits mass appreciation and niche interest. Frequently thought-provoking, though never abstruse, often sophisticated, but never pretentious, Demy's films are both entertaining and informed.

Although this is not the first book-length study of Jacques Demy's cinema (Duggan's monography on queerness in the fairytales of Demy was published in 2013), it considers his oeuvre as a whole body of work. Additionally, it engages with and builds on existing studies, in both French and English, by providing a sustained analysis of his films in the light of relevant debates on temporality, affect, subjectivity, self–other relations and free will. It reads Demy's cinema through a perspective grounded in pre- and post-war philosophies on time and alterity, and their application in work on film. It contributes to a turn towards existentialism and phenomenology in film studies since the early 2000s by assessing the extent to which related ideas and ethics were already mobilised within the films of a director often overlooked as having little intellectual merit.

Chapter 1 examines Demy's relation to the French New Wave (Nouvelle Vague). It argues that, if the theme of the chance encounter performs a structuring function in Demy's films, his association with the movement was the product of coincidence. Chapter 2 probes Demy's 'musicals', *Les Parapluies de Cherbourg*, *Les Demoiselles de Rochefort* and *Une chambre en ville*. It shows how the films comply with and deviate from the codes and conventions of the Hollywood staple, producing a specifically Gallic and 'Demyesque' twist on the genre. It is a commonplace of writings on Demy to highlight his 'monde en-/

enchanté', meaning both 'expressed through song' and 'enchanted'. The third chapter concentrates on the latter, and examines Demy's adaptations of fairytale (*Peau d'âne*), fable (*The Pied Piper* (1971)) and myth (*Parking* (1985)). Chapter 4 analyses the representations of gender and sexuality in Demy's cinema, with particular attention to *Le Bel Indifférent* (1957), *La Naissance du jour* (1980) *L'Evénement le plus important depuis que l'homme a marché sur la lune* (1973, hereafter *L'Evénement...*) and *Lady Oscar* (1978). The fifth chapter considers Demy's legacy. It reveals how his final feature, *Trois places pour le 26*, establishes the foundations of his posthumous myth, which the work of Agnès Varda and other directors has affirmed and supplemented since his death.

The origins of the *Demy-monde*: the young Jacques, filmmaking and Nantes

Demy often claimed that his childhood was the inspiration for his cinema, and accounts present his early years as idyllic. He was born on 5 June 1931 near his paternal grandmother's bistro in the village of Pontchâteau, which was then in Brittany. His family lived at their garage at 9, quai des Tanneurs in Nantes. His father, Raymond, was a mechanic, while his mother, Milou, worked part-time as a hairdresser and pulled the petrol pumps. Milou took Demy to puppet shows at the Guignol des Créteur on the Cours Saint Pierre on Thursday afternoons and bought him his first puppet when he was four. Demy was fascinated by the way the shows were assembled, and he staged marionette versions of fairytales for his friends. Such a burgeoning love of spectacle was bolstered through regular family visits to the operettas at the Théâtre Graslin. Demy also developed a passion for music when listening to records on his parents' phonograph while they worked.

One event – the allied bombardment of Nantes on 16 September 1943 – ruptured the otherwise happy tranquility of his childhood, according to Demy. On that night, he, his family, their friends and neighbours endured the terrifying air raids in a shelter. He recalls: 'quand une chose aussi atroce est arrivée, on a l'impression que plus rien de plus atroce ne peut arriver. Et à partir de cela, alors, on rêve une existence idéale'.[1] Such a traumatic event informed Demy's conviction that happiness is something that we strive for, that to want happiness is to already experience happiness, a worldview that he would portray and express in *Lola* and which would be repeated through the words and actions of the characters that populate his cinema. Following the bombardment, Demy and his younger brother Yvon were sent to live at the home of a clog maker and his wife in the hamlet of La Pierre-Percée near La Chappelle-basse-Mer, where he had already spent the summers of 1942 and 1943. This period is also depicted as joyful in his recollections.

Demy developed a passion for film during regular visits with his parents to the Palace, Apollo and Katorza cinemas on Saturday evenings. *Snow White and the Seven Dwarfs* (Walt Disney, 1937), *Les Dames du Bois de Boulogne* (Robert Bresson, 1945) and *Les Portes de la nuit* (Marcel Carné, 1946) particularly impressed him. Again, he was drawn to the technical aspects of the productions and he would attempt to put them into practice in his first experiments with film. He dipped 9.5mm reels of old Charlie Chaplin and Harold Lloyd movies into hot water to remove the gelatine and then drew his reconstitution of an air battle, entitled *Le Pont de Mauves*, which he screened to his family. In 1945, he exchanged a Meccano set for a 9.5mm Pathé-Baby manual camera in a second hand shop in the Passage Pommeraye and embarked on his first non-animated production, *L'Aventure de Solange*, about a young girl kidnapped by fairground workers who is rediscovered by her parents twenty years later. Sadly, the reel was returned from the developers blank due to overexposure. Undeterred, two years later, Demy convinced Milou to buy him an Ercsam 9.5mm camera with a motorised spring and 1.9mm lens for Christmas and, later, an automatic Ercsam projector. Milou thus played an instrumental role in supporting his passion. She contrasted with Raymond who prohibited Demy from enrolling at the Lycée Clemenceau and the Ecole des Beaux Arts and forced him to learn mechanics, electricity, woodwork, wrought iron work and boiler making at the Collège Technique Launay between 1945 and 1949. Demy's relationship with his father was thereafter marked by ambivalence, while his proximity to his mother endured until his death (Taboulay, 1996: 10).

1 'When something so dreadful has happened, you think that nothing more awful can happen. And from that point, therefore, you dream an ideal existence into effect.' (*L'Univers de Jacques Demy* (Agnès Varda, 1993/95))

Demy devoured the film magazine *L'Ecran français* and regularly attended the *ciné-club* L'Ecran nantais, where he nurtured an admiration for the films of Marcel Carné, Jean Delannoy, Robert Bresson and Jean Cocteau. After the War, American releases flooded the market and the young Demy was captivated by the musical, but it was to animation that he first aimed to apply his creative talents. He admired Paul Grimault's films and George Pal's advertisements for Philips, with their bright colours, sailors, dancing women and allusions to Busby Berkeley musicals, plus the magical world of the early shorts of Jiří Trnka (Berthomé, 1996: 35). At the Ecran nantais, he screened films of his trips to Amsterdam and La Rochelle, but, tired of discussions about adherents' holiday footage, he devoted himself to making animated films in his attic studio (Taboulay, 1996: 13). He modelled characters and sets from cardboard and plaster, and painstakingly shot each minuscule bodily movement frame-by-frame.[2]

La Ballerine (date unknown) features a composer and a ballerina performing the splits, a pirouette, a turn and two bows against a backdrop of a medieval castle perched atop a hill. *Attaque nocturne* (1947–48), which required two years to complete, focuses on a thief who steals a woman's bag and is chased by two passers-by before disappearing into a manhole. The sophisticated decors in the reconstituted version combine recognisable Nantes locations, including the quai de la Fosse and the transporter bridge, with roofs inspired by stills from *Sous les toits de Paris* (René Clair, 1930). *Attaque nocturne* foreshadows Demy's predilection for setting his narratives within compressed space, and his use of a tracking shot offers an early illustration of his proclivity for mobile camerawork.

Demy screened his short to director Christian-Jaque who had come to present *D'Homme à hommes* (1948) at the Apollo on 23 November 1948. Jaque showed it to Christian Matras, a teacher at the École technique de Photographie et de Cinématographie (ETPC) on the rue de Vaugirard in Paris. Meanwhile, one of his instructors at the Collège Launay recognised his talents as a painter, discovered his passion for filmmaking and encouraged him to attend evening classes at the Beaux Arts. It was here that he developed a sophisticated knowledge of and admiration for art and painting, which would inform many

2 Varda and researcher Mireille Henrio discovered two such characters and strips of 9.5mm film reel in the Demy garage during the filming of *Jacquot de Nantes*. They were able to recreate *La Ballerine* and *Attaque nocturne* (1947–48).

of the aesthetic choices he made in his films, and where he met his future decor and costume designers Bernard Evein and Jacqueline Moreau. Evein moved to Paris to study at the prestigious Institut des Hautes Etudes Cinématographiques (IDHEC), followed one year later by Moreau. Christian-Jaque convinced Demy's father to allow him to enrol at the ETPC. In 1949, he chanced upon Evein outside the Galléries Lafayette department store and was reunited with Moreau and future filmmaker Bernard Toublanc-Michel, whom he had met at the Coiffard bookshop in Nantes in 1948.

At the end of his second year Demy presented his first non-animated short *Les Horizons morts* (1951, discussed below). Following his graduation, he assisted Paul Grimault on advertisements, including one for Lustucru pasta. After unrealised projects, including a planned puppet adaptation of Jean-Paul Sartre's *Les Faux Nez*, Demy began writing as a novel the story that he would, almost three decades later, recount through film, *Une chambre en ville*. He also appeared as an extra in Richard Pottier's *Les Révoltés de Lomanach* (1954). In 1953, he began penning the script for his acclaimed documentary, *Le Sabotier du Val de Loire* (1955), which portrays a week in the lives of the clog maker and his wife to whom Demy had been evacuated. Demy invited Georges Rouquier[3] to direct his detailed script: although he declined, he contributed one million old Francs to the budget. *Le Sabotier du Val de Loire* won the prize for Best Short Documentary at the Berlin Film Festival in 1956. Demy assisted Rouquier on *SOS Noronha* (1957) and, when awaiting the first day of shooting, helped Jean Masson with his official commemoration of the wedding of Grace Kelly to Prince Rainier of Monaco. For Rouquier's film, Demy suggested Jean Marais as protagonist, who would later be cast in two of his productions: *Peau d'âne* and *Parking*. Through Marais, Demy met Cocteau, who gave him the rights to adapt his short play *Le Bel Indifférent* to the screen. Masson then offered Demy two further commissions: *Musée Grévin* (1958) and *La Mère et l'enfant* (1959). Both contain stylistic and thematic markers of his future work. *Musée Grévin* plays with the distinction between reality and dreams, the self and its representation, through its narrative about a man (Michel Serrault) who fantasises about bringing the models of the famous waxworks museum to life and allowing them to escape.

3 Demy assisted Rouquier on his documentaries *Arthur Honegger* (1954) and *Lourdes et ses miracles* (1955).

La Mère et l'enfant explores the relationship between a mother and her child. Demy made his first full-length feature, *Lola*, in 1960. A year later, producer Joseph Bercholz approached him to direct a short as part of his *film à sketch* entitled *Les Sept Péchés capitaux*.

Demy's career is marked by both acclaim and disappointment. His most famous films were made and released between 1960 (*Lola*) and 1970 (*Peau d'âne*). *Les Parapluies de Cherbourg*, which won the Palme d'Or at Cannes in 1964, is his most celebrated production, while *Lola* is popularly recognised as a flagship release of the Nouvelle Vague. However, Demy had to abandon projects (*Carmen, Anouchka, Louisiane*), struggled to secure funding for films (*Une chambre en ville* and *Trois places pour le 26*), and had to downsize or modify his aspirations (*Lola* and *Parking*) and censor his intentions (*L'Evénement...*). The 1970s were characterised by an inability to find French producers willing to support his projects, which led him to accept commissions from abroad (*The Pied Piper* and *Lady Oscar*) and an adaptation for the television (*La Naissance du jour*). During the 1980s, he achieved critical praise (*Une chambre en ville*) and condemnation (*Parking*), while audiences stayed away from his films. In 1987, Demy shot a homage to Grimault's animations in *La Table tournante*. His health deteriorated, forcing prolonged absences from the shooting of *Trois places pour le 26*. On 27 October 1990, Demy died from an AIDS-related condition. Eighteen years passed before the cause of death was confirmed in Varda's *Les Plages d'Agnès* (2008).

Demy's affinity with his home city of Nantes is evident throughout his cinema. Both *Lola* and *Une chambre en ville* are set in the city, and Nantes is evoked allegorically in many of his other films located in ports/seaside towns: Nice (*La Baie des Anges* (1962)), Cherbourg (*Les Parapluies de Cherbourg*), Los Angeles (*Model Shop* (1968)) and Marseilles (*Trois places pour le 26*). Moreover, *Model Shop*, *Les Parapluies de Cherbourg* and *Les Demoiselles de Rochefort* conjure Nantes in verbal recollections and/or photographs. Elsewhere, the main character of the original screenplay of *Trois places pour le 26* was to arrive in Marseilles from Nantes and, while Demy considered shooting his unmade *Kobi des auto-tamponneuses* in Orange, Béziers or Montpellier, according to his collaborator Patrice Martineau, he would have set it in Nantes (in Berthomé, 2011: 32).

With posthumous retrospection, Demy's cinema is recognised as constituting the work of a veritable *auteur* (Rosenbaum, 2011: 50).

To achieve his objectives, he controlled all aspects of the production process, including casting, choice of decors and costumes, and the recording of the music and songs (Rabourdin, 2011: 13), and he also wrote his own scripts and lyrics. Demy represented for many critics, scholars and admirers a screen poet whose films, as the next section affirms, project a peculiarly lyrical take on the world.

Poetic perceptions: time, space and self–other relations in the *Demy-monde*

Critics, scholars and spectators have derived a dreamlike quality from Demy's poignant narratives, alluring locations, wistful characters and moving scores. For Demy, dreams are not detached from the materiality of everyday life, and his films illustrate that it is through the affective and imaginary that we apprehend reality. Accordingly, his embellishments of space and verbal discourse coalesce the 'real' with the 'poetic' (Rabourdin, 2011: 10). A modern-day Orpheus, then, it is of little surprise that he adapted and updated the original Greek myth for the cinema in *Parking*, and, to a degree in *La Baie des Anges* and *Model Shop*. Scholar Gerald L. Bruns argues that Orpheus and poets in general do not imitate or reflect the environment around them, but build the world up through their poems (1970: 264). Poets reveal the role of intuition in how external matter is apprehended and experienced. Such engagement allows poets not only to interpret meaning, but also to convey meaning (1970: 270). Bruns sources the 'epistemological ground' of the poet's 'building up' of the world in the phenomenology of Edmund Husserl and Martin Heidegger (1970: 271–4). As Bruns observes 'a world … comes into appearance before man [*sic*] – a world which is present to human consciousness, and which consciousness cannot escape, except by adopting attitudes … which orient it away from the world' (1970: 273). In phenomenology, consciousness is marked by intentionality; we are always conscious of something. Moreover, as David R. Cerbone summarises, phenomenology displaces the emphasis from the 'worldly objects' and 'causal underpinnings' of experience to the experience itself, that is, the 'presentation of the world around me' (2006: 23).

Like Orpheus, Demy brings his intuitive apprehension of the world to his audience. Moreover, while he only occasionally films through the first person perspective, he nonetheless recurrently draws our attention to his characters' apprehension of the objects that surface on their perceptive horizons. Through stylistic tools, including overexposure, fluid camera movements, lyrical dialogues, wordplay, songs, musical arrangements and locations transformed by bright colours, he brings this constitution of the world through experience to the fore. Demy often places his characters in-situation, gesturing to the 'being-in-the-world' of Heidegger and Maurice Merleau-Ponty. His characters are feeling, emotional beings. Their bodies serve as a sensory medium through which they apprehend the world. Such embodiment intensifies the mobilisation of affect that traverses Demy's oeuvre. He underlines the emotional and relational connections and disconnects between his characters, both within each narrative, and across his films, his original intention being to create a cinematographic *comédie humaine*.[4]

In interpreting Demy's cinema, some scholars have invoked the work of Henri Bergson (Marshall and Lindeperg, 2000; Herzog, 2010). According to Herzog, for Bergson, 'perception is a reflective interaction between the perceiver and the perceived, a reciprocal exchange that takes place in the space between them' (2010: 115). Perception 'originates within the object itself' (2010: 115). It pertains to the present and is concerned with action. As complex sensory organisms, we have the power to touch, taste, smell, see and hear, but sight and hearing perceive at a distance and introduce a 'zone of indeterminacy' in which memory is activated (Bergson, [1896] 2004: 38). Perception is partial, interested or what Gilles Deleuze refers to as 'subtractive' (1985: 63–4); it takes that which is useful to it. The spontaneous memories invoked in the time-delay between the perceiver and the perceived object inform voluntary action; they allow us to select from a range of possible acts. Bergson's work on perception, memory and time is central to Deleuze's influential writings on cinema, and Demy's films lend themselves to analysis informed by both Bergson and Deleuze partly because they involve the representation of subjective time, a temporality constituted of perceptions, memories and fantasies. Authenticity is undermined or sidelined in Demy's play with recollections, affective duration and the rendering of the everyday through a dream-like or theatrical lens. Deleuze mentions Demy as an example

---

4 In 1964, Demy declared that his aim was to make fifty films that would be inter-connected via their shared characters (Taboulay, 1996: 5).

of a director interested in time-image cinema,[5] a cinema that is not dependent on deterministic relations between perceiver and object, cause and effect. As Marshall and Lindeperg summarise, such 'logics are replaced by ... "pure" sound and optical images that emphasise the simultaneity of past, present and future and the indiscernibility of "real"/"non-real", "truth" and "falsehood"' (2000: 103).

Deleuze was sceptical about the usefulness of phenomenology in understanding the cinema, partly because it posits as a norm 'la "perception naturelle" et ses conditions' which are 'des co-ordonnées existentielles qui définissent un "ancrage" du sujet percevant dans le monde, un être au monde, une ouverture au monde' (1983: 84) ('"natural perception" and its conditions ... existential coordinates which define an "anchoring" of the perceiving subject in the world, a being in the world, an opening to the world') (Tomlinson and Habberjam, 2005: 59). For Deleuze, informed by Bergson, the relation between subject/being and the world is in flux, that is not anchored, and this is more suited to the cinema, which can both bring us near to objects and distance us from them, as well as revolve around them (1985: 84). In the case of Demy, however, it is precisely this situated perspective, this individualised engagement with the world that his cinema often privileges, explicitly and/or implicitly. Although his characters tend towards flux, their environment is often delimited and/or enclosed. In such potentially stifling physical settings, they are forced to adopt attitudes through which they embrace or turn away from the people and objects that surround them. The sung dialogues, musical arrangements, costumes, character movements and settings transformed by the play on light and bright colours thus serve as examples of where his characters' subjective apprehension of the material world is sewn into the film's form.

Drawing on Bergson, Deleuze argues that the pure optical and sound image in time-based cinema mobilises 'attentive recogni-

---

5 Specifically on Demy, Deleuze writes in the second volume of his work on cinema 'on assiste ... à des situations optiques et sonores incarnées par les décors-descriptions colorés, et qui ne se prolongent pas dans des actions, mais dans des chants opérant en quelque sorte un "décrochage", un "décalage" de l'action' (1985: 91) ('we witness optical and sound situations realized by coloured set descriptions, which no longer extend into actions but into songs, producing in some sense an "unhooking", a "discrepancy" of the action' (Tomlinson and Habberjam, 2005: 64) For a reading of Demy using Deleuze's crystaline effect see Jean-Marc Lalanne (2013: 226–9).

tion' (1985: 64). Automatic recognition involves recollection images (memories) filling the gap between stimulation and response. In attentive recognition, we actively seek to draw recollection images from a pure recollection – that is a past event or virtual image – that enables or prevents recognition of what we see in the present or actual image. Flashbacks, when undertaken in the mainstream mode, serve the forward progression of a linear narrative. Meaning is more contingent in the unconventional flashbacks that pertain to time-image cinema. Reflection rather than action is triggered. For Deleuze, the proper equivalent of the optical-sound image derives from the falsification of memory and inaccuracies of recognition (1985: 75). Demy often invokes the past in his cinema, although he rarely deploys flashbacks and, when he does, uses them to question the veracity of the character's present and past. Habitually, modifications in a familiar character, costume changes, recurring themes, memories – false and true – that span his films and beyond, motifs, lighting, colour schemes, locations and musical arrangements invoke the past within the present and, in some cases, anticipate the future. Demy not only emphasises the importance of the past and future for the present, but also questions the reliability of memory, perception and subjectivity. Moreover, he utilises form, notably colour and music, both to corroborate the narrative events and undermine them.

As argued above, while Demy emphasises his characters' subjective encounter with the world, he inscribes his audience as onlookers and therefore maintains his characters, not as surrogates of ourselves, but as others. Via music, lighting, colour, costume and decor, as well as dialogues and gesturality, he heightens our ability to observe their apprehension of the world while underlining their status as subjects of their own consciousness. Demy's cinema can thus be said to nod to the 'inviolability of the other' as described by Emmanuel Levinas: 'autrui demeure infiniment transcendant, infiniment étranger – mais son visage ... rompt avec le monde qui peut nous être commun et dont les virtualités s'inscrivent dans notre *nature* et que nous développons aussi par notre existence' (1971: 211–12, emphasis in original).[6] His stronger protagonists ignore or refute the judgements of the other, averting and/or defying their attempts to impose their values. He

---

6 'The Other remains infinitely transcendent, infinitely foreign; his face ... breaks with the world that can be common to us, where virtualities are inscribed in our *nature* and developed by our existence.' (Lingis, 1969: 194)

occasionally replaces the shot/reverse-shot exchange with a face-to-face encounter in which the interlocutor-other addresses the self and the camera directly. While for Levinas the face is an abstract term that signifies the alterity of the other, and can neither actually be seen nor touched, here the face serves as phenomenon to depict the ethical value of the other as infinitely transcendental and irreducible to the self. In other words, the face of the other functions as a barrier against my totalising desire to possess them through my vision. It shields the other from being reduced to a state of pure object of my consciousness and from becoming totally knowable to me, partly because I assume that the other is the same as myself (see Davis 1996: 25–33).

Demy distinguishes between ethics – the impossibility of self-sameness – and received morality. Many of his strong characters, particularly his women, disregard dominant values; his films prominently feature flirtatious women, single mothers, erotic dancers, female gamblers, prostitutes and incestuous daughters (and fathers). These characters assume responsibility for their choices and lifestyles and, in this, they conform to one of Demy's principal ethics: fidelity. They are true to themselves by virtue of being true to their desires and passions. Although passion is multiform in Demy's cinema, it is most often associated with love. Here, once again he inflects the object – love – with his own perceptions. Successful love in Demy's universe should be reciprocal and faithful, and yet it is almost always depicted as transient and doomed.

Chance encounters structure Demy's films, and predestiny is constantly evoked. Demy's narratives often appear circular, the futures of his protagonists fated, and this provides the source of the melancholy that lies beneath the surface of his films. Yet, it is how his characters respond to and overcome their situation that becomes so meaningful and, at times, uplifting. Though by no means an avid reader of Heidegger, Maurice Merleau-Ponty, Jean-Paul Sartre or Simone de Beauvoir, through his characters and narratives, Demy implicitly reminds us that we can determine our own existence. Those who succeed in achieving autonomy tend to be romantic figures that acquire agency while remaining true to their core values. Such individuals do not suspend their happiness for a willed, yet indeterminate future, nor do they live in their dreams, but their fantasies form an integral part of their existential reality, rounding off the harder edges of their encounter with materiality and providing the necessary fuel to move forward. Moreover, their choices are informed, yet unbound by their past. Consequently, while Demy's cinema is anything but utopian, it nonetheless accentuates poignancy by highlighting the struggles his characters endure in their pursuit of happiness.

Demy suggests a similar ethics of hope and self-determination with regards to the local and global politics of his period. His cinema questions traditional provincial moralities, challenges Catholicism, undermines patriarchy, is sceptical towards modernity, Western imperialism and capitalism, and, above all, it confronts bourgeois privilege and morality. Demy's films thus contain a philosophical and ethical depth that belies their surface characterisation as light and sugary, and yet they remain appealing, entertaining and accessible. The next section will reveal how some of these aesthetic and ethical concerns materialise in his shorts *Les Horizons morts*, *Le Sabotier du Val de Loire*, *Ars* (1959) and *La Luxure* (1961). The first three were made before *Lola* (1960) while the fourth was shot shortly afterwards.

Transposing the poetic to celluloid: Demy's non-animated shorts

Concerns that would run through Demy's cinema are in evidence in *Les Horizons morts*. Demy cast himself as the protagonist, a shy, morose young man who considers suicide after being rebuffed by a woman and assaulted by her lover. The narrative unfolds in an attic room (where Demy lived as a student), with one scene depicting a feud in a meadow on the fringes of a town. What appears to be a flashback of the altercation ruptures the present. Shots of the protagonist as he stares into a broken mirror, and off-screen sounds of footsteps in the stairwell convey his anxiety and alienation, and serve as intertextual nods to Cocteau's *Le Sang d'un poète* (1930). The score juxtaposes classical violin instrumentation with jazz and rhythmic percussion arrangements. The protagonist embodies Demy's male archetype of a forlorn and melancholy young man, who bears a more than passing resemblance to Jean-Baptiste Deburau (or Baptiste (Jean-Louis Barrault) from *Les Enfants du paradis* (Carné, 1943–45)). During the assault scene, he is distanced from the couple, forced to watch as they embrace. His light trench coat, buttoned to the neck, accentuates his slender form and lack of assurance, while his rival's dark overcoat, open, with the collar turned up and padded shoulders, emphasises his strength and confidence. Demy's character emerges as lost and vulnerable, and fails to retaliate when his adversary assaults him. Patriarchy and the Church are depicted as the barriers to his self-determination. An aggressive male rival prevents him from loving the woman, and the sight of a cross on his bedroom wall stops him from drinking a seemingly deadly liquid. He is trapped, unable to break free from his melancholy existence, hence the dead horizons of the title.

Le Sabotier du Val de Loire marks a shift from fiction to documentary filmmaking. Direct speech is superseded by a voiceover narration, expressed in the third person and read by Rouquier. The clog maker is defined by his craft and differentiated by his region, while his wife is presented through her relationship to her husband. Neither is named, referred to in the voiceover as 'il/lui' or 'elle', while peripheral characters, such as their adopted son Claude (actor unknown), are identified. In accordance with Demy's burgeoning interest in setting his narratives within confined spaces, the story unfolds within the clog maker's hamlet and nearest village on the banks of the Loire. The voiceover and image track portray a celebration of fidelity and pastoral tranquillity. Dialogues convey the proximity of the couple even when they are not in shot together. For instance, while 'il/lui' toils, 'elle' can be heard feeding the chickens and she features constantly in his reported thoughts. Their complicity is projected early on. In a medium shot of 'elle' fanning the fire and peeling vegetables, the narrator informs us 'elle aime mieux quand il est là ... parce qu'elle entend son pas ... et elle y tient' ('she prefers it when he is there ... because she hears his footsteps ... and she needs to hear them'). Moments later, when he hacks through a block of poplar to carve a clog, we are told 'c'est là qu'il est heureux ... il pense à elle qui est là-haut. Il l'a bien aimée, elle' ('that's where he's happy ... he thinks of her upstairs. He has really loved her'). The voiceover turns momentarily to their past, recounting his proposal and explaining that, despite her sterility, he decided to wed her anyway. Later, when apprised of his friend Joubert's death, the narration turns to the couple's future: 'il sait bien que le jour où sa vieille le laissera, il ne tardera pas non plus. Si c'est lui qui part le premier, il sait alors qu'il ne l'attendra pas longtemps'.[7] Death appears to be the film's focus, evident in the references to the clog maker

---

7 'He knows very well that the day his old lady leaves him, he won't hang around either. If he goes first, he knows that he won't wait long before she joins him.'

and his wife's inevitable passing, and the loss of bucolic lifestyles and traditions.

The discursive turns allow Demy to figure time in two ways. External time progresses chronologically. The narrative opens on a Monday morning, ends on a Sunday evening and is structured by routines and isolated events: Joubert's death, Claude's failure to visit, the purchase of a new wheelbarrow. The very first words of the voiceover situate us in objective time and transmit the ritualistic and repetitive chores of daily life: 'quand la semaine commence, dans la saison d'automne, c'est toujours la même chose ... il faut qu'il soit prêt au premier coup de corne, et le premier coup de corne, dans la saison d'automne, c'est toujours vers les 7 heures 10'.[8] The final words of this quotation are repeated to end the film. Subjective time is represented via the relationship between the clog maker's actions and his reported thoughts. *Le Sabotier du Val de Loire* evokes the time-consciousness of phenomenology, that is as consciousness apprehends time. The narrator recounts the clog maker's past and comments on his future as he toils in the present, portrayed visually in his physical movements. The words 'il l'a bien aimée' gesture towards the 'no longer', but, rather than describing a love that has now terminated, convey the intensity of the clog maker's affections over a duration. Moreover, each subsequent invocation of their love and life stories serves, not as a recollection of a now expired experience, neatly packaged into a historical archive, but as a retention, an originary moment that forms a pivotal, though discreet, event in the progressive flow of his conscious life. Each retention is framed as if it were 'now' via a shift to direct speech: 'il lui a dit: "on pourrait se mettre ensemble. Moi, je connais bien le métier. Toi, ben toi, tu ferais ce que la femme doit faire". Elle avait fait "oui". Il avait bien eu un petit regret quand elle lui avait dit "je pourrai pas avoir d'enfants" mais ça, elle le lui avait prévenu'.[9] These retentions are synthesised according to the flow of their passing. When we are told that she had accepted, we retain his just-experienced proposal and, when he conveys his

8 'When the week begins, in the autumn season, it's always the same ... he has to be ready for when the first toot of the horn sounds, and the first toot of the horn, in the autumn season, is always at 7.10 am.'

9 'That's why he said to her: "we could get together. I know the trade. You, well you'd do what a woman must do". She said "yes". He regretted it a little when she said "I won't be able to have children" but she had at least warned him about it.'

regrets at her revelation, we already know the still-to-be-experienced of their lives because they are happily married.

Later, the clog maker apprehends his future as it appears to him in the present. In town on Sunday, he notices Claude talking to a young woman, and the voiceover portends: 'il sait aussi que, bientôt, ils resteront seuls parce que le fils commence à s'agiter. Il ne les abandonnera pas tout à fait, bien sûr, mais ça ne sera plus pareil'.[10] Like Joubert's death, such a development arises from the 'natural' order of events. *Le Sabotier du Val de Loire* thus illustrates another of Demy's preoccupations – destiny – although this is not accepted passively. Claude breaks the cycle of inherited lifestyles by moving to the town, and the film focuses not on the events, but on the clog maker's perception of them. Of Joubert, the voiceover states in free indirect discourse 'on a beau se dire que c'est dans l'ordre, ça vous fout quand même un sacré coup' ('you can tell yourself that it's the natural order of things, it nonetheless shakes you up badly'). Similarly, Claude's departure elicits the clog maker's melancholy: 'le fils n'est pas venu. C'est la première fois qu'il les laisse un dimanche ... il fallait bien que cela aussi arrive' ('the son didn't come. It's the first time that he has left them alone on a Sunday ... that too had to happen').

By emphasising the subjective and experiential, *Le Sabotier du Val de Loire* renders the moribund reality of its characters' existence poetic. Moreover, the shift through indirect, direct and free indirect discourse merges the voice of the narrator with the thoughts and feelings of the clog maker, as well as those of Demy, who had observed him in real life and had earlier attempted to make a film about him. Yet, the clog maker is maintained as separate from the speaking and viewing subject, underlined in the final shot when the backward tracking camera swiftly transports the narrator, filmmaker and us away from his pastoral idyll.

The film's lyricism is further enhanced by shots and editing. Images are connected via dissolves. For instance, following a period of sustained silence as the clog maker hollows out a clog, a close up of his face dissolves into a medium close up of his hands as he washes them under a tap and a further medium close up of him turning a tap on a cask and pouring himself a glass of wine before drinking it. The voiceover is suddenly interrupted as if in respect of his need to grieve

10 'He knows also that, soon, they will be alone because the son is getting restless. He won't abandon them completely, of course, but things won't be the same.'

in silence. Non-diegetic music heralds a change in mood, confirmed by the narration 'il faut profiter du moment, c'est tout simple' ('you have to make the most of now, it's very simple'). Because of the inevitability of death, we must take full advantage of the present. The clog maker achieves this leap as an act of will, his success confirmed by the words that open the next sequence: 'après la peine, la joie, un jour, et puis un autre jour, et aussi le dimanche' ('after sadness, joy, one day, and then another, and also Sunday'). Continuity and habitual pleasures resolve momentary sorrow. The film's final shot, of the couple on the riverbank, the clog maker peacefully fishing while his wife knits, transfers melancholy onto the spectator. The contrapuntal sounds of a train leaving the station as the camera tracks away from the river bank implies the viewer's regret at being forced to abandon this tranquil simplicity.

In *Ars*, Demy superimposes one temporal moment, recounted in the voiceover narration, over another, depicted in the image-track. *Ars* focuses on the final section of the life of Jean-Baptiste-Marie Vianney, a Catholic priest, canonised by Pope Pius XI in 1925, who led the parish of Ars-sur-Forman from 9 February 1818 to his death on 4 August 1859. Demy recounts his transition from humble servant of the Christian God to a tyrannical fanatic who alienates his congregation, with his death and supposed 'afterlife' forming the focus of the last minutes of the film. The priest's lifestyle and teachings are recounted in the third person, although the voiceover also cites from his spiritual writings. The present tense is deployed, thus placing us in the now of the priest's experiences. Yet, *Ars* juxtaposes the audible with the visible, the said with the seen, since the image track is situated within the contemporary moment of the film's production. Hence, as the voiceover informs us that the priest lambasts the congregation for frequenting bistros, attending village dances and working on Sundays, the villagers are dressed in 1950s clothes, situated in contemporary surroundings, and work with the tools of the period. Moreover, although the spaces in which Vianney chose to incarcerate himself are described verbally, no human inhabits the bare kitchen or bedroom full of religious relics that we see.

By juxtaposing the voiceover of the priest's life with the images of the present of the village, *Ars* reveals and then questions the transformation of Ars into a shrine to Catholic penitence. The voiceover is the official story of the past as it is seized and preserved, corresponding to what Laura U. Marks describes as 'the institutionalised representation of the moment', while the visual images contain the unpreserved 'present-that-passes' (2000: 40). Hence, although we are informed that everyday two hundred people will descend on the confessional, the image track shows a small boy, a young woman and a nun in the congregation, and no-one queues to confess. Through its form, *Ars* challenges Catholic doctrine about repentance for sins committed. Such scepticism towards Catholicism, already obliquely implied in *Les Horizons morts*, would return later in Demy's career, most obviously in his adaptation of *The Pied Piper*.

La Luxure revisits the theme of Catholic guilt, and focuses on lust. Interestingly, Vianney had written about lust in the 'Explanations and Exhortations' part of his 'Catechetical Instructions': 'no sins, my children, ruin and destroy a soul so quickly as this shameful sin'. *La Luxure* provides an antidote to Vianney's evangelism. Like *Ars*, both past and present time is presented, though less experimentally. The present opens and closes the film, framing a central flashback. Young flirt Jacques (Laurent Terzieff) bumps into his friend Bernard (Jean-Louis Trintignant) in the street. Bernard purchases a book on the paintings of Hieronymus Bosch and they flick through the pages in a cafe, enraptured by the portraits of female nudes. One, illustrating 'la luxure', elicits Bernard's childhood memory of being misled about the meaning of the French word for lust. The image track then turns back to when he and his classmates were asked to study the seven deadly sins as part of their Catechistic education. Bernard's friend Paul (actor unknown) misconstrues 'la luxure', telling him it signifies luxury. As Paul answers Bernard's bemused questions about why a luxurious existence should merit an afterlife of purgatory, two cutaways to Bernard's perception of hell, triggered by Paul's comments, are inserted. Bernard returns home where his confusion and curiosity spark a family dispute. Bernard looks up 'la luxure' in the dictionary, bizarrely misconstruing the references to flesh and the exuberance of physical strength as describing the craft of a butcher. We then return to the present, as both men laugh at Bernard's childhood naivety. The final section also includes three cutaways, though this time depicting Jacques's imagination as he imprints the nude portraits he sees onto the women and men in the cafe.

La Luxure bears the hallmarks of its director. As Demy observes, the central anecdote is, autobiographical (Berthomé, 1996: 140), a claim visually supported by the use of a market closely resembling the Marché Talensac in Nantes. An intertextual reference to *Les Enfants du paradis* is included, although, typical of Demy, it is revised to evoke one of his thematic preoccupations: incest. Jacques' attempt to chat up a female passerby (Corinne Marchand) recalls Frédérick Lemaître's (Pierre Brasseur) endeavours to charm Garance (Arletty), but he tells her that she has rekindled his repressed pre-Oedipal desires for his cousin. Moreover, *La Luxure* illustrates Demy's interest in the individuality that inheres in perception. The construction of hell we witness, though informed by Paul's descriptions, arises from Bernard's consciousness. We see men and women naked, eating off flaming plates or lying around in jewels and furs. Neither Paul nor Jacques have access to these images since they pertain to Bernard's imagination.

La Luxure highlights alternative perceptions of the world. During the flashback, Bernard's parents argue after he asks his father (Jean Dessailly) to define 'la luxure'. Demy films their dispute via six face-on shots rather than the standard shot reverse-shot structure. Bernard's father accuses his mother (Micheline Presle) of daydreaming and not paying enough attention to her children's education, to which she retorts that they are also his. The form of the exchange emphasises resistance to the co-option of the other within the self's discourse, since the mother's face and reaction surge up to defy her husband's attempts to subject her to his judgements, to subordinate her as an object of his – and by extension our – consciousness. The incompatibility of the perceptions of the same object from two subjects of consciousness is brought to bear on the theme of lust itself. Jacques conjures lustful images from the paintings of naked women he sees, which prompts the three dissolves to women and men being undressed in front of his eyes. Point-of-view shots allow us to see what Jacques is imagining, but this access to his consciousness serves to underline the singularity of his perceptions as opposed to those of Bernard, who is less driven by prurience.

La Luxure provides an early example of the playful irreverence and self-parody which becomes prominent later in Demy's career. Much of the humour emerges from the wordplay. For instance, Jacques asks 'tu peins' ('are you painting at the moment?') to which Bernard replies 'je peine' ('I am suffering').[11] Jacques then advises 'bois' ('drink') to

---

11 A play on the similar sounds of the French verbs peindre (to paint) and peiner (to suffer).

which Bernard retorts 'je peux pas, j'ai mal au foie' ('I can't, my liver hurts').[12] At times these puns are unsuccessful; when Bernard decides to purchase the book on Bosch, Jacques declares 'tu te débauches' ('you're letting your hair down') which Bernard dismisses with 'si on veut' ('if you say so'). When the two men enter the cafe, Jacques asks the waiter 'un demi, Jacques, bien frais avec de la mousse' ('a half, Jacques, very cold and with a frothy head'), ironically attaching Demy's name to the French word for 'froth', almost as if the director is pre-empting later caricatures of his work by critics. Such irreverence extends beyond the creative self and targets misconceptions of art. Undoubtedly, the references to Bosch, and a passing nod to Pieter Bruegel, project Demy's knowledge of painting. Yet, they are overturned to mock art criticism. Purely motivated by his lustful appreciation of the paintings of female nudes, Jacques claims that artists from the period were all geniuses, to which Bernard contends 'n'exagérons rien' ('let's not exaggerate'). More than enabling displays of esoteric discernment, painting serves a more visceral function of sparking spontaneous memories and lustful fantasies.

La Luxure complies with many aspects of Nouvelle Vague film-making. It offers a gritty depiction of childhood and thus nods to one of the movement's pioneering releases, François Truffaut's *Les 400 coups* (1959). Moreover, concordant with many Nouvelle Vague films, the youth are depicted as bohemian and hedonistic. Elsewhere, the film is set in real locations; natural lighting and sound are deployed; jazz-based partitions provide the soundtrack; and young, emerging actors are cast', including Marchand who had already played Daisy in *Lola* and who later played Cléo/Florence in Varda's *Cléo de 5 à 7* (1962). Such qualities are no doubt influenced by the imperatives that guided the production as a whole; *Les Sept Péchés capitaux* also includes contributions by Jean-Luc Godard and Claude Chabrol. It is to Demy's association with the Nouvelle Vague that the next chapter will turn.

12 A play on the similar sounds of the French verb 'boire' and noun 'foie'.

References

Bergson, Henri (1896) *Matière et mémoire*, Paris, Librairie Félix Alcan, transl. Nancy Margaret Paul and W. Scott Palmer, *Matter and Memory*, Mineola, New York, Dover Publications, 2004.

Berthomé, Jean-Pierre (1996) *Jacques Demy et les racines du rêve*, 2nd Edition, Nantes, L'Atalante.

—— (2011) 'La Nantes de Demy: Repères pour une géographie amoureuse', in Jérôme Baron (ed.), *Jacques Demy, 303: arts, recherches, créations*: 22–33.

Bruns, Gerald L. (1970) 'Poetry as Reality: the Orpheus Myth and its Modern Counterparts', *ELH*, 37 (2): 263–86.

Cerbone, David R. (2006) *Understanding Phenomenology*, Durham, Acumen.

Colomb, Philippe (1998) 'L'Etrange Demy-monde', in Marie-Hélène Bourcier (ed.), *Q comme Queer*, Paris, Cahiers Gay, Kitsch, Camp: 39–47.

Davis, Colin (1996) *Levinas: an Introduction*, Cambridge and Malden, MA, Polity.

Deleuze, Gilles (1983) *Cinéma 1: l'image mouvement*, Paris, Les Editions de Minuit, transl. Hugh Tomlinson and Barbara Habberjam, *Cinema 1: the Movement-Image*, London and New York, Continuum, 2005.

—— (1985) *Cinéma 2: l'image temps*, Paris, Les Editions de Minuit, transl. Hugh Tomlinson and Barbara Habberjam, *Cinema 2: the Time Image*, London and New York, Continuum, 2005.

Duggan, Anne E (2013) *Queer Enchantments: Gender, Sexuality and Class in the Fairy-Tale Cinema of Jacques Demy*, Detroit: Wayne State University Press.

Herzog, Amy (2010) 'En Chanté: Music, Memory and Perversity in the Films of Jacques Demy', in *Dreams of Difference, Songs of the Same*, Minneapolis and London, University of Minnesota Press.

Lalanne, Jean-Marc (2013) 'Pièges de cristal', in Anon. (eds) *Le Monde enchanté de Jacques Demy*, Paris, Skira Flammarion, La Cinémathèque Française and Ciné-Tamaris: 226–9.

Levinas, Emmanuel (1971) *Totalité et infini: essai sur l'extériorité*, Paris, Le Livre de Poche, transl. Alphonso Lingis, *Totality and Infinity: An Essay on Exteriority*, Pittsburgh: Duquesne, 1969.

Lingis, Alphonso transl. (1969) *Totality and Infinity: An Essay on Exteriority*, Pittsburgh: Duquesne.

Marks, Laura U. (2000) *The Skin of the Film: Intercultural Cinema, Embodiment and the Senses*, Durham NC, Duke University Press.

Marshall, Bill and Lindeperg, Sylvie (2000) 'Time, History and Memory in *Les Parapluies de Cherbourg*', in Bill Marshall and Robynn Stilwell (eds), *Musicals: Hollywood and Beyond*, Chicago, University of Chicago Press: 98–106.

Paul, Nancy Margaret and Palmer, W. Scott transl. (2004) *Matter and Memory*, Mineola, New York, Dover Publications.

Rabourdin, Dominique (2011) 'Cette émotion appelée poésie', in Jérôme Baron (ed.), *Jacques Demy, 303: arts, recherches, créations*: 8–15.

Rosenbaum, Jonathan (2011) 'Two or Three Things I Know about Demy', in Quim Casas and Ana Cristina Iriarte (eds), *Jacques Demy*, Donostia-San Sebastián, Festival de San Sebastián S.A./Filmoteca Española/ICAA/ Ministerio de Cultura: 49–60.

Taboulay, Camille (1996) *Le Cinéma enchanté de Jacques Demy*, Paris, *Cahiers du Cinéma*.

Tomlinson, Hugh and Habberjam, Barbara transl. (2005) *Cinema 1: the Movement-Image*, London and New York, Continuum.

Tomlinson, Hugh and Habberjam, Barbara transl. (2005) *Cinema 2: the Time Image*, London and New York, Continuum, 2005.

Internet sources:

www.crossroadsinitiative.com/library_article/698/Catechetical_Instructions_St_John_Vianney.html, accessed 3 December 2012.

1

Jacques Demy, the Nouvelle Vague and beyond

Film scholars have struggled to place Demy in relation to the Nouvelle Vague. Richard Neupert describes him as 'one particularly important figure from the era who has never fit in comfortably with everyone's definition of the New Wave' (2002: 360). Similarly, Naomi Greene positions him within a peripheral group of what Michael Witt and Michael Temple describe as '"satellite" figures' (Greene, 2007: 4; Witt and Temple, 2004: 183). Demy's preoccupation with musicals and fairytales distinguishes him from his Nouvelle Vague contemporaries and, while he did not eschew their transformative strategies, his associations with them are the product of happenstance. He encountered Jacques Rivette, Alain Resnais and Godard at the Tours Film Festival in 1956 at which he presented *Le Sabotier du Val de Loire* (Taboulay, 1996: 19). He joined them at the offices of *Cahiers du Cinéma* in Paris where he met Chabrol, Truffaut and Eric Rohmer, among others from the movement. They watched films at cinemas on the Champs-Elysées and the *Cinémathèque* and discussed them afterwards. In 1958, Godard introduced Demy to Georges de Beauregard who agreed to finance *Lola* and, later, Truffaut aided Demy in securing the funds for *Les Parapluies de Cherbourg* (Hill, 2008a: 27).

This chapter nonetheless discusses *Lola* and *La Baie des Anges* in the light of Nouvelle Vague techniques and concerns, plus the aesthetics and themes that are specifically associated with Demy's personal filmmaking. It then examines how Demy's sequel to *Lola*, *Model Shop*, exported some of the iconic practices of the movement to Hollywood in a remarkable act of singular vision that countered the expectations of his Universal Studios financiers.

Contemporary fairytale: *Lola*

Lola is often perceived as an archetypal Nouvelle Vague film since it is the product of a filmmaker involved in all aspects of its construction and who wrote the original screenplay (Hill, 2008b: 385). Demy worked with a small crew, including set designer Evein, director of photography Raoul Coutard, and Michel Legrand who composed the score.[1] *Lola* is also partly autobiographical: it was shot on location in Nantes; Jeanne (Margo Lion) and Claire (Catherine Lutz), who work in the Café Naval, are inspired by Demy's aunts; Lola (Anouk Aimée) is modelled on a fusion of a friend of the same name[2] and a neighbour called Reine; while Roland Cassard (Marc Michel) is, according to some critics, Demy's alter-ego (Berthomé, 1996: 122). *Lola* is also read as a condensed version of Demy's oeuvre as a whole, containing all the elements – stylistic and thematic – that would return throughout his cinema.

Congruent with many Nouvelle Vague films, *Lola* pays homage to cinematic antecedents, particularly Max Ophüls to whom it is dedicated. Lola's name and profession recall the main protagonist of *Lola Montes* (1955), while the *belle époque* interior of the Eldorado club and Lola's costume allude to *Le Plaisir* (1952). The narrative structure evokes the cyclical form of *La Ronde* (1950), although, as Berthomé remarks, in *Lola* the circle is not closed, but opens outwards (1996: 126). Beyond Ophüls, the central theme of fidelity in the absence of a lover recalls Luchino Visconti's *Le Notti Bianche* (1957) while Bresson's *Les Dames du Bois de Boulogne* is conjured in the figure of Elina Labourdette, recast from the young dancer Agnès to the single mother Madame Desnoyer. Furthermore, the MGM musical *On the Town* (Stanley Donen and Gene Kelly, 1949) is referenced in the sailors who roam the streets. Allusions to filmgoing are also part of the self-reflexivity that characterises Nouvelle Vague productions. Roland watches the Gary Cooper classic *Return to Paradise* (Mark Robson, 1953). Moreover, the self-referentiality that links Nouvelle Vague films emerges as Roland tells Claire about his friend Poiccard who had turned bad and was shot dead, thus recounting the demise

---

1 This collaboration with Legrand was the product of coincidence since Quincy Jones had already started working on the score, but was forced to return to the USA.

2 Lola went to Paris to dance in a cabaret and, later, Demy gave her a role as an extra in the film.

of Godard's hero (Jean-Paul Belmondo) in *A bout de souffle* (1960).

Yet, like much of the Nouvelle Vague output, *Lola*'s fresh and casual tone is the result of limited finances. Demy's original vision bore little resemblance to the grittiness of the movement's staple output. He intended to make an exuberant musical, entitled *Un billet pour Johannesbourg*, and asked Beauregard for a budget of 250,000,000 old French Francs.[3] He was only offered 38,000,000 and was thus forced to discard colour, elaborate costumes, all musical numbers bar one and had to film in silence before adding the voices in post-synchronisation. Moreover, although *Lola* embraces the modernity cherished by the Nouvelle Vague directors, it also conveys a fondness for the past.

Lola rehabilitates a classic form: the fairytale. Single mother Lola works in the Eldorado club as an erotic dancer. After a seven-year absence, her lover Michel (Jacques Harden) returns and drives them off in his white Cadillac convertible, this icon of post-War Americana an updated version of the classic steed of medieval knights. However, *Lola* is far more than a boy-saves-girl story. It offers a fictional insight into the lives and aspirations of a group of individuals in a provincial city at a time when history, society and culture are evolving at breakneck speed. Lola sleeps with American sailor Frankie (Alan Scott) because he reminds her of Michel. Roland dreams of relocating abroad, but lacks self-determination. Desnoyer suffers from loneliness and seeks Roland's affections, while her daughter Cécile (Annie Dupéroux) runs away in search of Frankie who has left for the United States. *Lola* is thus a snapshot of a town in transition, the present within the film constituting the confluence of longstanding customs and aspirations (romance, affection and fidelity) with modern values and lifestyles (adventure, materialism and freedom).

Lola's narrative is structured around a complex series of chance encounters and missed connections. Michel almost runs over a group of sailors, including Frankie. Jeanne informs Claire and Roland that she has just seen her son Michel. The sailors casually pass Roland outside the Katorza cinema. He encounters Desnoyer and Cécile in a bookshop and tells Cécile that she reminds him of a Cécile he had known ten or fifteen years earlier, whom we later discover is Lola. Lola bumps into Roland in the Passage Pommeraye and, later, recounts her love for Michel. Roland enters the Café des Caboteurs without

---

3 *Jacques Demy: L'Art en tête*, 25 May 1987, www.ina.fr/media/television/video/ CPC87004652/jacques-demy.fr.html, accessed 15 June 2012.

knowing that the diner dressed in white is Michel. Lola leans against Michel's white Cadillac, unaware that its owner is her absent lover just a few metres away. Michel sees a poster of Lola outside the Eldorado and drives off seconds before she and Frankie exit. Cécile meets Frankie when she buys her favourite comic, *Meteor*. Roland spots Lola returning home with Frankie and enters the Café Naval just after Michel has left to find Lola. Lola notices Roland walking along the road as she leaves with Michel and her son Yvon (Gérard Delaroche).

While each encounter is depicted as coincidental, collectively they constitute a reflection on the themes of chance, fate and free will. As the story develops, we learn that Desnoyer and Cécile are possible derivations of Lola. Cécile symbolises what Lola used to be. She aims to be a dancer and goes to the fairground with Frankie on her fourteenth birthday as Lola had with Michel. Desnoyer represents what Lola may become, a single mother raising her teenage child alone. By suggesting that Cécile is Lola's past and Desnoyer her future, *Lola* nods to the idea of fatalism: while time may be boundless, our options are not. This sense of predestiny and repetition is extended into the film's structure. Scenes depicting Desnoyer berating Cécile or Cécile enjoying her date with Frankie are preceded or succeeded, moments earlier or later, by those portraying Lola dancing in the club, running around town and lamenting Michel's absence. Lola's past, present and future thus appear alongside each other, like the retentions and portensions witnessed in *Le Sabotier du Val de Loire*. Such pre-destiny is humorously reflected through rhyming dialogue when Lola is offered a dancing contract in Marseille: 'on sait ce que c'est, on part pour Marseille et on se retrouve en Argentine' ('everyone knows what it's like. You leave for Marseilles and you end up in Argentina'), a line Roland repeats during his last meeting with Lola.

And yet, *Lola* reveals that, although similar, all three characters differ significantly. Lola and Desnoyer are marked by: their divergences in attitudes (Desnoyer is conservative and considered while Lola is free and spontaneous); their experiences (Desnoyer fled from Cécile's father, Aimé, a hairdresser from Cherbourg, to raise her daughter alone whereas Lola brings up her son in the absence of his father); and their status (Desnoyer has become relatively affluent, while Lola dances for a living). Consequently, Lola, Desnoyer and Cécile symbolise the impossibility of repeating the experiences of the other, which is reinforced by the extra-diegetic associations that connect and misconnect the characters to and from other films. The photograph Cécile shows Roland of Desnoyer as a young dancer – an occupation she denies – is a still of Labourdette as Agnès in Bresson's film, while Lola wears a version of Labourdette's costume when she performs *La Chanson de Lola*. Such disruptive associations extend further back; Lola's name and occupation although based on Demy's childhood friends, also recall those of Lola Lola (Marlene Dietrich), in *Der blaue Engel* (Josef von Sternberg, 1930), whose costume, with top hat, strappy top and stockings, is a precursor of that of both Agnès and Lola. These nods also provide an early indication of Demy's concern with portraying the falseness and contingency of memory; recollections of Agnès/Labourdette in the earlier film are elicited when Lola performs, which extend back to Lola Lola/Dietrich, but the character we now see is Lola/Aimée.

While *Lola* posits the possibility of pre-destiny, it also emphasises the importance of self-determination in mapping out our life paths. Despite their seemingly limited options, Lola and Desnoyer strive to control their present and determine their future. Such agency eludes Roland, a dreamer who complains about his life rather than resolving to change it. He is chided for his inactivity in his first dialogue with Claire. After declaring, 'moi, ce que j'aime par dessus tout, c'est la liberté' ('what I like more than anything else is freedom'), Roland complains 'les gens m'ennuient', 'tout m'écoeure', 'je suis désespéré' ('people bore me', 'I'm sick of everything', 'I'm without hope'), and the following exchange ensues:

> *Claire*: Un bien grand mot. Réagissez. Je réagis. Est-ce que je me laisse abattre moi?
> *Roland*: Je me laisse pas abattre, je pense.
> *Claire*: Pensez un peu moins et agissez davantage.[4]

This short extract illustrates how *Lola* engages with the existentialist philosophy that captured popular consciousness in the post-war years and which is mobilised in key Nouvelle Vague films, including Truffaut's *Tirez sur le pianiste* (1960) and Varda's *Cléo de 5 à 7*. According to its most famous proponent, Jean-Paul Sartre, because there is no divine power to guide our actions, we are condemned to be free (1946: 295). Our 'abandonment' implies that we determine our

---

4 'That's a big word. React. I react. Do I allow myself to get discouraged?' 'I don't let myself get discouraged, I think', 'Think a little less and act more.'

being (1946: 297–8). Sartre famously declared that existence precedes essence (1946: 290); what we are is achieved when we have purposed to be what we are (1946: 291). And yet, as William C. Pamerleau notes, awareness of our freedom can cause anguish about the choices we make and will make, and despair about the choices we have made (2009: 17). Existentialism sees humans as 'being-in-situation', which emphasises a being-in-the-present, although we remain aware that what we are now is informed by our past decisions and the choices we make in projecting ourselves in the future. We become situated beings when our freedom intersects with the facts of our lives that we have not selected and cannot be altered (referred to as facticity). As human beings, we have consciousness; we differ from the immanent object that only exists in and of itself (être-en-soi) and can exist for ourselves (être-pour-soi). Existentialists refer to this as transcendence – our capacity to step back and contemplate ourselves, to negotiate the facts of our existence.

For Sartre in *L'Etre et le néant*, facticity and transcendence constitute the double property of the human condition (1943: 91). In *Existential-isme est un humanisme*, he urges us to choose freedom (1946: 297–8). Not acknowledging our freedom and ability to make creative choices is to act in 'bad faith'. Sartre identifies two forms of 'bad faith': to allow the facts of our lives to control our present and future existences or to live for the benefit of others ('être-pour-autrui'), and to exist in a fantasy world and deny our facticity (1943: 89–101). Sartre states 'l'ambiguité nécessaire à la mauvaise foi vient de ce qu'on affirme [...] que je *suis* ma transcendance sur le mode d'être de la chose' (1943: 92; emphasis in original).[5] Such bad faith is portrayed through Roland who claims he can have freedom, but does nothing practically to achieve it, behaviour that alienates him from his existential reality.[6]

The scene depicting Roland being dismissed by his boss provides further evidence of his bad faith. Roland admits that he is late because he is reading André Malraux's *La Condition humaine* about the plotting of a communist uprising in Shanghai in 1927. He passes it to his boss, citing his favourite excerpt from page 55: 'il n'y a pas de dignité

---

5 'The ambiguity necessary for bad faith comes from the fact that I affirm here that I *am* my transcendence in the mode of being a thing.' (Barnes, 2000: 57)

6 After having seen *Return from Paradise*, Roland claims that travelling is the only remedy for his ennui. Matareva, the island on which Cooper's film is set and to which Roland dreams of escaping, was Michel's first destination after having left Nantes.

possible, pas de vie réelle pour un homme qui travaille douze heures par jour sans savoir pourquoi il travaille' ('there is no possible dignity, no true life for a man who works twelve hours a day without knowing why he works'). *La Condition humaine* combines an awareness of the absence of a metaphysical reason for existence with a belief in self-determination. Yet, Roland fails to put such self-making into practice. Again, he is transcendence in the mode of facticity; he proclaims that he can be so much more than he is, but fails to prove it. This is underlined later in that he is forced to rely on the help of others; Claire and Jeanne inform him of a trip organised through their friend M. Favigny, the shoe shop owner, which involves transporting a briefcase containing diamonds to Johannesburg.

Roland's inability to seize his freedom has ethical repercussions for those around him. Sartre argues that 'man' is responsible for all 'men': that is, in choosing freedom for himself, 'he' chooses for all 'men' (1946: 291). In complaining rather than acting, Roland denies the transcendence so fundamental to human existence, not only for himself, but also for others. Ethical issues of a different type are conveyed in Michel's choices. Although he embodies drive and ambition, he has acted as if in a vacuum. His departure, seven years before the beginning of the film, conveys his indifference to the implications of his actions for those around him. In abandoning Lola, Yvon and Jeanne, Michel denies the facts of his existence and risks stymieing their potential for achieving freedom for themselves.

Demy favours characters that engage intuitively with the world over those who subject themselves and others to self-reflexive cogitation. His strong protagonists often act on impulse, responding to whims, and shifting their moods and opinions unexpectedly. Intuition is portrayed as a means through which his protagonists act spontaneously for themselves and achieve agency, liberated from the paralysing effects of ennui and procrastination. Demy's oeuvre constitutes a cinema of emotions and feelings, a label he vigorously defends against what he characterised as American-inspired intellectualism after the release of *Une chambre en ville* in 1982: 'je ne vois pas au nom de quoi il faut se priver du coeur ... c'est un peu une réaction intellectuelle mais c'est une maladie américaine' (in Daney, Narboni and Toubiana, 1982: 57).[7] Narrative, characterisation and tenor emphasise

---

7 'I don't know in what name we must ignore our hearts ... it's an intellectual reaction, but an American illness.'

poignancy and elicit endearment. Laughter and affect are mobilised, prefigured by the proverb with which Demy opens *Lola*: 'pleure qui peut, rit qui veut' ('cry if you can, laugh if you want'). The instinctive and the banal render extraordinary events touching and humorous. For instance, when Lola bumps into Roland in the Passage Pommeraye after an extended separation, she suddenly interrupts their salutations and declares 'ô, attends, je t'ai mis du rouge' ('oh, hold on, I've got lipstick on you'). At times, her spontaneous remarks serve to highlight Roland's passivity. For example, after Roland declares his past love for Lola, she nonchalantly enquires 'je mets une veste ou j'en mets pas? Hop si j'en mets une' ('shall I wear a jacket or not? Oh yes, I'll wear one').

Such shifts between the extraordinary and the anodyne are common in Demy's films and allow him to stage another of his concerns: the blurring of the boundaries between authenticity and theatricality (or often reality and cinema; when Claire says that life is always more beautiful in films, Jeanne replies that life is cinema). When Lola tells Roland she has got some lipstick on him, her intonation is melodic, constituting a rapidly descending trill that lends a lyrical tenor to her banal comment. For critic Jean-Marc Lalanne, the enchantment attributed to Demy's cinema is found in his particular way of portraying the world as a theatre without limits, in which the boundaries between stage, backstage and auditorium are constantly transgressed (1997: 62). The authentic and the theatrical cannot be distinguished, which Matthew Lazen relates to the approach to subjectivity in *Lola* (2004: 192). The blurring of the theatrical with the everyday is illustrated in Lola's rehearsal performance of *La Chanson de Lola*. Paradoxically, her intonation is flat and her articulation rapid, lazy and unclear, and yet her smile is broad and her dance, though amateur, is choreographed.[8]

Aesthetically, *Lola* achieves a poetic sensibility despite its budgetary constraints. Demy composed the dialogues as if they constituted a musical arrangement (Berthomé, 1996: 113), as in the alexandrine rhyming lines of Desnoyer after her first meeting with Roland: 'sa

---

8 This seemingly nonchalant delivery also has a material explanation since the film was shot in silence. Hence, Aimée had to read the lyrics as a poem, written by Varda, without knowing the musical phrasing that would accompany her performance in the soundtrack, with a record by the Platters playing in the background. Legrand then had to compose the music based on Aimée's articulation, which was dubbed by Jacqueline Danno (Legrand in Lerouge, 2013: 80).

figure est plaisante, il s'exprime avec aisance, je m'demande ce qu'il peut bien faire dans l'existence' ('his face is pleasant, he expresses himself with ease, I wonder what he really does in life'). The images extend the film's poetic grace. *Lola* shifts between casual aesthetics and a slick style, and nowhere is this more evident than in the sequence showing Cécile and Frankie's date at the fairground, which Demy had originally intended to be filmed as a dance, an idea he was forced to abandon because of the budget restrictions. Fixed and handheld camerawork interchange as Cécile and Frankie ride the dodgems and waltzer. The image-track is slowed as Frankie jumps off, turns to catch Cécile as she leaps into his arms and they both run through the crowds. Camerawork, editing and music portray time as it appears to consciousness. At first, the quick cuts, pans, abrupt shifts through points-of-view and fast movement within the shot transmit Cécile's excitement. The emotional significance and magic of the encounter for Cécile is then transmitted via the slow-motion shots. However, typical of Demy, euphoria is tinged with melancholy, here conveyed via the narrative as Frankie has to return to the US, and underscored by Johann Sebastian Bach's *Das Wohltemperierte Klavier*, played in the soundtrack, which underlines Cécile's sadness at having to leave her American sailor.

In as much as Demy's cinema is one of affect, it is specifically about love and its effects. Lola's devotion to her absent lover appears self-delusory since Michel has abandoned her twice, once after their first date and again when she fell pregnant. For Roland Barthes in *Fragments d'un discours amoureux*, absence exists as a result of the actions of the other: 'l'autre est en état de perpétuel départ, de voyage; il est, par vocation, migrateur, fuyant; je suis, moi qui aime, par vocation inverse, sédentaire, immobile, à disposition, en attente, tassé sur place' (1977: 19).[9] Traditionally, such a discourse of absence is attributed to woman: 'la Femme est fidèle (elle attend), l'homme est chasseur (il navigue, il drague). C'est la Femme qui donne forme à l'absence, en élabore sa fiction, car elle en a le temps' (1977: 20).[10]

9 'The other is in a condition of perpetual departure, of journeying; the other is, by vocation, migrant, fugitive; I–I who love, by converse vocation, am sedentary, motionless, at hand, in expectation, nailed to the spot, *in suspense*.' (Howard, 2002: 13)

10 'Woman is faithful (she waits) man is fickle (he sails away, he cruises). It is Woman who gives shape to absence, elaborates its fiction, for she has time to do so.' (Howard, 2002: 14)

However, Lola is far more than a destitute servant girl awaiting her prince charming. She does not allow the challenges of her situation as a single mother to have mastery over her, but does what she can, within the constraints of her situation, to determine her own existence. Instead of finding a surrogate male protector, she fends for herself and Yvon alone. Rather than a sedentary abandoned lover, Lola is mobile, hurrying around the streets with purpose. She curtails her encounters with Roland to take Yvon to school and to perform at the Eldorado. Although Lola's moods vary (she breaks down after telling Roland about Michel and when Roland declares his love for her), she exclaims rhetorically 'c'est beau de vivre, non!' ('it's great to be alive, isn't it?'). Of Michel, she predicts 'peut-être qu'il reviendra ... j'ai confiance ... un premier amour c'est tellement fort' ('perhaps he'll come back ... I believe it ... A first love is so strong'), uttering the line Roland later repeats to Cécile and Desnoyer. Moreover, the gender relations at the heart of Barthes's account are revised since Lola tells Roland that she is always travelling and that she has only been in Nantes for three days, while he has remained in the city for ten years.

Lola provides an example of a life structured around absence that is neither passive nor pessimistic. Lola does not embark upon a self-delusory attempt to forget her past, but constantly recalls and affirms it. Although she tells Michel that, at times, his memory poisoned her existence, she chooses to continue loving him. She is candid about her emotions and takes responsibility for her choices. After Roland lambasts Michel, Lola defends her ex-lover, telling him that he could not accept having a child without being able to raise it correctly. Lola does not internalise Roland's morality. Moreover, she illustrates how hope that a past love will return does not preclude happiness in the present. Roland claims to understand this: 'ce qui compte, c'est ... vouloir quelque chose à tout prix. Par exemple ... vouloir le bonheur, c'est déjà un peu le bonheur. Avant de te retrouver, je voulais rien et maintenant ... je te comprends. Tu as raison, c'est beau de vivre'.[11] Nevertheless, when Lola suggests that they meet after her time in Marseilles to see whether they can form a couple, he replies that it would be two wasted months, thus falling back into his morose passivity. Roland does leave Nantes, but only thanks to the contacts

11 '... what matters is ... to want something at any price. For example ... to want happiness is already to have a taste of it. Before meeting you, I wanted nothing and now ... I understand you. You're right, it's great to be alive.'

of others and because Lola insists on departing for Marseilles. His acts, then, are not the product of choice and his plans are subject to sudden change.

Lola is constructed as an embodied subject. When we first see her emerging from the dancing girls and sailors in the Eldorado her body dictates her actions; she notices a fold in her tights and lifts her leg to smooth them. In many ways, Lola illustrates one of the premises of corporeal phenomenology as outlined by Merleau-Ponty: 'nous sommes au monde par notre corps, en tant que nous percevons le monde avec notre corps. Mais en reprenant ainsi contact avec le corps et avec le monde, c'est aussi nous-même que nous allons retrouver, puisque, si l'on perçoit avec son corps, le corps est un moi naturel et comme le sujet de la perception' (1945: 249).[12] Lola is her body, she encounters and apprehends the world through her corporeality. She tells Roland 'je tremble', 'je suis comme un frisson' ('I'm shaking', 'I'm like a shiver'), orders him to feel her chest because her heart beats so fast, and urges Daisy to touch her freshly washed hair that feels like silk. The instinctive surges up from within her body, interrupting her discourse, often in the form of the aforementioned spontaneous exclamations. Moreover, the self and the world merge through her body. When Lola tells Frankie about her love for Michel, dressed in his white tunic and leaning against the window, the warm sunlight blends with the contours of her hair and face, blurring the lines between self and environment. By contrast, the exterior world subsumes Roland. When he stands in profile against the bookshop window and tells his story of his past love for Lola, the bright daylight obscures his features, transforming him into a dark silhouette. Lola's love for Michel is thus symbolically figured as symbiotic and sublime while Roland's love for Lola is portrayed as disjointed and condemned.

Like Lola, Desnoyer also transcends her situation. Rather than allow Roland's rejection of her advances to destabilise her, she determines to search for Cécile. We learn that Cécile's father Aimé is not her late husband, but his brother (thereby introducing a subtle touch of incest into the story) and she chooses to raise her daughter alone, despite the challenges of her existence. She tells Roland that she lost

---

12 'We are in the world through our body, and in so far as we perceive the world with our body. But by thus remaking contact with the body and with the world, we shall also rediscover ourself, since, perceiving as we do with our body, the body is a natural self and, as it were, the subject of perception.' (Smith, 2002: 239)

everything during the War and found herself alone and penniless because her husband was a gambler. Although Cécile berates her for seeing negativity everywhere, she advises her daughter not to believe that all humanity is rotten. Here, then, *Lola* articulates how, however challenging our circumstances, we must retain faith. *La Baie des Anges* develops these concerns by setting its narrative within constricted spaces – Nice and casinos – and by depicting further the need to claim freedom and assume responsibility for personal choices. Provocatively, such traits are embodied by Desnoyer's *bête noire*: the gambler.

Modernising myth: *La Baie des Anges*

Shot in real locations with natural sound and lighting, and featuring actual casino croupiers, *La Baie des Anges* achieves a style akin to the gritty realism often associated with the Nouvelle Vague. Its casual feel may be explained by the rapidity of its production, from inception to distribution. The project was conceived at the Cannes film festival in May 1962. Demy attended to support Varda who was presenting *Cléo de 5 à 7*. He also sought funding for *Les Parapluies de Cherbourg*, of which the dialogues had been written and music arranged. After having no luck in finding a financier, Mag Bodard, the producer of *Les Parapluies de Cherbourg*, took Demy to a casino to cheer him up. Demy recalls 'quand on entre dans un tel lieu … on a l'impression de pénétrer dans un autre monde' (in Mardone, 1963) ('When you go into such a place … you feel as if you've penetrated another world').

La Baie des Anges recreates this otherworldliness. Like *Lola*, it is informed by stories from Demy's past. The relationship between the male protagonist Jean Fournier (Claude Mann) and his father (Henri Nassiet) is inspired by a tale his own father had recounted to him about a man who committed suicide because he could not reimburse his son's gambling debts. Accordingly, Jean's father tells Jean that he does not want to be responsible for his debts and that he does not want a gambler in his house. Demy wrote the screenplay in a few days and found a producer, Paul-Edmond Decharme, keen to work with the directors of the new French cinema. He offered the key role of Jacqueline Demaistre to Jeanne Moreau who, having admired *Lola*, wanted to collaborate on one of his projects. Filming started in mid-September and was completed in six weeks.

The plot is simpler than that of *Lola*. Jean is a young impression-able bank clerk, inveigled into gambling by his friend Caron (Paul Guers). On his first visit to a casino at Enghien-les-Bains, he spots Jackie, the wife of an industrialist, who is being expelled, probably for trying to coerce punters into parting with their money. Jean wins 480,000 old French Francs. This success and his burgeoning attraction for gambling trigger his desire to continue. On Caron's advice, he takes his summer holiday in Nice – hence the Bay of Angels of the title – where he (re-)encounters Jackie at a casino. The narrative there-after focuses on their relationship, structured around Jackie's passion for gambling and Jean's infatuation with Jackie. The film ends with Jackie – seemingly at least – succumbing to Jean's affections, the final shot from inside the casino showing them walking away, arm-in-arm, into the bright sunlight of the Côte d'Azur, heading for the railway station and Paris.

Though more naturalistic than *Lola*, *La Baie des Anges* nonethe-less obtains a lyrical quality that aligns it with Demy's personal style. Its very title is inspired by a Raoul Dufy painting of the same name. *La Baie des Anges* shows, once again, that reality and dreams are two co-constitutive facets of human existence. Exaltation is immediately conveyed in its incredible opening sequence. An iris shot opens on Jackie walking towards the camera on the Promenade des Anglais. The camera then tracks back rapidly, distancing us from the advancing protagonist. The spiralling chords of Legrand's cyclical main musical theme, 'Le Jeu', played on two pianos, supersede the natural diegetic sound. Its increasingly high chord elevates the film from the drab platitude of reality into an exalted realm. Camera movement and soundtrack are misleading, creating the impression of a tumultuous climax. 'Le Jeu' returns throughout. It provides the soundtrack to the dissolve on Jackie and Jean as they walk away from the casino at the end; it accompanies their arrival in their luxurious suite at the Hôtel de Paris in Monte Carlo; and it synchronises with their wins. It transmits the characters' anticipation and euphoria as the image track dissolves between their faces and the ball spinning around the rotating roulette wheel. Yet, its hyperbolic tones amplify the transience of such oneiric interludes, which serve as momentary suspensions of the accruing tensions and conflicts that structure Jean and Jackie's existence.

As in *Lola*, lighting and black-and-white are manipulated to create an iambic aesthetic. Both are deployed to convey differences in time and space and the shifts and tensions in Jean and Jackie's relationship. For Berthomé, Jean Rabier's cinematography highlights the distinction between Paris and Nice (1996: 151–2). In Paris, the light and dark shades are pronounced and rigid, while in Nice, incandescent natural light floods the shots, blurring the boundaries between bodies and environment. The opposition between Michel and Frankie dressed in white and Roland dressed in black in *Lola* is revisited in *La Baie des Anges*, although here it transcends gender. Until their phenomenal wins in Nice take them to Monte-Carlo, Jean is dressed in his dark suit; he and Caron, wearing black, travel to the casino at Enghien in a black Citroën DS, while Jackie is dressed in white. After their success, Jackie convinces Jean to purchase lighter clothes, including a grey jumper and white smoking jacket, and a white MG convertible. She buys three Pierre Cardin dresses, two with either white or black backgrounds, and contrasting shades in floral motifs, and one completely black. This shift from opposing to matching tones suggests a rapprochement between the two characters, although tensions continue. It is by contrasting and merging light and shade, then, that Demy projects his characters' apprehension of their environment and of the other. Demy is thus able to gesture towards a phenomenological conceptualisation of the encounter of the self with the world without having recourse to first-person camerawork and editing.

A degree of enchantment and fantasy can also be found in the film's evocation of ancient and modern myths. The narrative recreates the classic story of Orpheus's descent into the underworld, the entrance of which is represented by the mirrored porches and lobbies of the casinos. Just like Charon in the original Greek myth, Caron serves as the 'ferryman', responsible for transferring Jean to the intoxicating subaltern world of gambling. Jackie is already trapped in this thrilling inferno, and thus functions as a Eurydice surrogate whom Jean attempts to rescue. Hill suggests that *La Baie des Anges* transforms the Greek myth's conclusion by ending 'hopefully', although he questions the plausibility of such an ending (2008b: 393). Indeed, Demy claimed that Jackie and Jean save each other from their anxieties and moral decline (in Baby, 1963).

Yet, it is precisely the implausibility of the final images that aligns *La Baie des Anges* with the elegiac outcome of the original myth. Jackie's presage in the penultimate scene – 'bien sûr nous pouvons vivre ensemble et pourquoi pas être heureux quelque temps, mais pourquoi faire? Je ne m'arrêterais jamais de jouer et ça recommencera, alors à quoi bon?'[13] – hangs as a menace over their final reconciliation. Moreover, just as Orpheus defies the gods' orders and looks at Eurydice at the very moment they are about to leave Hades's realm, Jean, it seems, condemns his romance to certain annihilation by prematurely glancing at Jackie as she runs up to him from behind, still cast in the shadows of the palm trees. Consequently, the unpredictability of Jackie's sudden change of heart renders the idealism of the film's improbably romantic finale obvious, and therefore undermines it.

Modern myths are conveyed in the depictions of Jackie's lifestyle, appearance and gesturality. While his contemporaries Truffaut and Godard revere and mock Hollywood by accentuating the weaknesses of the 'gangster' character, as in Charlie Kohler (Charles Aznavour) in *Tirez sur le pianiste* and Michel Poiccard, Demy venerates and satirises not just the *femme fatale* figure, but also the female star that played her. Having sacrificed her husband and three-year-old son Michou to reside and gamble in the seductive surroundings of the Côte d'Azur, Jackie evokes the extraordinary existences of classic stars. Her bleached blond hair, white Chanel suits, boas, basques, feathered dressing gown and cigarette holder render her exceptional, recalling fabled Hollywood female icons such as Veronica Lake, Marilyn Monroe and Marlene Dietrich. Her gestures, which include chain-smoking, slowly passing her hands through her hair, caressing her calf, and her mincing walk (self) fetishise her body parts (lips, hair, legs, hips) for her diegetic and non-diegetic onlookers. Jean tells Jackie 'je croyais même que cette existence ... n'existait plus qu'au cinéma ... ou dans certains livres américains' ('I even thought that this existence ... only existed in films these days ... or in some American books'). And yet, Jackie also illustrates the inescapable precariousness of the female star whose extraordinary lifestyle is predicated upon the wonder her image generates among her admirers. Here, then, the film alludes to the illusion of agency produced through narcissism, which actually depends, for its power, on the validation of the self by the other. *La Baie des Anges* highlights this paradox by troubling the image of

13 'Of course, we will be able to live together and, why not, be happy for a while, but what for? I would never stop gambling and it will all start again. So what's the point?'

Jackie's extraordinary existence with her, at times, shabby appearance and crude, antipathic personality. Her hair is often unkempt, her clothes creased, her behaviour aggressive and her language vulgar.

Demy could be criticised for portraying Jackie in compliance with the cold, monstrousness of the *femme fatale*, who leads the impressionable young male astray from the course of righteousness. Her haggard face and blond hair at times render her visually grotesque. She defies bourgeois morality: not only is she a gambler, liar, drinker, chain-smoker and 'failed mother', she also steals money from Jean in Monte Carlo and flirts with older men, leading Jean to dismiss her as a 'whore' and someone who would not hesitate to walk the streets for a chip. She is often brutal, dismissing Jean's affections and telling him that she drags him around like a dog or a lucky horseshoe, thus abandoning nothing of herself to her lover. She acts in 'bad faith'; while she claims she is free, her existence is contingent upon the kindness of others, including her friend Marijo, to whom she is in debt.

As in many Nouvelle Vague films, *La Baie des Anges* centres on the aspirations for a hedonistic existence that were assumed to drive the post-War middle-class and urban youth population. Roulette functions as a symbol of the profligacy wrought by modernity. When Jean's father dismisses gambling, Jean replies that everyone derives pleasure from wherever they can. This comment, expressed by a bank clerk and son of a watch and clock repairer, illustrates a shift in perceptions among petit bourgeois, urban young white men, to whom leisure pursuits hitherto exclusive to the rich seemed accessible. Via Jean's gradual awakening to the allure of gambling, *La Baie des Anges* depicts how middle-class young men were seduced by the dream of rapid acquisition of wealth. Jean refutes Caron's snipe that he lacked daring after his first visit to Enghien and joyfully acknowledges that he has won six months' salary in less than an hour. Modernity and affluence are symbolised by cars, including the DS and MG convertible, and by locations, both geographically and in the shiny interiors of the casinos. The depictions of Jean and Jackie's life on the Côte d'Azur nod to the intemperance celebrated in the Nouvelle Vague's literary and filmic precursors: Françoise Sagan's novel *Bonjour Tristesse* and Roger Vadim's film *Et Dieu créa la femme* (1956). Yet, *La Baie des Anges* films the Côte d'Azur through a realist lens by portraying how the dreams of new arrivals can soon be destroyed. Tensions mount when

Jean and Jackie lose, and are forced to return to a more banal existence in Paris, the money for their train fare loaned by Jean's father.

La Baie des Anges is less about gambling than passion, chance and destiny. Agency is suspended once the chips are placed, the croupier announces 'no more bets' and the roulette wheel starts to turn. For a few seconds, the futures of the players are solely contingent upon where the ball lands. *La Baie des Anges* reveals that financial gain is not the true gambler's objective; Jackie affirms that she is driven by luck and the precariousness of her existence. The submission of her existence to chance, the surrender of herself to her passion, is how Jackie achieves fulfilment. She proudly proclaims that gambling has become her religion. Her addiction to chance leads her to relinquish care for her own wellbeing and that of others. She gleefully boasts to Jean that she has only eaten part of an ice cream in two days.

However, while she places her immediate future in the hands of chance, this is an act of will. Her passion for gambling might constitute a pseudo-religion for her, but it is one she wittingly selects. While she occasionally claims that she needs Jean to help her stop gambling, in the cold light of day, she declines such assistance until the unlikely ending. Although controlled by her addiction, for Demy, she represents the bravery of those who choose an unorthodox life path (in Mardone, 1963). Jackie acknowledges the ethical implications of her choices, and assumes responsibility for them, admitting that she feels that she has gambled her son away. And yet, awareness of her flaws does not prevent her from playing. In a key diatribe, she defends her lifestyle choices to Jean: 'je ne dois rien à personne. Puisque cette passion m'aide à vivre, pourquoi m'en priverais-je? Au nom de qui, de quoi, de quelle morale? Je suis libre ... Je n'ai pas besoin de ta pitié'.[14] Although she states that gambling keeps her alive, she acknowledges that this life path is the product of her own choices.

Jackie embodies the distinction, often raised in Demy's films, between externally imposed morals and personal ethics. Jackie withstands attempts by others to judge her life choices, while never hiding the truth of her emotions, desires and lifestyle, either from herself or Jean. While she incarnates a narrative of failed motherhood, her decision to relinquish the raising of her son reflects her authenticity,

14 'I don't owe anyone anything. Since this passion helps me to live, why should I deny myself it? In the name of who, of what, of which morality? I'm free ... I don't need your pity.'

since it demonstrates an awareness of her freedom to choose her existence and recognition of her incapacity to adequately perform maternal duties. In her apparent selfishness, she echoes Michel, but she takes responsibility for her actions. Jackie refuses to be co-opted within the value systems of the other, here implied and expressed through Jean.

By contrast, Jean is depicted as acting inauthentically. At times, his words claim to reject a traditional life path, but elsewhere, his comments and actions convey his conformity. After his first win at Enghien, he tells his father 'j'étais assez bête jusqu'à aujourd'hui pour vivre comme un petit garçon studieux et pensif' ('I was stupid enough to live here like a little boy, studious and thoughtful, until now'). Moreover, he later recounts to Jackie that he almost married once, but stopped everything because he could not face a conventional future, thus implying that his rebelliousness preceded his initiation into gambling and his relationship with Jackie. However, his choices are influenced by others: Caron and Jackie. His infatuation with Jackie drives him. He is almost willingly blinded to the inescapable truth of the imbalances in their relationship, opting to ignore Jackie's portension that she will eventually leave him because of her passion for gambling.

Unlike the almost blanket acclaim that followed the release of *Lola*, the critical reception of *La Baie des Anges* was mixed. Although some reviewers praised it for its realistic and original approach to gambling (Siclier, 1963; Sadoul, 1963), others argued that it revealed Demy's limitations as a filmmaker (Rochereau, 1963; Magnan, 1963). A particularly virulent critique by Claude Tarare used the film to illustrate what he viewed as a fundamental flaw of the *politique des auteurs* associated with the Nouvelle Vague directors: 'ils se veulent auteurs complets et uniques, ce qui est une ambition louable mais fréquemment démesurée. Beaucoup savent tourner, très peu savent écrire, mais ils refusent de le savoir' (1963).[15] Demy's most celebrated production, *Les Parapluies de Cherbourg*, suggested the contrary since it was acclaimed for both its mise-en-scène and dialogues. That Tarare is the pseudonym of Jacques-Laurent Bosch, a screenwriter, may indicate his agenda.

---

15 'They believe that they are complete and unique authors, which is a laudable ambition, but often an exaggeration. Many know how to shoot films, very few know how to write them, but they refuse to acknowledge it.'

Whether celebrated or dismissed, though, *La Baie des Anges* bears the hallmarks of its director in its focus on strong-minded women, weak-willed men and intense passion. Moreover, through the motif of roulette, it depicts how fantasy and reality coalesce. Furthermore, in the background of the shots and in the costumes, familiar iconography, already seen in *Lola*, re-surface, including basques, boas and sailors. Finally, *La Baie des Anges* is a narrative satellite of *Lola*, which Demy confirms in his first film's sequel, *Model Shop*.

Poetic reality: *Model Shop*

Shot in Los Angeles and made in English, *Model Shop* applies Demy's thematic and stylistic sensibilities to a Californian setting. Demy first visited the United States in April 1965 for the Oscars ceremony, where *Les Parapluies de Cherbourg* was nominated, and returned after he had made *Les Demoiselles de Rochefort* in October 1967. On this second visit, he was reunited with Michel Legrand who was writing the score for *The Thomas Crown Affair* (Norman Jewison, 1968) and Gerry Ayres, a young executive producer who Demy had encountered on his first trip. Ayres promised a contract with Columbia Pictures if Demy devised a project. Inspired by a visit to the hippy area of Haight-Ashbury in San Francisco, Demy wrote about twenty pages of *Model Shop* in eight days. Offered a budget of $1,000,000, he agreed to make it for $700,000 and spent two years in Los Angeles with Varda and their daughter Rosalie. Paradoxically, Demy forewent the opportunity to make an expensive musical, opting for a naturalistic movie. *Model Shop* was shot in the streets of the Venice quarter of Los Angeles and on Santa Monica Boulevard in less than thirty days.

Model Shop is the culmination of Demy's dual attraction for and scepticism of American culture. References to the United States abound in his earlier films. In *Lola*, beyond Frankie, the Americana iconography and jazz-based score, Roland recounts how he had been stateside at the age of five and dreams of returning, uttering the words 'Salt Lake City' as he gazes at his wall map of the world. In *La Baie des Anges*, Jackie evokes Hollywood female screen legends, as mentioned. Allusions to the United States also emerge strongly in *Les Parapluies de Cherbourg* and *Les Demoiselles de Rochefort*. We learn that Roland has just returned from the States in the former, and

American composer Andy Miller, played by MGM musical icon Gene Kelly, returns to France in the latter. The United States symbolise the birthplace of consumerism and the site of emancipation in Demy's cinema, pursued further in *Lady Oscar*. In all these films, though, the United States are conjured externally, via the fantasies of distant admirers. *Model Shop* constituted Demy's opportunity to depict American culture from within.

Demy was impressed by the freedom of expression in the press, on the radio and television that he witnessed in California (Langlois, 1969). He admired the emerging civil rights and anti-Vietnam War movements, and appreciated new art trends, including those emanating from Andy Warhol's *The Factory* (Langlois, 1970), diverse musical forms and the underground press. He praised the bold fusion of art with entertainment he encountered and was inspired by the energy and enthusiasm of his American friends. A paradox thus emerges. While he decried an American-inspired relegation of emotions, he celebrated the free spirit of many young Americans, which he saw as approximating his own attitude towards life.

Model Shop centres on a twenty-six-year-old, unemployed architecture graduate from Berkeley, George Matthews (Gary Lockwood),[16] who falls on hard times. His relationship with Gloria (Alexandra Hay) is failing and bailiffs threaten to confiscate his vintage MG convertible. When he asks his friend, a car park attendant, to lend him some cash, he encounters Lola (Anouk Aimée), the heroine of *Lola*, now living in Los Angeles. Entranced, George embarks on a twenty-four hour odyssey during which he follows Lola to the hills and the model shop where she works, a peep show in which paying male customers take photographs of scantily clad women. Meanwhile, George receives his call-up papers to fight in Vietnam. These two dejected souls chat about their past disappointments and future anxieties at Lola's apartment. The film ends when Lola returns to Paris, Gloria leaves George, his car is repossessed and he faces his imminent despatch to Vietnam.

Model Shop is overtly critical of American foreign policy with regards to Vietnam. This is explicitly depicted in the scene in the offices of the *Free Press*, a newspaper written by young, male journalists, that George visits. The young columnists talk openly about how they intend to escape or defy conscription. One states that he is exempt

---

16 Demy had originally wanted Harrison Ford, but the producers refused.

because he must care for his mother, while another recounts how he was declared psychologically 'off type' and a third confesses that he is awaiting his papers, but refuses to fight. Although the spatial, temporal and cultural contexts are unmistakably American, this critical stance with regards to war mirrors a recurrent theme in French Nouvelle Vague cinema, in which the conflicts of French decolonisation are questioned (*Ascenseur pour l'échafaud* (Louis Malle, 1958), *Cléo de 5 à 7* (Varda), *Muriel ou le temps d'un retour* (Alain Resnais, 1963), *Le Petit Soldat* (Jean-Luc Godard 1963) and Demy's own *Les Parapluies de Cherbourg*). Moreover, the journalists' stories and George's experiences bear an autobiographical connection to Demy's life as a young adult in France. Called up to serve in a parachute regiment in Vannes, Brittany as part of his military service, Demy simulated depression and managed to avoid serving in Algeria.[17] A Nouvelle Vague stance is thus transposed into this American production to give an alternative and critical view of the United States.

Model Shop counters the dominant image of a successful, ambitious modern America. George and his peers are not interested in achieving the American dream, but are concerned with the State's insidious control. They read newspapers that openly defy censorship and legislation. In the diner scene, George glances at the lead article calling for the decriminalisation of marijuana and indifferently peruses sex advertisements. American critics received the film's politics with scepticism, dismissing *Model Shop* as too personal and *auteuriste* (Langlois, 1969).

A French cinematographic legacy is also manifest in the film's form, style and aesthetics. The reflexivity of the Nouvelle Vague is in evidence when George speaks to his father on the telephone: he gazes at a poster of Jean-Paul Belmondo as Michel Poiccard in *A bout de souffle*. Reminders of the film as text emerge when George peruses Lola's photograph album in her apartment. The images are all stills from *Lola*. To the right and top of the shot can be found confirmation that the images are publicity shots and stills from the shoot of the earlier film, and that *Model Shop* is nothing more than a construct. The right-hand page shows an image of Lola and Roland walking around the Passage Pommeraye during their last meeting; to the top, we see a copy of *Le Monde* magazine with an image of Catherine

---

17 *Il était une fois* les Parapluies de Cherbourg (Marie Genin and Serge July, 2008).

Deneuve on the cover, her name in yellow capitals – the actress who achieved international stardom because Demy had cast her in *Les Parapluies de Cherbourg*.

Just as the Nouvelle Vague filmmakers had famously taken their hand-held equipment into the streets and rendered a gritty image of the French capital, Demy filmed what he saw as an authentic vision of Los Angeles. Demy enjoyed almost total control as director, screen-writer and producer. The images of Los Angeles are filtered through a soft haze that transforms the streetscape into a pastelised decor. The proximity of the ocean is conveyed by this slightly grainy aesthetic, *Model Shop* thus capturing the physical reality of Los Angeles. The city's immense sprawl across the lower slopes and flat lands that connect the Santa Monica and San Gabriel mountains to the Pacific mean that the ocean's presence can be felt many miles from its shore. In focusing his action within a small part of the city, Demy also portrays the paradox of Los Angeles as an enormous metrop-olis, but which is nonetheless constrained by its sea and mountain borders. Its peculiar allure is portrayed and enhanced by the wide lens and the eye-level angle of the camera, which shows the predomi-nance of signage within the streetscape. Almost every exterior shot along Sunset and Santa Monica Boulevards is crammed with signs adorning shop frontages or billboards advertising products.

Consonant with Demy's cinema, shot composition, angle, distance and sound are deployed to place the characters firmly in-situation. They serve to underline the connection between their bodies and their environment, their mood and their habitat, the self and the surrounding world. George and Gloria's situation is defined by their small and modest dwelling; an actual house that Demy insisted on leaving as he had found it (Langlois, 1969), it is constructed from rough wood, its cramped interior packed with objects and its confine-ment underlined by the proximity of the oil drills seen through the windows. Repetitive and continuous ambient sounds, such as the incessant drone of the drills and planes taking off from nearby LAX airport, interrupt and muffle the verbal exchanges between the characters. Engines, horns, sirens, as well as news announcements and music airing on the radio accompany George as he wanders and drives around the streets. However, whereas in *Lola* the blurring of the boundaries between body and world served to underline Lola's poignant optimism, the ordinary and tawdry streets and rooms in

Model Shop induce and mirror the characters' frustrations, anxieties and melancholy. Rather than adopting stances through which they turn away from their environment, they appear resigned to personal and social injustices.

Beyond its politics and style, the narrative of *Model Shop* explicitly draws on and develops *Lola* and *La Baie des Anges*. *Model Shop* recounts the next chapters in the lives of Lola, Frankie, Michel and Jackie. The pro-filmic narrative is contained within Lola's account of her life in the United States. She tells George how she, Michel and Yvon had moved to New York from Paris three years previously and that she discovered that Michel had met another woman, Jackie Demaistre, now living in Las Vegas. Consequently, Jackie's escape from the space that defines her – the casino – was transitory, even if she changes a Provençal metropolis for a Nevadan city. Michel never loved Jackie, Lola says, and unlike his mentor, was more interested in money than gambling. She adds that Michel lost all their money, thereby forcing her to work and send Yvon back to Paris. She describes how they fought constantly in their hotel room on 44th Street and consequently parted, which she qualifies as the 'greatest disappointment' of her life. Lola also tells George that she had attempted to contact Frankie, but he had been killed in Vietnam, a fate that, as George admits, possibly awaits him. Lola's aim is to return to France and be reunited with her son. By contrast to her lightness in Nantes, Lola in Los Angeles is dejected and taciturn. She rarely smiles and bears a distant sadness in her eyes, accentuated by the thick black mascara that covers her upper lashes, making her eyes appear heavy and downturned. Where in *Lola* she remains upbeat, in *Model Shop* she is cynical: 'Michel took everything. I am empty. I have no strength left. I don't want to love anyone, ever again'.[18]

Lola's despondency echoes George's disenchantment. He refuses to ask his ex-boss to re-employ him, asserting to Gloria 'I didn't waste seven years in college to end up designing gas pipes that won't ever be seen'. George tells Lola that his future is all mapped out; he knows he is going to Vietnam, if he does not desert, and that his return is not guaranteed. His perceived fate impacts on his view of life. Although he asks rhetorically 'what's more beautiful than life?' and responds

18 The relationship between Demy and Aimée was fraught. Aimée's arrival was delayed because of the events of May 1968 and she almost withdrew from the project (Berthomé, 1996: 220–1).

romantically 'maybe the reflections of life in a book, a quartet, film, painting, sculpture', he gloomily adds 'I decided to become an architect because I wanted to build, construct, but what a hideous job when you consider that man's only driving passion is to destroy, it's pointless'.

Yet, despite such despair, *Model Shop* conveys moderate hope. The encounter between George and Lola is portrayed as cathartic, showing how the self acquires strength to face up to situations through her/his relations with the other. Although Lola informs George that she spent six months in her hotel room crying after Michel had left, living like a dead person, she asserts 'I was very unhappy and yet I never thought of killing myself'. In a key line, she adds, 'I've spent my whole life struggling, hoping, and life has tried to destroy those hopes, but it doesn't matter, I never gave up'. The tragedy of her situation notwithstanding, Lola retains her resolve to fight on. Her situation is economically arduous; she offers her body for erotic gratification to live and pay for her return ticket to France. However, George reveals the contradiction between Lola's words and her actions, accusing her of allowing her past disappointments to have mastery over her present and future; because of her romantic breakdown with Michel, she refuses to love again. Initially, Lola counters George's claim, rejects his pleas to spend the night with her and tells him that she does not love him. And yet, in a fleeting echo of Jackie running to Jean at the end of *La Baie des Anges*, she calls him back just as he is about to leave and they sleep together.

Lola's assertion that she is able to retain some hope inspires George. Her legacy is depicted in the final sequence. George returns home to discover that Gloria is leaving him and learns that Lola has departed for France. Demy exploits visual planes and shot composition to place George in-situation. He films George from within his wooden house and intercuts close-ups of his face with longer shots of his empty bedroom and, through the windows, Gloria's departure in her male friend's Porsche Carrera convertible, plus the bailiffs' repossession of his MG. As the men hook his car up to their truck and tow it away, George tells Lola's flatmate Barbara (Carole Cole) on the telephone that Lola had made him 'very happy'. He then adds insistently 'I just wanted to tell her that I loved her. I just wanted her to know that I was going to try and begin again'. At the very moment he is being abandoned to his fate of combative service in Vietnam,

George portrays his desire not to be a prisoner of his situation. He may be forced to face a harsh and terrifying future, but he can adapt his attitude, signified by his final words 'a person can always try'. By situating this emphasis on agency within the contexts of the characters' existence and the realms of narrative plausibility, *Model Shop* accentuates its affective impact.

According to Lazen, *Lola* 'casts doubt' on its fairytale 'sense of plenitude at the end' by portraying Roland's 'dejected departure' (2004: 195). In fact, the happy ending is almost entirely absent from Demy's cinema, as will be seen, and this is manifest in *La Baie des Anges* through the suggestions that Jackie's relationship with Jean is doomed, despite the fact that the pair walk off together. *Model Shop* is somewhat nuanced since, although alone, Lola and George adapt their attitudes so that their situation does not have complete mastery over them, but none of the films is joyful. As the next chapter will reveal, the melancholy conclusion of Demy's narratives is accentuated in *Les Parapluies de Cherbourg* and *Une chambre en ville*, in particular, and also to a degree in *Les Demoiselles de Rochefort*.

References

Baby, Yvonne (1963) '"Un film de moraliste" nous dit Jacques Demy', *Le Monde*, 7 March.

Barnes, Hazel E. transl. (2000) *Being and Nothingness: an Essay on Phenomenological Ontology by Jean-Paul Sartre*, London and New York, Routledge.

Barthes, Roland (1977) *Fragments d'un discours amoureux*, Paris, Seuil, transl. Richard Howard, *A Lover's Discourse: Fragments*, London, Vintage, 2002.

Berthomé, Jean-Pierre (1996) *Jacques Demy et les racines du rêve*, 2nd Edition, Nantes, L'Atalante.

Daney, Serge, Narboni, Jean and Toubiana, Serge (1982) 'Le Retour au pays des rêves: Entretien avec Jacques Demy', *Cahiers du Cinéma*, 341, November: 6–13, 56–66.

Greene, Naomi (2007) *The French New Wave: a New Look*, London and New York, Wallflower Press.

Hill, Rodney (2008a) 'The New Wave Meets the Tradition of Quality: Jacques Demy's *The Umbrellas of Cherbourg*', *Cinema Journal*, 48 (1): 27–50.

—— (2008b) 'Demy-Monde: the New-Wave Films of Jacques Demy', *Quarterly Review of Film and Video*, 25 (5): 382–94.

Howard, Richard transl. (2002) *A Lover's Discourse: Fragments*, London, Vintage.

Lalanne, Jean-Marc (1997) 'Noirceur et féerie de Jacques Demy', *Cahiers du Cinéma*, 511, March: 60–3.

Langlois, Gérard (1969) 'Entretien avec Jacques Demy', *Les Lettres françaises*, 7 May.

—— (1970) 'Jacques Demy, *Peau d'âne*: La féerie existe-t-elle?', *Les Lettres françaises*, 23 December.

Lazen, Matthew (2004) '"En perme à Nantes": Jacques Demy and New Wave Place', *Studies in French Cinema*, 4 (3): 187–96.

Lerouge, Stéphane (2013) 'Michel Legrand, la moitié Demy', *Le Monde enchanté de Jacques Demy*, Paris, Skira-Flammarion, La Cinémathèque Française and Ciné-Tamaris: 80–2

Magnan, Henri (1963) '*La Baie des Anges*', *Libération*, 9 March.

Mairet, Philippe transl. (1948) *Existentialism is a Humanism*, London, Methuen.

Mardone, M. (1963) 'Interview with Jacques Demy about *La Baie des Anges*', *Les Lettres françaises*, 28 February.

Merleau-Ponty, Maurice (1945) *La Phénoménologie de la perception* (Paris: Gallimard, 1945), transl. Colin Smith, London and New York, Routledge, 2002.

Neupert, Richard (2002) *A History of the French New Wave Cinema*, Madison, University of Wisconsin Press, 2nd Edition.

Pamerleau, William C. (2009) *Existentialist Cinema*, Basingstoke, Palgrave Macmillan.

Rochereau, Jean (1963) '*La Baie des Anges*', *La Croix*, 15 March

Sadoul, Georges (1963) '*La Baie des Anges*', *Les Lettres françaises*, 17 March.

Sartre, Jean-Paul (1943) *L'Être et le néant* (Paris, Gallimard), transl. Hazel E. Barnes, *Being and Nothingness: an Essay on Phenomenological Ontology by Jean-Paul Sartre*, London and New York, Routledge, 2000.

—— (1946) *L'Existentialisme est un humanisme* (Paris, Nagel), transl. Philippe Mairet, *Existentialism is a Humanism*, London, Methuen, 1948.

Siclier, Jacques (1963) '*La Baie des Anges*', *Télérama*, 17 March.

Smith, Colin transl. (2002) *Phenomonology of Perception*, London and New York, Routledge.

Taboulay, Camille (1996) *Le Cinéma enchanté de Jacques Demy*, Paris, Cahiers du Cinéma.

Tarare, Claude (1963) 'Funeste passion: Une bicyclette à roues octogonales', *L'Express*, 28 February.

Witt, Michael and Temple, Michael (2004) 'A New World', in Michael Witt and Michael Temple (eds), *The French Cinema Book*, London, British Film Institute: 183–93.

2

Melodic reconfigurations: Demy's musicals

The qualification of Demy's films as a 'cinéma en-chanté' receives its formal justification in his 'musicals', the genre for which he is most famous. Demy reconfigures the classical musical film in order to transmit his creativity, defy audience expectations and convey, either implicitly or explicitly, his concerns and preoccupations, mainly around subjectivity and affect. *Les Parapluies de Cherbourg* and *Une chambre en ville* avoid set-piece numbers, constituting a continuous recitative, while in *Les Demoiselles de Rochefort*, songs advance the narrative flow and characters address the audience directly.[1] Song and sung dialogues are deployed to express the encounter between the self and the world, as Raphaël Lefèvre rightly remarks (2013: 106). The 'gleeful outcome' or 'happy end', ubiquitous in dominant Hollywood musicals, is elided or subverted, through either the portrayal of dystopian situations or the deployment of parodic humour.

Musical melancholia: *Les Parapluies de Cherbourg*

Les Parapluies de Cherbourg comprises many of the defining features of Nouvelle Vague filmmaking (Hill, 2008a: 27). Its sung dialogues mark it as one of the most unique films of the 1960s and, alongside its palette of variegated colours, convey Demy's inventive approach to musical film. It disturbs from the outset. The slow strains of the

---

1 Although also musical, *Peau d'âne* and *Parking* are adaptations of fairytale and myth, and are discussed in chapter 3. Similarly, while *Trois places pour le 26* is a musical, its qualities as an affirmation of Demy's legacy render it suitable for study in chapter 5.

'Thème des amants', which accompanies the opening credits, shift abruptly to fast paced jazz rhythms. A customer at the Garage du Port Aubin sings 'c'est terminé?' ('is it finished?'), to which mechanic Guy Foucher (Nino Castelnuovo) intones 'oui, le moteur cliquette encore un peu à froid, mais c'est normal' ('yes, the engine rattles a little when cold, but that's normal'). The musical mode of delivery is manifestly not normal, however. The juxtaposition between extraordinary form and ordinary dialogues is the premise of an entire film. Moreover, the opening question is self-parodic, inscribing within the film the reluctant spectator's discomfort at its unconventional form, a technique repeated moments later as another mechanic declares 'je n'aime pas l'opéra, le ciné c'est mieux' adding 'tous ces gens qui chantent … ça me fait mal' ('I don't like opera, I prefer cinema. All those people who sing … it's painful').

For Laurent Jullier, the sung dialogues elicit the *Verfremdungseffekt* (2007: 40); that is, they surprise the audience by making them aware, on a conscious level, of the constructedness of the story and characters. In his detailed study of the formally similar *Une chambre en ville*, Lefèvre notes that both films assume a 'distanced effusion'; the songs implicate the spectator emotionally while their stylisation prevents total identification with the characters (2013: 104). For Herzog, the poignancy of the narrative mitigates the alienating effects of the film's peculiar form (2010: 120). The extreme fluidity of the narrative structure aids the spectator's potential involvement in the film. Each scene is seamlessly attached to the one that follows it via instrumental bridges, repeated colours in costumes or decors, portended dialogues and objects.

Les Parapluies de Cherbourg portrays the doomed romance between seventeen-year-old Geneviève Emery (Catherine Deneuve) and twenty-year-old Guy Foucher. It is structured into three sections: 'le départ', 'l'absence' and 'le retour' ('the departure', 'the absence' and 'the return'). 'Le départ' establishes the intensity of their love and their disconsolation when Guy receives his call-up papers to fight in the Algerian War of Independence. Geneviève's mother, Madame Emery (Anne Vernon) learns that she is in debt and attempts to sell her pearl necklace to jeweller M. Dubourg (Harald Wolff). Here, she and Geneviève chance upon the very same Roland Cassard (Marc Michel) from *Lola* who, having made his fortune in Paris and London, offers to purchase Emery's pearl necklace and falls for Geneviève. 'L'absence' depicts Geneviève's revelation that she is pregnant, her distress at Guy's silence and her surrender to Roland's advances. 'Le retour' follows Guy's troubled reintegration, dejected by war, abandoned by Geneviève and bereft at his aunt Elise's (Mireille Perrey) death. He purchases a service station with his inheritance and proposes to Elise's nurse, Madeleine (Ellen Farmer). Geneviève bumps into Guy at his garage. The former lovers chat briefly before saying their farewells, their passion having seemingly waned, stifled by the pressures of bourgeois social morality and the class differences that separate them. Despite its musical form and bright colours, then, *Les Parapluies de Cherbourg* is unequivocally disenchanting.

Les Parapluies de Cherbourg is intrinsically linked to Demy's earlier films through its shared themes and motifs. Love, separation, fidelity, teenage pregnancy, single-motherhood, fate, chance encounters, modernity, social class and consumerism all feature. The story unfolds in a port town – Cherbourg – where sailors wander the streets and hang out in cafes. To the sailor, Demy adds the umbrella, recycled from *Singin' in the Rain* (Stanley Donen and Gene Kelly, 1952). Mobile camerawork abounds in the frequent panoramic, crane and tracking shots, exemplified immediately in the opening aerial image of sailors and single mothers crossing the wet portside cobbles. *Les Parapluies de Cherbourg* is partly autobiographical: Guy shares the same occupation as Demy's father; like Roland, Demy adopted his wife's daughter, although unlike Guy, he escaped being despatched to Algeria. Narrative derivations link *Les Parapluies de Cherbourg* to *Lola*, even if Demy claimed that they were unintended (in Berthomé, 1996: 182). Cherbourg is the town to which Cécile escapes and Desnoyer follows, in which her biological father lives and from which Frankie returns to the United States and Roland hopes to travel to Johannesburg. Such textual reciprocity is immediately evident; the customer arriving in his Mercedes at the Garage du Port-Aubin in the opening sequence is Roland. Later, Geneviève tells Guy that she used her friend Cécile as an alibi to meet him; Emery and Geneviève's encounter with Roland recalls Desnoyer and Cécile's meeting with Roland in the bookshop; and their Twelfth Night dinner evokes the meal at Desnoyer's apartment with Roland and Cécile. Such close associations are visually confirmed when Roland describes Lola to Emery, which elicits a tracking shot of an empty Passage Pommeraye.

Les Parapluies de Cherbourg is the product of a team of determined entrepreneurs, artists and technicians. Producer Mag Bodard raised the finances, and music editor Francis Lemarque paid the musicians. The musical dialogues and extraordinary decors are the fruits of two pivotal creative collaborations, with Legrand and Evein respectively. Legrand would pen the music for all bar four of Demy's films: *Model Shop*, *The Pied Piper*, *Une chambre en ville* and *La Naissance du jour*. He and Demy were complicit in their objectives to encourage large audiences to appreciate their taste for lyrical and musical cinema (Ancelin, 1964). Harmonising the score, editing and shots required eight months of painstaking close collaboration. While, according to Demy, notes and syllables guided him in writing the screenplay (in Bellour, 1964), for Legrand, close-ups, tracking shots and a detailed scene-by-scene breakdown influenced the structure of the score (in Ancelin, 1964). A jazz-inspired composition was selected because its harmonies approximate verbal intonation. Jazz and *variété* singers provided the voices, which were superimposed onto the instrumental soundtrack. Actors attended the recordings to facilitate the conso-nance between sung dialogue and character, and Demy and Legrand spent a month working with the cast to synchronise sound and mime. The opening credits pay homage to their creative reciprocity, placing the names of both men in the same shot, while the film's awards recognise the mutual value of their respective contributions.[2]

For Marshall and Lindeperg, the 'musical form' of *Les Parapluies de Cherbourg* emphasises the 'question of time, this over and above the film's self-conscious temporal markers' (2000: 101). They reveal how the musical dialogues invoke Bergson's concept of duration. For Bergson, 'real' or 'pure' duration pertains to time as it unfolds within the psyche. Composed of the flow of our 'affective states', duration is – as Herzog summarises – 'indivisible, multiple and conditional' (2010: 124). Within 'immediate consciousness', time is not config-ured as juxtaposed succession, but our affective states overflow from one to the other. Aptly, Bergson uses melody as a figure of duration

---

2 In addition to the Prix Louis Delluc in 1963, the *Palme d'Or* and Technical Grand Prize at Cannes in 1964, and the award for best film by the French Syndicate of Cinema Critics, *Les Parapluies de Cherbourg* received nominations for the Academy Award for Best Foreign Language Film in 1965 and four Academy Awards in 1966, three for music and score and one for writing and screenplay. It was also nominated for a Golden Globe in the Best Foreign Language Film category as well as a Grammy for its score in 1966.

(1908: 91). Melody is constituted of notes that flow from those that precede, coincide with and succeed them. As such, melody figures duration as a heterogeneous multiplicity of nows that pass. Similarly, according to Marhsall and Lindeperg, because it constitutes one piece of continuous music, *Les Parapluies de Cherbourg* is able to 'juxtapose past and present, recall the past in the present, anticipate the future, accompany the protagonists' hopes, contrastively undermine their reality' (2000: 103).

The score conveys moods and emotions, and reflects shifts in relations. Guy and Geneviève's romantic bond is expressed through long notes within a medium range with slight pitch deviations. Discord between Emery and Geneviève is transmitted via rapidly ascending scales of pizzicato chords and occasional held notes. At times, the instrumentals soar, as in the 'Thème des amants' when Guy leaves for Algeria. Music situates the characters. A fast jazz arrangement introduces Guy, while clarinets, flutes and violins create a swooning composition to accompany Geneviève. Distinctions in style emphasise differences in status. Emery is attached to Geneviève via an instrumental bridge, the air symphonically richer and deeper, situating both within an established *petite bourgeoisie* while Guy's jazz tones align him with a dynamic and aspirational young generation. Emery's compositions vary in range and rhythm, presenting her as unpredictable, while Roland's theme, taken from *Lola*, is a medium-pitched string, brass and woodwind instrumental, with minimal orchestration and melodic variation that underlines his status as an outsider. The other marginalised character is Madelcine, whose low partition comprises extended notes, transmitting her isolation as Guy's distant admirer.

For Herzog, the repetition of Roland's theme links the Roland of *Les Parapluies de Cherbourg* to the Roland of *Lola*, but it also serves as one device among many that illustrates how recollections 'are always marred by their profound difference' (2010: 128). The immediately apparent associations are questioned by their implausibility. In *Lola*, we are told that Roland and Lola reunite after a separation of ten to fifteen years since the end of the War. Roland recalls that Lola used to wear her hair in plaits, to which she replies that she must have been ten years old. As she recounts that she met Michel on her fourteenth birthday and that seven years separate their reconciliation, this would take us to Spring/summer 1955/56. However, Lola remembers that, after their first meeting, Michel did not return for a long time and, when he did, Yvon was conceived on the Pentecost. By beginning in November 1957, *Les Parapluies de Cherbourg* leaves but a few months for Roland to tour the world and make his fortune. Such disparities provide illustrations of how the film invokes the falsity of the 'recollection image' (Deleuze, 1985: 75). As Herzog observes, 'the past is drawn into an active engagement with the demands of the present, the conditions that cause us both to recall and to falsify' (2010: 129). The flashback of an empty Passage Pommeraye illustrates this as it contrasts with the shots of a busy shopping arcade in *Lola*. Roland claims that he has recovered emotionally, hence the absence of people and, particularly, Lola, in the mall, but his willed rehabilitation is fantasy. He affirms that his encounter with Geneviève has given his life the meaning it lacked, thus repeating a sentiment he had expressed to Lola. As in *Lola*, his love is not reciprocated. So, despite evolutions in appearance, status and standing, Roland fails to transcend his earlier existence as an unrequited lover.

The colourful decors also function to situate the characters and convey their emotions. Evein's contribution to Demy's cinema is as important as Legrand's. He created the decors for all of Demy's films bar *Model Shop, Peau d'âne, The Pied Piper* and *Parking*. Demy and Evein were inspired by the art of Henri Matisse. The most striking visual feature of *Les Parapluies de Cherbourg* is the wallpapers with their complex motifs, which extend into or contrast with Jacqueline Moreau's costumes. As Stephen Peacock notes, the 'intensity, range, and placement of colours on display shift the meaning of any given scenario' (2010: 95). Sensations – concordant or discordant – are elicited and projected through the 'contiguity or separation' of the palette, music and settings from the dramaturgy of each scene (2010: 95). Affect is extended into, reflected by and contrasted with the colours. Muted hues complement the tragedy of the situation depicted, as in Guy's departure and the ending in which the monochromatic scheme confirms the gloomy dilution of the couple's passion. Bright tones are contrasted with pastel shades to project Geneviève's initial resistance to and eventual cooption within Emery's plans to marry her off to Roland. It is in the colours and music, then, that emotions and affect are expressed and transmitted.

Given that the film is contained within an enclosed townspace and that most of the scenes unfold in a delimited set of interiors, *Les*

Parapluies de Cherbourg gestures towards a phenomenological conceptualisation of subjectivity. As outlined in the introduction, according to phenomenology, identity is constructed through the encounter between the self and the outside world. The world appears as I apprehend it. It surges up within my consciousness in the form of objects that figure on my perceptive horizons. My consciousness is intentional; it apprehends the environment as inviting and welcoming or as hostile and alienating, and I adapt my response accordingly. In *Les Parapluies de Cherbourg*, as argued, music and colour demarcate certain spaces as pertaining to specific characters and they also convey how other characters apprehend those spaces, the people that inhabit them and the values and judgements that circulate within them. In this, then, they function as the outward extension of embodied emotions. The hiatus between the melodic mode of delivery and brightly colourful decors and the narrative of doomed love and a pregnant teenager left behind as her lover fights in Algeria serves to emphasise the sense of entrapment and powerlessness through paradox.

By contrast to Lola, the external world traps Geneviève. Her consciousness apprehends it as inhospitable, unsympathetic and alienating, figured aurally in the increasingly discordant and melancholy melodies, and visually in the clashes between the shades of her costume and those of the wallpapers that accompany her arguments with Emery. She is unable to adopt constructive attitudes that allow her to flee her environment or circumvent its oppressive control over her. She is forced into a compromise marriage partly because she is denied legal and social assistance as a soon-to-be single mother in late 1950s provincial France[3] and she lacks the obstinacy necessary to affirm mastery over her existence. Unlike Lola, she loses faith, succumbs to external pressures and morals and accepts her status as Roland's trophy wife. Her union is presaged from early on. When Geneviève first meets Roland, his theme plays in the background, signalling her entrance, as an object, into his realm of consciousness. In fact, Geneviève's fate is foreshadowed in the preceding scene in which Emery agrees to sell her necklace. As mother admires her necklace in the mirror, daughter moves into shot via a ricochet of reflections across wall and wardrobe mirrors, symbolically mapping jewels onto Geneviève. At Dubourg's, Emery confirms Geneviève's

---

3 Single mothers were not granted the right to a 'livret de famille' or family register until 1960 (Jullier, 2007: 72).

commodification; as she bids goodbye to Roland, she rearranges Geneviève's collar as if to guarantee the wealthy entrepreneur's interest in her additional merchandise.

And yet, if *Les Parapluies de Cherbourg* portrays Geneviève's material capitulation, it also highlights her resistance to Roland and her mother, and thus conveys the injustice of her situation. This is first implied in the Epiphany dinner scene. A cruel irony ensues as Geneviève finds a lucky charm in her slice of King's Cake and, according to the custom, must nominate a king. The subsequent exchange is filmed via four face-on shots: of Geneviève declaring 'je n'ai pas le choix, vous êtes mon roi' ('I don't have a choice, you are my king') to Roland; of Roland handing her the crown; of Geneviève reluctantly wearing it, encouraged by Emery, and then of Roland again who tells her that she reminds him of the painting of the *Virgin and Child* that he saw in Antwerp (probably Jean Fouquet's *Le Nu sacré – la vierge à l'enfant* (c. 1450)). Here, then, the film reproduces the *face à face* encounter through which, according to Levinas, the alterity of the other is signified. For Levinas, the other is always infinitely distinct from the self because their reaction can never be predicted or fully known (1971: 217). Their opposition to the self is confirmed in the figure of the face, which stands for the absolute difference and separateness of the other (1971: 215). Rather than an object of my perception, as Libby Saxton summarises, the face is able to express, convey and signify meanings that I cannot know when I encounter it (2010: 99). The face therefore signifies the alterity or difference of the other precisely because it cannot be fully represented through its material form, it cannot fully be given to vision. When the face of the other is but its representation or image, according to Levinas, it is stripped of any expression of its alterity and transcendence (1984: 108). We recall from chapter 1 that transcendence, in the existentialist sense, is the human ability to negotiate the facts of their existence (être-pour-soi). In the painting, the crowned Virgin is silenced, her eyes turned downwards, tacitly accepting of her subjection to the masterful gaze of her patriarchal onlooker – accepting, that is, of her 'divinely ordained' immanence (être-en-soi). By contrast, Demy has Geneviève confront her observer – Roland/us – with her melancholy look, and express her defiance of his/our gaze. Although we see Geneviève through the eyes of Roland, we also witness and hear her protestations that she cannot choose her own destiny. As Sarah Cooper argues, language allows the 'totalising gestures' of sight and touch to be transcended

(2007: 69). Language in *Les Parapluies de Cherbourg* is visual as much as verbal, seen as much as it is heard. Colour visually confirms Geneviève's affective resistance to Roland and Emery at precisely the point when she is forced to verbally declare her surrender. Her predicament as undesiring of, but dependent upon Roland, already suggested in her resigned gesturality, language and intonation, is affirmed in the tonal dissonance between her deep pink dress and the pastel pink and black stripes of the wallpaper, Roland's black suit and Emery's black dress and pastel pink shawl.

For Levinas, the face of the other bears an ethical responsibility for the self. It invites my vision, but prohibits the reduction of the other to the status of pure object of my vision. Levinas bases his philosophy of alterity figured in the face in the commandment 'thou shalt not kill'. The consequences of not assuming this ethical responsibility are dramatically suggested through Geneviève, whose look back at the camera and vocalisation of her lack of choice extends, through Roland, to the audience. *Les Parapluies de Cherbourg* does not suggest that Roland is responsible for Geneviève's misery, but holds the imagined audience – French society more broadly – to account, for failing to modernise in terms of the position and status of women while embracing other aspects of modernity (see Jullier, 2007: 71). *Les Parapluies de Cherbourg* dramatises the situation of the single pregnant young woman in late 1950s France, who needs that which she does not desire. It portrays her emotional resistance to a world that compels her union with an unwanted partner because of her situation, and which seeks to deny her the freedom to determine her own existence, while, at the same time, reminding us that she is dependent upon that union in order for her child to be officially recognised, and, possibly, to avoid destitution. This is illustrated later through Geneviève when she worries that Roland will rebuff her once he realises that she is pregnant. Consequently, the Epiphany dinner scene, and the other face-on shots, transmit Geneviève's struggle, an effect emphasised in the two further direct looks to camera: when she tries on the bridal gown and then, via a direct cut to the church, when she is praying at the altar during her wedding.

The graphic representations of the trauma caused to Geneviève by Guy's absence, the fact that life continues without him and the waning of her passion underline the sense of injustice transmitted by the film. Guy's perceived silence overwhelms Geneviève, its emotional impact revealed when she faints after her mother cruelly claims that he has forgotten her. For Barthes, because of its apparent banality, emotional implosion is more abject than graphic depictions of sex (1977: 210). *Les Parapluies de Cherbourg* confronts its audience with this form of abjection. On carnival day, the camera tracks Geneviève in medium close-up as she pushes against the shop window, juxtaposing her with the happy revellers marauding in the street (furnishing a further reference to *Les Enfants du paradis*). Increasingly distraught, she implores 'pourquoi Guy s'éloigne-t-il de moi?' and 'moi qui serais morte pour lui, pourquoi ne suis-je pas morte?' ('why is Guy drifting away from me?' 'I who would have died for him. Why am I not dead?'). When she reaches the door, she turns her back to us. By having her face away from Emery and the audience, Demy underlines the unseemliness of displays of affective breakdown. Rather than attenuate the drama, her shaking shoulders accentuate the intensity of her emotional disarray.

However, *Les Parapluies de Cherbourg* also suggests that Geneviève is complicit in her situation because, at precisely the moments when she should assert her agency, she acquiesces. The 'Thème des amants' reaches a sharp crescendo as we shift from Geneviève's breakdown in the shop to the next scene, one month later, in which she receives Roland's ring. The score, which bridges the two temporal moments, suddenly softens and, when metal comes into contact with skin, the bass tones of Roland's theme commence. Geneviève's lack of resolve to await her true love is thus confirmed. She has ultimately failed in reaffirming her alterity, in acting from her own free will. As for Guy, he settles for a marriage to Madeleine, an act that lacks authenticity. Although he tries to convince Madeleine of the truth of his feelings for her, when she asks if Guy still thinks of Geneviève, he responds 'je ne veux plus penser à Geneviève' ('I don't want to think about Geneviève anymore') thus framing his recovery, not as acquired, but desired.

The ending confirms the consequences of not standing up to external morality and asserting free will. Ambiguity is strongly suggested. Although Guy embraces Madeleine, he remains silent when she declares her love for him. Moreover, when Geneviève enters the garage, Guy reaches for a cigarette and smokes nervously. While he declines the invitation to meet his daughter and advises Geneviève that she can leave, he seems resigned, his words unconvincing. Yet, as she drives off, Guy runs smiling to hold Madeleine, while his son

François (Hervé Legrand) plays in the snow. Such apparent familial harmony implies that Guy is happier than Geneviève, who wears the accessories (fur coat, sophisticated hairstyle) of the trophy wife status that incarcerates her. For both partners, though, a passionate encounter has been superseded by two compromise marriages. The two lovers' lack of courage to overcome the class differences and provincial morality that opposed them has cost them dearly, an outcome portended at the end of the first section, before Guy departs for Algeria. As they return to Elise's apartment, a backward tracking camera shows Guy and Geneviève as immobile, yet carried along by the seemingly moving pavement.[4] They are transported towards certain annihilation, figured in the right-to-left orientation of the moving ground. The tragedy of such a conclusion is emphasised by the score. The 'Thème des amants' builds to a euphoric crescendo, hummed by a choir. Unlike in a Hollywood musical in which it would signify the reunification of the original couple, the epic final partition confirms the sad loss of a passionate love.[5]

In addition to its critique of France's inability to extend the freedoms achieved in modernity to young women, *Les Parapluies de Cherbourg* also challenges the increasingly consumerist culture that was taking over provincial France at the time of its production. The car symbolises the surreptitious reach of consumer culture into the provinces. For Kristin Ross, while ownership was by no means commonplace, 'the car had become a project: what one was going to buy next' (1996: 29). Taking up the left panel of the garage façade in the opening shot is a large advertisement for the American multinational Chrysler. The jazz score aligns machine with modernity. Despite his expertise, Guy's blue-collar status constrains him within a relation of servant to his white-collar masters, who are endowed with the financial means to own a car, but are ignorant of its mechanics. The ending of the film depicts a transition in which car ownership is shown to have impacted on the configuration and experience of provincial space, as illustrated in the name of Guy's garage, L'Escale Cherbourgeoise; no longer a destination, Cherbourg functions as a

4 Cocteau used this technique in *La Belle et la bête* (1946), when Beauty enters the Beast's castle for the first time.

5 Comparisons have been be made with the ending of *Splendor in the Grass* (Elia Kazan, 1961), although Geneviève and Guy's feelings are portrayed as ambiguous, the ending more morose.

stopover. The Cherbourg we witness lacks its earlier multidimensionality. The setting has shifted to the periphery, visually dominated by global branding, as seen in the Esso sign on the garage forecourt and the oil can François uses as a drum. Moreover, the homogenisation of the town centre is depicted when Guy visits Emery's umbrella shop, now occupied by a washing machine outlet.

Not without controversy, *Les Parapluies de Cherbourg* also depicts the anxieties triggered by the conflicts of French decolonisation. The Algerian War bears a constant presence, but in absentia. For Guy Austin, 'the war ... exists only insofar as it tells a tale about French lovers; Algerians remain invisible, always off-screen' (2007: 185). Austin is right in questioning the film's lack of representations of the conflict and the terrible effects it had on Algerian people, but *Les Parapluies de Cherbourg* addresses the trauma of the war for provincial French communities. When it was released, the conflict weighed heavy on popular consciousness;[6] as Gérard Vaugeois recalls, it constituted an open wound.[7] For historian Benjamin Stora, in simply referring to the War with a section title ('l'absence'), Demy states that the story of the conflict is marked by its absence from discourse.[8] The film engages with the effects of war through what is and is not said. Guy predicts, when bidding farewell to Elise, 'je rencontrerai la mort avant toi' ('I will meet my death before you'), which she instantly dismisses by affirming 'le régiment n'est pas la guerre' ('serving in the army does not mean serving in war'). His letters recount the realities of serving on the front line; he describes soldiers being caught in an ambush, and sustains a knee injury in a grenade attack. Guy's cold, distant look after returning conveys the irreversible impact of military action for those forced to fight. The views of others illustrate society's difficulties in dealing with the returnees and responding to their trauma. Aubin describes Guy as a delinquent, while Madeleine refers to him as a man with no aims. His reply encapsulates the disorientation of the returnee: 'depuis que je suis revenu, je ne comprends plus ce qui se passe' ('since I came back, I no longer understand what's going on').

---

6 The film's production, from May 1961 to June 1962, underlines its near contemporaneity with events. The narrative also unfolds over the final years of the conflict. *Les Parapluies de Cherbourg* opened on 19 February 1964, less than two years after the declaration of independence.

7 *Il était une fois* les Parapluies de Cherbourg, 2003.

8 *Il était une fois* les Parapluies de Cherbourg, 2003.

Euphoria in excess: *Les Demoiselles de Rochefort*

If the mood of *Les Parapluies de Cherbourg* is morose, the tenor of *Les Demoiselles de Rochefort* is its polar opposite. It is the type of film Demy had envisaged for *Lola*. Following the international success of *Les Parapluies de Cherbourg*, he was given a budget of 6,000,000 French Francs, 50 per cent of which was assured by American backers provided that he cast Gene Kelly and George Chakiris, and make an English language version.[9] By featuring Kelly and Chakiris, and Grover Dale, Demy acknowledges the classical musical and more modern permutations, particularly the trailblazing *West Side Story* (Jerome Robbins and Robert Wise, 1961), in which Chakiris played Sharks gangster Bernardo, while Dale was cast as Snowboy in its Broadway adaptation. Classic film icon Danielle Darrieux, admired by Demy, also stars, alongside Nouvelle Vague actor Michel Piccoli. In the roles of the central twins, Demy cast sisters Françoise Dorléac and Catherine Deneuve.[10] The songs were dubbed, apart from those performed by Darrieux, and Kelly choreographed his own routines.

However, *Les Demoiselles de Rochefort* is far more than a celebration of the Hollywood musical. It constitutes the adaptation of Demy's proclivity for the intuitive to a highly coded genre. Its location in an actual provincial town is its most obviously revolutionary feature.[11] Evein spent three months repainting 40,000 square metres of Rochefort's facades in white, adding pastel colours to more than 10,000 shutters and doors. Legrand's compositions juxtapose symphonic and jazz styles, while British choreographer Norman Maen, alongside his assistant Maureen Bright, combined the American dance vernacular of syncopated jazz moves with the French idiom of classical ballet. Elsewhere, the numbers are fully integrated, articulating the

---

9 The French version screened at cinemas in the USA, while the English copy was destined for television. The dialogues were translated into English, but the songs were left in the original.

10 Brigitte Bardot and Geraldine Chaplin, and Audrey Hepburn and Jeanne Moreau had been considered. Tragically, Dorléac died in a car accident close to Nice on 26 June 1967, a few months after the film's premiere on 8 March 1967; she was late for a flight for its premiere in London.

11 Avignon, Hyères, Tarascon, Narbonne, Beaucaire, Toulouse and La Rochelle had been considered. Rochefort was chosen for its rigid militaristic architecture and large square. The inclusion of Avignon illustrates further the intended link with art in Pablo Picasso's cubist *Les Demoiselles d'Avignon* (1907) (*The Young Ladies of Avignon*).

characters' experiences, regrets, hopes and aspirations, and holding their past and future in a dynamic relationship with the present, depicted in the image track.

Les Demoiselles de Rochefort unfolds over a four-day weekend in high summer, and, just as in *Lola,* opens with the arrival of outsiders, here itinerant fairground workers Bill (Dale) and Etienne (Chakiris), and their entourage. The plot comprises a sophisticated mosaic of chance encounters, missed opportunities and romantic intrigues. Solange (Dorléac) and Delphine Garnier (Deneuve) work as music and dance teachers who dream of moving to Paris and meeting male suitors. Their mother, Yvonne Garnier (Darrieux), manages a cafe in the place Colbert and regrets leaving Simon Dame (Piccoli), the father of her son Boubou (Patrick Jeantet), ten years earlier. Maxence (Jacques Perrin), a young conscript, fantasises about his ideal woman and paints a portrait of her that he hangs in Guillaume Lancien's (Jacques Riberolles) gallery. Delphine discovers that Maxence's painting resembles her and promptly falls for its unknown artist. American composer Andy Miller (Kelly) and Solange fall in love when they meet in the street. Bill and Etienne recruit Solange and Delphine to perform the big number at the fair. Andy seduces Solange, and Yvonne is romantically reunited with Simon. The film's final long shot shows Maxence climbing into the lorry cab transporting Delphine to Paris, provocatively denying the audience visual confirmation of their encounter. A sub-plot coincides with the film's main narrative. Ex-dancer Lola Lola is discovered murdered and dismembered. Her killer is the Garnier family friend, Subtil Dutrouz (Henri Crémieux).

Joy was the guiding principal in making *Les Demoiselles de Rochefort.* Enchantment exists in abundance and Rochefort is saturated in a carnival atmosphere,[12] temporarily colonised by musicians, dancers, sailors and artists. Brightly painted buildings and gleaming sunlight suffuse the town with vitality. It is as if the film is unable to contain the exaltation held within it, which seeps through the seams, appealing to the spectator's senses. *Les Demoiselles de Rochefort* invites us to feel the warmth exuding from the sun's rays as they bounce off the bright, pastel facades, windows, zinc counters, shiny floors and costumes. Everything works to sweep us up within its thrall, to instil within us a sense of euphoric plenitude, a successful strategy according to

12 The film transformed the town, which had stagnated since the closure of the dockyards in 1927 and its bombardment during the Second World War.

reviewer Michel Capdenas, for whom the film 'réussit à nous communiquer ce plaisir sensoriel, à nous envoûter par son charme plastique' (1967) ('succeeds in communicating this sensorial pleasure to us, in bewitching us with the charm of its formal beauty').

Art and life are fused to the extent that art becomes life and vice-versa. Maxence declares that 'Braque, Picasso, Klee, Miró, Matisse' are life itself. Evein used the pastel palette of Dufy paintings as inspiration for his transformation of the Rochefort townscape, which is juxtaposed with the colder, avant-garde art that hangs in Guillaume's gallery, inspired by the works of Niki de Saint Phalle, Alexander Calder, Auguste Herbin, Georges Mathieu, Jean Dewasne, Yves Klein and Lucio Fontana (Joséphine Jibokji Frizon, 2013: 99). The accessible is preferred over the abstruse. Although normally an abstract painter, Maxime's portrait of his ideal woman is figurative, its bold and naive lines nodding to the work of Bernard Buffet.

Dance amplifies the sensory connection between characters and environment, spectator and film. For Bergson, dance can illustrate pure duration (1908: 9–10). Visual pleasure in watching dance emanates from an ability to predict future movements from within the present (1908: 9–10). Choreography, rhythm and music mobilise a kinaesthetic empathy between viewer and film. The flowing and predictable jazz ballet moves serve to aid the spectator's sensory engagement with the film. The sequence in which Delphine walks to Guillaume's gallery depicts how the exaltation projected by the sun-blessed facades and leaping dancers reflect and amplify her joyful insouciance. Everything is designed to uplift. Women dressed nymph-like in diaphanous costumes perform high-kicks, while others spring into the air, and sailors lift Delphine. Ghislain Cloquet's cinematography is composed of tracking and panning shots, one from a low angle, that accentuate character spontaneity, movement and lightness, while Legrand's arrangement of accelerated jazz chords and ascending choir harmonies supplement the elation depicted.

Yet, *Les Demoiselles de Rochefort* is far more than a sugary depiction of life in the provinces. Demy remarked 'je voudrais qu'on accepte cette légèreté mais qu'on ne la prenne pas à la légère' (in Taboulay, 1996: 93) ('I would like people to accept this lightness, but not take it lightly'). Happiness is portrayed as contingent, vulnerable to temporary curtailment or permanent loss: 'ce sentiment de joie ... n'était valable que s'il était lui-même susceptible, d'un instant à l'autre, de "craquer"' (in Sadoul, 1967) ('this feeling of joy ... was only valid if it were susceptible to "break" at any moment'). *Les Demoiselles de Rochefort* illustrates that elation is inherently threatened by despair, that to experience euphoria requires a familiarity with woe. Yvonne's regret at having abandoned Simon purely because of her fear of assuming his surname conveys, through absurdity, the past sorrows that inflect present happiness.

The camera's movement assumes, in some sequences, a phenomenological mode of organic, gradual presentation. As Cerbone summarises, phenomenological constitution brings 'into view the systematic nature of objects at the level of appearance or experience' (2006: 31). In phenomenology 'objects are constituted as systems of adumbrational presentations' (2006: 31). When we observe an object, only certain aspects present themselves to us. When looking at the front of a rock, for instance, the back and some of the sides are obscured. Yet, we recall what we have seen and imagine what we have yet to see and these retentions and portensions contribute to what we see now (2006: 29). This 'adumbrational approach' is illustrated in an early sequence in *Les Demoiselles de Rochefort*, which serves the transition from the background contexts (the arrival of the fair) to the foreground narrative (the main protagonists). A crane shot slowly completes a half rotation from the dancers in the square to the Garnier sisters' studio. The camera tracks backwards, moving behind ladders and past Yvonne's cafe. The jazzy non-diegetic score dissolves into soft diegetic piano scales as the camera passes Etienne and Bill, crosses the street and, tilting slightly upwards, reveals young girls pirouetting behind open windows. Solange is seen to the left of the screen, playing the piano and singing 'do-re-mi' chords, and Delphine is to the right, instructing her girls' ballet moves. The object of the sequence (the introduction of Solange and Delphine) is constituted cumulatively through our perceptual experience of these 'adumbrational presentations'. To connect the contexts to the narrative, we must hold onto what we have just witnessed in conjunction with what we see now, while anticipating what will come.

Les Demoiselles de Rochefort fluctuates between implicating its spectator via its emotive storyline, endearing characters, effervescent aesthetics, uplifting choreography and fluid camera movements, and rendering them an accomplice in its connivances. The spectator is positioned as omniscient, able to map out the complex connections between the characters, gradually revealed through the songs and actions, and constantly made aware that the lamented past or anticipated/fantasised future lover is metres away, despite the characters' obliviousness. Access is restricted to certain locations: the place Colbert, Yvonne's cafe, outside Boubou's school, Guillaume's art gallery, Simon's music shop, the Garnier sisters' studio and the surrounding streets. The film's contrivances to keep the future lovers apart become obvious. Inter-titles serve as a chronometer of objective temporality, while subjective time emphasises the affective impact of external events. While Solange, Delphine, Bill and Etienne practice their routine for the main performance, a sequence of dissolves shows Guillaume, Yvonne, Andy, Simon and Maxence conjuring their absent/imagined love object, figured in the lyrics of their songs and their airs, which replicate the partitions that unite each coupling. The flow of objective time is thus arrested as we witness what appears to be the same moment being lived by each character. Elsewhere, suspense is undermined by the excessive deployment of missed connections. In a key sequence, Solange chances upon Maxence at the murder crime scene, who immediately encounters Andy in the street, who instantly bumps into Delphine as she returns from shopping, who promptly meets Solange near Boubou's school. However, disbelief is suspended in the penultimate scene. Maxence collects his duffle bag from the cafe seconds after Delphine exits to take the newspaper to her grandfather. When she returns, Maxence has gone. By situating this missed encounter towards the resolution, the film seeks to draw the spectator back into the narrative and sets up the potential of disappointment at not actually seeing the couple's encounter on screen.

Les Demoiselles de Rochefort is also highly self-reflexive. Direct camera address is deployed regularly, both during performances and natural conversations. References to the film as text abound. After listing classical and jazz musicians, Delphine asks Etienne and Bill if they would prefer some Michel Legrand. Tongue-in-cheek self-reflexivity recurs.[13] After Solange and Delphine's performance of 'Les Marins

---

13 The original idea for the screenplay parodied *Les Parapluies de Cherbourg*. Bill was to be Guy Foucher who becomes a fairground worker after Madeleine's death. Geneviève was to attend the Garnier sisters' performance with Roland and Françoise, and would miss Guy by seconds. Guy was to chance into Delphine outside Boubou's school and, struck by her close resemblance to Geneviève, show her a photograph of his lost love, to which she was to comment ironically that she is better looking. However, Nino Castelnuovo returned to Italy to make films for television (taken from Demy quoted in Berthomé, 1996: 201).

d'Hambourg', Bill complains that he has had enough of sailors, girls and boats. The film's wordplay is explicitly mocked. Subtil Dutrouz is an oxymoron combining the terms 'subtle' and 'hole', which can both mean mouth and anus. After explaining his name to Bill and Etienne, he asks his friend Pépé (René Bazart), who is building a model airplane, 'alors ça colle?' ('so does it work?') Maxence's pun 'je vais en perm' à Nantes' ('I'm going on permission to Nantes') amuses Yvonne and Andy, but is absurd to Solange.

As in *Les Parapluies de Cherbourg, Les Demoiselles de Rochefort* portrays the fallibility of memory that pertains to Deleuze's recollection image (1985: 52). The present image approximates and diverges from Demy's earlier films. During a dinner party at Yvonne's cafe, in which the characters speak in Alexandrine rhyme, Etienne recounts how he met Bill when he was being thrown out of a bar in Cherbourg. Instantly, recollections of Guy are triggered, but the character we see is different. The falsity of this perceptual *déjà vu* is inscribed into the dialogues. Dutrouz maintains that he recognises Delphine, much to her consternation, but the audience knows that the only image he has seen of her is Maxence's portrait (which he had already confused with an ex-dancer he had known forty years prior and who had short dark hair). Dutrouz talks of a hairdresser friend in Cherbourg called Aimé who married Madame Desnoyers, a widow and ex-dancer, he says, from Tours or rather Orléans. Recollections are sparked, then blurred until Dutrouz confirms that she was from Nantes. Such recognition/misrecognition extends to the antecedents of Demy's films. Yvonne reads about Lola Lola's murder, which instantly conjures the heroine of *Lola*, but reveals that the victim was in her sixties. For Herzog, a more plausible source is Lola Lola in *Der Blaue Engel*, thus making *Les Demoiselles de Rochefort* an oblique and ironic derivation of this earlier film (2010: 130), although the remarks also conjure Desnoyer, through association. Such manipulation of memory is also sewn into the film's form. Characters repeat enunciations already expressed by others and hum airs that later provide the instrumental for their individual songs. Moreover, musical partitions often incur disconcerting modifications when repeated. For instance, Solange plays her concierto in a lower key when recounting her meeting with Andy to Delphine, while Andy chooses a higher range and unfamiliar note sequence when performing it to Simon.

Cinephilic memory is invoked in the intertextual allusions to iconic French films. When Solange opens the door to Etienne and

Bill, she exclaims 'Jules et Jim'. Guillaume owns a convertible resembling the Ford Mustang driven by Michel Poiccard in *A bout de souffle*. The opening of *Les Enfants du paradis* is repeatedly referenced in the complicated crane shot showing the excited crowd at the fete, which includes young girls performing can-can kicks, *demi-pliés* and pirouettes in *pointe*, and a reveller dressed as Pierrot. The shot of Dutrouz meandering through the jostling crowd, and cuts to Guillaume and Simon among the revellers, recall Baptiste engulfed by the carnival goers in Carné's climactic ending. Guillaume's attraction to Delphine evokes Lacenaire's fetishisation of Garance. The knowing reflexivity of these intertextual connections is amplified by his remark to Delphine, which cites Prévert's most famous line when Garance rebuffs Frédérick's advances: 'comme disaient les poètes, "Paris est tout petit pour ceux qui s'aiment comme nous d'un aussi grand amour"' ('as the poets said, "Paris is so small for those who love each other as we do, with such an immense love"'). Another direct citation comes when Solange meets Simon; 'on m'appelle Solange' ('they call me Solange'), she declares, conjuring Garance's interrogration by a policeman in the earlier film. A complex dynamic between past and present films is thus marshalled. Our recollections are falsified by what we see in the present and, at the same time, our ability to invest in what we currently witness is affected by our memories of the past film.

A similar process occurs in the many allusions to Hollywood musicals. The aforementioned fair scenes also reference *West Side Story*, particularly in the basketball teams that evoke the street gangs of the Sharks and the Jets. Solange and Delphine conjure Rose and Esther Smith (Lucille Bremer and Judy Garland) from *Meet Me in St Louis* (Vincente Minnelli, 1944) who, like the Garnier sisters, play the piano, sing and dance. Yet, rather than simply paying homage to past images, *Les Demoiselles de Rochefort* revisits them. Instead of an exotic elsewhere,[14] France is represented by a provincial town during a summer fair. As critics have noted, Andy's dance number in the street replicates some of Kelly's routine for 'I Got Rhythm' in *An American in Paris* (Vincente Minnelli, 1949) and his sword fights as D'Artagnan in *The Three Musketeers* (George Sidney, 1948). The dos-y-dos moves, ballet turns and the steps hand-in-hand of his routine with Solange

---

14 Kelly's character lives as an artist in Paris in *An American in Paris*, Monroe and Russell travel to France on a luxury liner in *Gentlemen Prefer Blondes* and Kelly's first talkie is set in pre-revolutionary France in *Singin' in the Rain*.

in the music shop recall Kelly's seduction of Leslie Caron in 'Our Love is Here to Stay'. The conclusion of 'Good Mornin'' in *Singin' in the Rain* is evoked by Solange, Delphine, Etienne and Bill as they fall exhausted to their seats after their medley of songs. Solange and Delphine's set-piece performance of 'Aimez la vie' conjures Marilyn Monroe and Jane Russell's rendition of 'Little Rock' in *Gentleman Prefer Blondes* (Howard Hawks, 1953). However, French children replace Hollywood extras, actual streets supersede studio reconstitutions, and amateurish choreography substitutes slick dance moves. *Les Demoiselles de Rochefort* thus hints at the surreptitious means by which Hollywood abstractions of France are projected and reified by the MGM musical.

This challenge to dominant Hollywood representations also targets the formation of the heterosexual couple. On the surface, the film celebrates heterosexual love, while lustful desire fails, as evidenced in Bill, Etienne and Guillaume. Love is depicted in three ways: a melancholy yearning for a past beloved, an instant attraction, and faith in a romantic ideal. Simon believes that Yvonne abandoned him to live on the Pacific Coast of Mexico with her new husband, while Yvonne is left with her regrets at having forsaken Simon. Solange and Andy experience enamoration during which, as Barthes remarks, the subject is enraptured by the love object (1977: 223). For Barthes, such ravishment is always expressed in the historic past as an immediate anterior (1977: 229). Accordingly, Solange re-enacts her encounter with Andy after the event to a captive Delphine, although the anterior is rendered even more immediate in that she relays it in the present tense. Of his image of feminine perfection, Maxence laments 'je ne connais rien d'elle, et pourtant je la vois ... son portrait et l'amour ne font plus qu'une image' ('I know nothing about her and yet I can see her ... her portrait and love are the same image'), which Delphine replicates almost identically when she pines after her unknown artist.

Yet, each display of hope, each recollection of euphoria, is undermined by flippant remarks that mock the intensity of such romantic investments. Of Maxence's ode to his feminine ideal, Yvonne casually observes 'c'est un joli portrait, mais je ne vois pas ça dans mon entourage' ('it's a pretty picture, but I haven't seen that in my entourage'). At times, the characters' own comments diminish the significance of their feelings. Solange tells an indifferent Yvonne 'je suis toute émue parce que j'ai rencontré l'homme de ma vie' ('I'm extremely emotional because I've met the man of my dreams') and then adds 'à part ça, on travaille' ('apart from that, we're working'). Rupturing the extraordinary with the banal can render it absurd, thus triggering laughter and defusing affect. According to Bergson, comedy 'exige ... pour produire tout son effet, quelque chose comme une anesthésie momentanée du cœur.' (1924: 11) ('to take full effect [comedy] requires something like a temporary numbing of the heart'). For Bergson, indifference is the natural arena of humour, which here is underlined in the flat and nonchalant tone of each character's verbal reaction to the extraordinary experiences of their interlocutor. We hear evidence of the selfishness that frames the construction of each character, preoccupied with their own narcissistic pursuit of happiness and lacking responsibility and compassion for others. Yvonne allows strangers Bill and Etienne to pick Boubou up from school, and Solange dismisses Delphine when she claims she is sad after rupturing her relationship with Guillaume. Such egotism is extended in the Garnier women's vanity; when flattered by Bill and Etienne, Yvonne and Delphine retort, separately, 'on me l'a déjà dit' ('I've already been told that').

Given its dual implication and distanciation of the spectator through its aesthetics, choreography, songs, narrative structure and humorous dialogues, *Les Demoiselles de Rochefort* lends itself well to a camp reading. Some have dismissed such an interpretation as superficial (Lalanne, 1997: 60; Rosenbaum, 2011: 54). Yet, beyond its gay cast members Chakiris and Dale, its mobilisation of camp affect and humour reinforces the film's challenge to normative heterosexuality. As Richard Dyer observes, camp unifies 'qualities that are elsewhere felt as antithetical: theatricality and authenticity', as well as 'intensity and irony' (1986: 154). In his analysis of the camp sensibilities elicited by the Hollywood musical, Steven Cohen reveals how iconic numbers, including 'The Trolley Song' in *Meet Me in St Louis*, simultaneously educe audience involvement and detachment (2005: 35). In Minnelli's famous sequence, Esther Smith takes the trolley bus when she sees John Truett (Tom Drake) running to catch it. As it pulls off, Esther sings of their love-at-first-sight as if it were unfolding on the bus, but John only reaches Esther at the end of the song and watches her as if a spectator of the story rather than its object. In accordance with Barthes's immediate anterior, Esther sings of her dreamed encounter in the past tense, but the events she recounts do not transpire. Camp affect arises from the scene's 'theatricalisation of authentic feminine desire' (Cohen, 2005: 35). By representing heterosexual romance as fantasy in such obvious ways, the film undermines the normative logic it appears to advance. Thus, the effect of the mobilisation of camp narrative and performance devices is anything but cursory.

Heterosexual enamoration is theatricalised and parodied in *Les Demoiselles de Rochefort* most explicitly in the encounter between Solange and Andy. The panning camera movements, editing, hazy filter and swirling instrumentals serve to render explicit the scene's machinations to exaggerate the affective impact of the encounter. Its obvious excess and hyperbole, evinced in the hackneyed ploy of the male helping the female to collect the spilled contents of a dropped bag, elicits the audience's involvement in the joke, a strategy intensified by the extravagance and reflexivity of the characters' actions. Solange slowly raises her eyes to meet Andy's face, which beams with inordinate elation after their hands touch, and she flashes a look to the camera when she vainly declines his request to meet up. While the implication of the spectator in its ironic strategies allows *Les Demoiselles de Rochefort* to further Demy's interest in portraying how reality and theatricality fuse in everyday apprehension of the world, the obvious slippage between self and performance explicitly figures the patriarchal concepts of femininity, masculinity and heterosexuality as constructs rather than essential realities. Such mischievous undermining of heteronormativity is implied earlier; the potential of an incestuous encounter between Solange and Simon is suggested, but invalidated when Yvonne confirms that her daughter is not Simon's progeny. Engagement with this irony is not necessary to derive pleasure, but camp modes of address contribute to the sense of fun and joy offered. Paradoxically given that camp is seen as both whimsical and alienating, here it serves to challenge gender hegemonies and intensify the impression of plenitude transmitted.

As in *Les Parapluies de Cherbourg*, *Les Demoiselles de Rochefort* also presents a critique of the reach of consumerism across provincial France and its ramifications for local cultures. The fair is a commercial enterprise dressed up as a popular fete. The opening sequence shows Bill, Etienne and their entourage transporting luxury boats and motorbikes into Rochefort. The symbolism is militaristic; their convoy and mini-cavalry of men on horseback – wearing beige shirts, Stetsons and cowboy boots, and on motorbikes, in white shirts and caps, pale blue trousers and black leather boots – conjure the arrival of an invading force. As it passes under the town's banner proclaiming the parochial *fête de la mer*, a battalion is seen departing on the left, symbolically surrendering Rochefort to its occupying forces. The heady carnival ambiance acts as a smokescreen behind which luxury goods corporations, including Shell (Johnson), Rocca, Nautilus and Honda, advertise their products. The townsfolk are portrayed as complicit in this capitalist territorialisation of their space. While the characters complain about certain signs of hegemonic control, they ignore others. Dutrouz bemoans the legions of soldiers in the street and yet fails to acknowledge the surreptitious means through which consumerism spreads its control, comically offering Boubou a model of a nuclear submarine as a gift. Yvonne and Dutrouz acknowledge that things are going badly everywhere, but the threat of consumerism and its consequent cultural homogenisation fails to surface in their consciousness. The Garnier twins' set-piece number encapsulates the paradox. While they urge us to embrace simple pleasures to be happy, the stage they perform on had, moments earlier, been occupied by Bill and Etienne promoting their luxury motorbikes.

Just as *Les Demoiselles de Rochefort* implies that the desire for material wealth deceives by offering ephemeral happiness, it also reveals how the profane and macabre become trivialised in modern society. When a violent and tragic event occurs, such as the murder of Lola Lola, the characters apprehend it with flippancy, transforming it into a source of salacious gratification. Yvonne and Josette (Geneviève Thénier) recount the gruesome details, stopping temporarily to joke with Maxence, who quickly departs for the murder scene, blithely declaring that he is enchanted by mystery. When the policeman states that the victim was grey haired, Maxence retorts that he only likes blondes, which offends Solange. The discovery that the assassin was a friend of the family leads Yvonne to predict Dutrouz's fury at the misspelling of his name in the newspaper. Consequently, the strategy of ironic humour that mocks heterosexual enamoration through a dynamic relation with the audience becomes troublesome when used by the characters and applied to social malice. Irony is shown to be subversive and oppositional in one area, and complicit and reactionary in another. The sense of plenitude that emanates from the film's ebullience is diluted by these critical sleights on post-War society and morality. *Les Demoiselles de Rochefort* encapsulates the proverb, adapted from Charles Perrault's *Peau d'âne*, and inscribed on Demy's original screenplay that 'un film léger parlant de choses graves vaut mieux qu'un film grave parlant de choses légères' (Garson and Zvonkine, 2010: 4) ('A light film about serious issues is of more value than a serious film about light things').

Musical Marxism: *Une chambre en ville*

By contrast to *Les Demoiselles de Rochefort*, *Une chambre en ville* is a serious film that tackles weighty issues. The two seem to constitute the opposite sides of the same coin, a dichotomy that, Demy claims, encapsulates his attitude towards life:

> je suis écartelé entre la joie et la tristesse, trop heureux dans le bonheur, trop malheureux dans le malheur. Il faut être ainsi pour avoir fait *Les Demoiselles de Rochefort* et aboutir à *Une chambre en ville*. (in Trémois, 1982)[15]

Une chambre en ville recounts a condemned heterosexual romance against the historical backdrop of a strike by dockyard metalworkers in Nantes in the summer of 1955. Its depictions of industrial unrest, which open, close and structure the narrative, are also informed by stories of social action from the 1920s, recounted to Demy by his father, who worked in portside factories, as did two of his uncles.[16] Like *Les Parapluies de Cherbourg*, its disenchanting narrative is expressed through sung dialogues, thus producing another film version of the recitative. However, its political contestation is explicit; *Une chambre en ville* openly challenges bourgeois hegemony and exploitation. The outcome, though, is similar; although briefly threatened, the status quo reaffirms its hold and the transcendent love affair is curtailed.

The two central storylines of social discord and condemned love intertwine. Metalworker François Guilbaud (Richard Berry) is an activist, fronting the stand-off between the strikers and riot police that opens the film. He lodges with an ex-Baroness and widow of a Colonel, Margot Langlois (Danielle Darrieux). His girlfriend, Violette Pelletier (Fabienne Guyon), proposes to him, but he does not reciprocate her love. Langlois's daughter, Edith Leroyer (Dominique Sanda),

---

15 'I am split between joy and sadness, too happy in happiness and too unhappy in sadness. You have to be this way to have made *Les Demoiselles de Rochefort* and to have finished with *Une chambre en ville*.'

16 Demy in *L'Univers de Jacques Demy* (Agnès Varda, 1993/95).

visits a clairvoyant who predicts that she will fall in love with a metal-worker. After a strike meeting, François encounters Edith, walking the streets following a fight with her husband Edmond (Michel Piccoli). In the film's most unexpected shot, Edith opens her fur coat to reveal her naked body to François. The two then spend the night together in a hotel room. As the lovers langour in post coital rapture, François reveals his occupation and Edith tells him that Langlois is her mother. Meanwhile, Violette discovers she is pregnant with François's child and confides in his best friend Dambiel (Jean-François Stévenin). When Langlois discovers her daughter's romance with François, she threatens to evict him. Desperate with jealousy, Edmond slits his throat in front of Edith. Industrial tensions peak as the conflicts between the central characters climax. Violette visits Edith while François and Dambiel riot outside. A policeman fatally wounds François who is trying to protect a fellow striker. Swiftly transported by Dambiel and another striker to Langlois's apartment, he dies. Unable to countenance a life without him, Edith shoots herself, and the penultimate shot shows both characters' lifeless bodies nestled together.

Demy had wanted to base a fictional narrative around the strike since he encountered a demonstration when walking in Nantes with his mother and baby brother.[17] He first considered writing the story as an opera, penned five or six chapters of a novel and finally decided to make a film. He struggled to find a satisfactory ending, though, because of the proximity with his father's experiences; François is partly inspired by Raymond who had lodged with the wife of a colonel in Nantes.[18] In 1974, he felt ready to shoot his film and eventually secured 500,000 Francs in *avance sur recettes* and the backing of Gaumont and Planfilm. Shooting was to commence on 15 June 1976. However, Catherine Deneuve and Gérard Depardieu, whom he had originally intended to play Edith and François, withdrew because they insisted on singing their own parts and Legrand declined to write the score, which Demy described as a betrayal (Berthomé, 1996: 291). Dominique Sanda accepted the role of Edith, but Gaumont backed out following the failure of risky ventures. Fresh from the flop of *L'Evénement...*, Demy faced hostile producers. Part of the reason, he surmised, was the theme of social class, which, it was feared, would scare Parisian office workers (in Berthomé, 1996: 292). Demy had

17 From *L'Univers de Jacques Demy* (Agnès Varda, 1993/95).
18 From *L'Univers de Jacques Demy* (Agnès Varda, 1993/95).

to await the election of a Socialist government before he could revive the project. In April 1981, he approached Christine Gouze-Rénal, François Mitterrand's sister-in-law, who, inspired by the euphoria of the Socialist candidate's victory, agreed to produce the film.

For Alain Badiou *Une chambre en ville* 'célèbre en vérité, au moment même de sa mort, le "peuple de gauche" rassemblé autour d'une classe ouvrière énergique et bon enfant' (2010: 109) ('celebrates, at the very moment of its death, the "people of the left" unified around an energetic and good natured working class'). On initial viewing, *Une chambre en ville* indeed seems nostalgic for a period when the battle lines of class politics were clearly marked. Yet, it also reminds its audience of the dangers of prematurely confining political struggles to history. Such resonance of past conflict for present injustices is conveyed in the opening and latter scenes. Shot composition pits strikers and riot police against each other. The chanting intensifies, while the editing and camera angles evoke the iconic montage sequences from *Battleship Potemkin* (Sergei Eisenstein, 1925). As the first line of riot police charge, the image transitions into colour. A striker brandishes a large *Tricouleur* flag, furnishing an oblique allusion to Eugène Delacroix's iconic *La Liberté guidant le peuple* (1830) (*Liberty Leading the People*). Shifting from black-and-white to colour brings the events firmly within the diegetic present and underlines their resonance for the now of the film's exhibition. May 1968 is recalled as the strikers throw cobbles and burn cars. The dockyard workers become revolutionary vanguards, cast in the dyes of epoch-changing uprisings, with François instated as ultimate martyr.

By setting its story of doomed love against a narrative of social unrest, *Une chambre en ville* complies with the melodrama genre. Consonant with melodramas, social contestation unfolds on the doorstep of the privileged domestic space and is literally brought into the bourgeois interior by the proletarian figure of François. The majority of the action occurs inside, mainly in Langlois's apartment, while the violent confrontations between strikers and police unfold directly in front of her building on the rue du Roi Albert in the bourgeois eastern side of central Nantes. However, unlike conventional melodramas, *Une chambre en ville* casts none of its protagonists in an unequivocally positive or negative light. While François embodies the paladin of the proletarian cause, he abandons his pregnant girlfriend who, although victimised by François's infidelity, is depicted as manipulative. Conversely, while Langlois is portrayed as duplicitous and spiteful, she elicits sympathy as a lonely widow. Edith is projected as self-centred, but tragically finds love too late, and Edmond garners compassion as a weak and chastised middle-aged man, despite his aggressivity. Classic figures from fairytales are thus revised; the princess and her prince are neither angelic nor charming, the servant girl lacks piety, and the spite of the ogre and wicked stepmother can be justified.

Une chambre en ville revisits and revises our knowledge of key spaces in Demy's cinema. The stifling surroundings of the bourgeois eastern end of Nantes contrast markedly with the light, modern and socially mixed western side seen in *Lola*. The Passage Pommeraye is transformed from an enchanted space into a site of morbidity, stripped of the lofty romantic resonance attached to it in *Lola*. We see it at night, thus lacking the diaphanous light, which, according to Demy's childhood recollections, transforms it into a magical space.[19] The camera remains fixed at the lower level of the passage where Edmond's television shop is located (incidentally, near the hairdresser's salon where Roland collects the briefcase of diamonds for his trip to Johannesburg in *Lola*).[20] Explicit nods to the early film are contained within the image's periphery; when Edith tries to escape from Edmond's shop after his suicide, the client names Cassard and Desnoyer are chalked up on the board behind her.

As in Demy's other films, the environment bears a constitutive and reflective relation to the characters' subjectivity. Their emotions and moods are extended in and triggered by their surroundings. Evein decorates Langlois's apartment in heavy, dark blues and reds, which enhance the sense of asphyxiation and entrapment. Similarly, Edmond's shop is painted in a dark green that externalises and accentuates his jealousy. The only bright interior is the apartment that Violette shares with her mother, decorated in pink and blue patterned wallpaper with yellow doorframes, but this is seen only briefly. An emerald green is used in the wallpaper of the hotel room where Edith and Edmond first make love, signifying the energy and reciprocity of their passion, underlined by the romantic motif of three pink roses,

19 *L'Univers de Jacques Demy* (Agnès Varda, 1993/95).
20 This locating of the scene on the lower level of the passage recalls André Pieyre de Mandiargues's surrealist short story, *Passage Pommeraye* in *Le Musée noir* (1946).

but, again, this only makes a cursory appearance. *Une chambre en ville* thus constructs a morose and oppressive environment from which its characters can escape only as a result of the acts of others, as in François's slaying by the riot police, and through extreme measures, as in Edith and Edmond's suicides.

In his discussion of the uses of melodrama in political and commitment films, Martin O'Shaughnessy argues, summarising Peter Brooks (1976), that 'realist and melodramatic drives can exist in complex and productive tension both to engage with and to give eloquence to the real' (2007: 131). In *Une chambre en ville* this giving 'eloquence to the real' is transmitted through its form. The opening credits avoid mention of dialogue or script, preferring *paroles* or lyrics, and the classical musical score compliments the action. Through its decipherable language, *Une chambre en ville* recalls the *opera verismo* that emerged from late nineteenth-century Italy, and which was typified by dramatic plots, everyday characters and, according to the Encyclopaedia Britannica, 'passionate declamation by solo voices and emotionally charged harmonies and melodies'.[21]

In *Une chambre en ville*, the verbal exchanges articulate raw emotions, creating a sense of realism, candour and authenticity admired by critics and viewers, including eminent novelist and filmmaker Marguerite Duras (1986). The language is brutal, full of expletives that project the characters' intense resentments and frustrations. Herein lies the film's most innovative feature, for it sets such crude verbal discourse to Michel Colombier's rich and melodic symphonic arrangements. A hiatus emerges between the epic score and gritty dialogues, which serve as the direct extension of authentic, embodied emotions. Language is portrayed as insufficient in encapsulating actual feelings. Such brutal honesty is evidenced most extremely in the first scene between Edith and Edmond. Edith attacks Edmond, dismissing him as 'coward', 'bastard', 'filth' and 'shit'. After a scuffle, Edmond burns Edith with his soldering iron. When she falls back against the window, her fur coat opens to reveal her naked body. Edmond demands angrily whether she is working as a prostitute and orders her to leave. When she turns towards the door, he falls to his knees and begs her to stay, uttering after she leaves: 'tu sais bien que

21 For a detailed study of the historical background of *Une chambre en ville* and *Les Parapluies de Cherbourg* in terms of their musical form in French, see Lefèvre (2013: 12–15).

je t'aime, tu feras ce que tu voudras, Edith, tu sais que je ne pourrai pas vivre sans toi, Edith, je souffre trop, ô je suis trop malheureux, Edith, Edith, Edith, je t'aime, Edith, je suis trop con'.[22] Edmond's repetition of the verb 'aimer', her first name, the intensifier 'trop', the non-vocable 'ô' and the expletive 'con' transmits his struggle to articulate his disarray in precise terms, even though the strength of his feelings is manifest.

A sense of doom and foreboding builds in intensity through *Une chambre en ville*, accelerating the characters and the audience towards its melancholy finale. This impression of precipitation is accentuated by the order of the scenes, which structure time in a series of episodes, while the musical themes that flow into, out of and across scenes heighten the sense of fluidity. The impression of a downward spiral, winding ever faster towards inevitable demise is triggered in the encounter between Edith and her tarot card reader, Madame Sforza (Marie-France Roussel). After Sforza foresees that Edith will meet her metal worker, she turns the cards once more and warns her to be terribly wary. Consequently, later, when we witness Edith and François's amorous euphoria as they lay in the hotel room, we know that their love is already threatened, not only by the card reading, which implies that Edmond is the menace, but also by Violette's pregnancy and Langlois's bitter hostility.

The presageing impact of Edith and François's affair for Violette, Langlois and Edmond is visually conveyed in a montage when the two lovers first embrace in the hotel room. As we witness François kissing Edith's naked neck from the street, the film cuts to a restless Violette turning in her bed, an oblivious Langlois applying her night cream and a troubled Edmond frantically pacing up and down. The forward flow of objective time is suspended as the same moment is revisited according to the different emotions and experiences of the characters. The significance of the lovers' encounter is accentuated by the music, which oscillates between a low and high string and woodwind partition, emphasising Violette's anticipation, Langlois's ignorance and Edmond's anxiety.

Unlike Guy and Geneviève, Edith and François choose to withstand external judgements. Their initial encounter is depicted as an instant

---

22 'You know I love you, you can do what you want, Edith, you know that I can't live without you, Edith, I'm suffering so, oh I'm so unhappy, Edith, Edith, Edith, I love you, I'm such an idiot'.

and sublime erotic connection. It appears initially as an exalted representation that contrasts with the realism conveyed by the film's language and images of social conflict. In Edith and François, Demy figures the coming together of carnal desire and projected romantic love. While medium shots show the two characters in their hotel bed, the camera fetishising their svelte, blemish-free torsos, their sexual encounter immediately triggers a desire to love the other as they have surged up in their lives. Herein, then, lies the film's apparent tragedy, for this *rencontre* is, once again, abridged by outside forces. As in *Les Parapluies de Cherbourg*, love's enabling capacity to unify people from very different class backgrounds is thwarted.

And yet, *Une chambre en ville* can also be read as undermining the narrative of condemned heterosexual romance it enacts. Sublime heterosexual love is portrayed as born out of a selfish preoccupation with one's own happiness to the detriment of others. Through their resolve to be together, Edith and François are shown to be insensitive to the plight of others, especially Violette, who is dismissed by both and abandoned to a possible miserable existence as a single mother in mid-1950s France. Strategies of audience distanciation, beyond the lyrical form, are also deployed, as in the occasional instance of self-parody; for example, when Langlois first spots Edith and François embracing, she asks angrily 'qu'est-ce que c'est que cette farce?' ('What is this farce?'). The ultimate heterosexual tragedy of the mutual suicide of star-crossed lovers is mocked through excess and lack. Excessive is François's death, which, coming as the result of a hit by a policeman's baton, does not comply with the valorous demise of traditional male heroes in battle. Excessive also is the expressionistic acting as François utters his last words. Muted, by contrast, are the reactions of the other characters beyond Edith, who passively look on. Muted also is the response to Edith's suicide. Again, the characters stand immobile as she slowly reaches for her gun and brandishes it, declaring that she cannot live without François. Langlois's feeble attempt at preventing her daughter from killing herself reinforces the incredulousness of the whole sequence. Narrative thus gives way to performance, which figures the heterosexual love-at-first-sight story as fantasy.

Sadly for Demy, *Une chambre en ville* was initially remembered more for the controversy it prompted than its originality. Despite its glowing critical reception, it managed a poor showing at the box office. Ironically on the day of a strike in the Paris transport system, more than 71,000 spectators went to see Gérard Oury's action comedy *L'As des as*, while only 3,165 chose Demy's film. A series of articles and reviews urged audiences to see the film, led by reviewers Gérard Vaugeois, Michel Boujut and Jean-Jacques Bernard. Twenty-six critics signed their name to an article/petition published in *Les Nouvelles littéraires* on 11 November 1982. They claimed that Oury's production enjoyed far greater success because it benefitted from an intense advertising campaign. Yet, as Berthomé observes, *Une chambre en ville* also enjoyed wide-scale billboard promotion and, ultimately, both the film and its campaign failed to attract audiences (1996: 348). Jean-Paul Belmondo, the main actor in *L'As des as*, vigorously defended Oury's production in an open letter to the press on 19 November and dismissed the critics' contentions as risible and sad. According to Gérard Lefort, who had authored one of the initial calls for audiences to watch *Une chambre en ville*, Belmondo was justified in challenging the critics who had wrongfully assumed that the French viewing public were too stupid to make 'correct' choices about the films they chose to see (1982). Demy distanced himself from this implied judgement in *Nouvelles littéraires* on 25 November, but nonetheless defended the critics' right to express their view. He also thanked them by name in a full-page advertisement supported by Progéfi, Top 1, TF1 Films Production and UGC (Berthomé, 1996: 349). The sad irony is that this polemic inadvertently positioned Demy alongside a group of critics seen as detached from the tastes of actual audiences, a categorisation he had been careful to avoid (Vaugeois, 2013: 75).

The musicals discussed here develop and intensify some of the themes and moods apparent in *Lola*, *La Baie des Anges* and *Model Shop*. Roland's forlornness inspires the atmosphere and outcomes of *Les Parapluies de Cherbourg* and *Une chambre en ville* and, while the protagonists in *Les Demoiselles de Rochefort* determine to be happy, and ultimately realise their aspirations, they are wilfully blinded to the obvious menaces wrought by modernity and capitalism. Chapter 3 will show how some of these notions are pursued in Demy's adaptations of fairytale, fable and myth. As will be seen, rapture and resolution are once again either illusory or absent.

References

Ancelin, Pierre (1964) '*Parapluies de Cherbourg*', *Les Lettres françaises*, 5 March.

Austin, G. (2007), 'Representing the Algerian War in Algerian Cinema: *Le Vent des Aurès*', *French Studies*, 61 (2): 182–95.

Badiou, Alain (2010) *Cinéma*, Paris, Nova.

Barthes, Roland (1977) *Fragments d'un discours amoureux*, Paris, Seuil, transl. Richard Howard, *A Lover's Discourse: Fragments*, London, Vintage, 2002.

Bellour, Raymond (1964) '*Les Parapluies de Cherbourg*, premier film "en chanté" français', *Les Lettres françaises*, 6 February.

Belmondo, Jean-Paul (1982) 'Bebel et les bêtes', *Libération*, 19 November.

Bergson, Henri (1908) *Essai sur les données immédiates de la conscience*, Paris, Félix Alcan.

—— (1924) *Le Rire: Essai sur la signification du comique*, Paris, Félix Alcan, transl. Cloudesley Berereton and Fred Rothwell, the Gutenberg Project (www.gutenberg.org/files/4352/4352-h/4352-h.htm, accessed 25 November 2013).

Berthomé, Jean-Pierre (1996) *Jacques Demy et les racines du rêve*, 2nd Edition, Nantes, L'Atalante.

Brooks, Peter (1976) *The Melodramatic Imagination: Balzac, Henry James, Melodrama and the Mode of Excess*, New Haven CT and London, Yale University Press.

Capdenas, Michel (1967) '*Les Demoiselles de Rochefort*', *Les Lettres françaises*, 9 March.

Cerbone, David R. (2006) *Understanding Phenomenology*, Durham, Acumen.

Cohen, Steven (2005) *Incongruous Entertainment: Camp, Cultural Value and the MGM Musical*, Durham and London, Duke University Press.

Cooper, Sarah (2007) 'Mortal Ethics: Reading Levinas with the Dardenne Brothers', *Film-Philosophy*, 11 (2): 66–87.

Deleuze, Gilles (1985) *Cinéma 2: L'image-temps*, Paris, Les Éditions de Minuit.

Duras, Marguerite (1986) 'Il n'est jamais trop tard pour découvrir Demy', *Libération*, 22 July 1976.

Dyer, Richard (1986) *Heavenly Bodies: Film Stars and Society*, New York and London, Routledge.

Garson, Charlotte and Zvonkine, Eugénie (2010) *Jacques Demy: Les Demoiselles de Rochefort*, Paris, Centre national du cinéma et de l'image animée.

Herzog, Amy (2010) 'En Chanté: Music, Memory and Perversity in the Films of Jacques Demy', in *Dreams of Difference, Songs of the Same*, Minneapolis and London, University of Minnesota Press: 115–53.

Hill, Rodney (2008a) 'The New Wave meets the Tradition of Quality: Jacques Demy's *The Umbrella's of Cherbourg*', *Cinema Journal*, 48 (1): 27–50.

Howard, Richard transl. (2002), *A Lover's Discourse: Fragments*, London, Vintage.

Jibokji Frizon, Joséphine (2013) 'La Peinture en fiction', in Anon. (eds), *Le Monde enchanté de Jacques Demy*, Paris, Skira Flammarion, La Cinémathèque Française and Ciné-Tamaris.

Jullier, Laurent (2007) *Abécédaire des* Parapluies de Cherbourg, Paris, Broché.

Lalanne, Jean-Marc (1997) 'Noirceur et féerie de Jacques Demy', *Cahiers du Cinéma*, 511: 60–3.

Lefèvre, Raphaël (2013) *Une chambre en ville*, Crisnée, Belgium, Editions Yellow Now.

Lefort, Gérard (1982) 'Ni "critique", ni "française"', *Libération*, 19 November.

Levinas, Emmanuel (1971) *Totalité et infini: essai sur l'extériorité*, Paris, Le Livre de Poche.

—— (1984) 'Interdit de la représentation et "Droits de l'Homme"', in Adélie and Jean-Jacques Rassial (eds), *L'Interdit de la représentation, Colloque de Montpellier, 1981*, Paris, Seuil: 107–13.

Marshall, Bill and Lindeperg, Sylvie (2000) 'Time, History and Memory in *Les Parapluies de Cherbourg*', in Bill Marshall and Robynn Stilwell (eds), *Musicals: Hollywood and Beyond*, Chicago, University of Chicago Press: 98–106.

O'Shaughnessy, Martin (2007) *The New Face of Political Cinema: Commitment in French Film since 1995*, Oxford and New York, Berghahn.

Peacock, Stephen (2010) *Colour*, Manchester, Manchester University Press.

Rosenbaum, Jonathan (2011) 'Pas le même vieux numéro', in Jérôme Baron (ed.), *Jacques Demy*, Revue 303, Nantes: 4–8.

Ross, Kristin (1996) *Fast Cars, Clean Bodies: Decolonization and the Reordering of French Culture*, Cambridge MA and London, The MIT Press.

Sadoul, Georges (1967) 'Les Demoiselles de Rochefort', *Les Lettres françaises*, 9 March.

Saxton, Libby (2010) 'Levinas, Ethics, Faciality', in Libby Saxton and Lisa Downing, *Film and Ethics: Foreclosed Encounters*, London and New York, Routledge: 95–106.

Taboulay, Camille (1996) *Le Cinéma enchanté de Jacques Demy*, Paris, Cahiers du Cinéma.

Trémois, Claude-Marie (1982) *Demy de Nantes*, *Télérama*, 27 October.

Various (1982) 'Un appel des critiques de cinéma: Pourquoi nous louons "Une chambre en ville"', *Les Nouvelles littéraires*, 11 November.

Vaugeois, Gérard (2013) 'Le Combattant', interview, in *Jacques Demy: L'enchanteur, Les Inrockuptibles – hors série*: 75.

Internet sources:

www.britannica.com/EBchecked/topic/626111/verismo, accessed 15 June 2012.

3

Fantasy and its disenchantments: fairytale, fable and myth in the *Demy-monde*

'Enchanté', which, as seen, is the most commonly used adjective to describe Demy's musical cinema, also applies to varying degrees to his adaptations of fairytale, fable and myth. Yet, congruent with his defiance of expectations, he fuses the beguilement anticipated of such forms with disillusionment. On the surface, his screen adaptations of Charles Perrault's *Peau d'âne*, Robert Browning's *The Pied Piper* and Robert Graves's version of Orpheus's descent into the underworld appear distinct. *Peau d'âne* flouts historical accuracy, *The Pied Piper* expands upon the contexts of its period and *Parking* sets a story from ancient Greece in the present day of its production. And yet, all three convey, in different ways, Demy's scepticism towards bourgeois privilege, and anxieties around the erosion of affect in the modern world.

In this, Demy modifies the original text to serve, not simply the ideology of the film he is directing at the time, as Christopher Orr remarks in his intertextuality approach to adaptations (1984: 72), but that of his cinema. Since *Peau d'âne*, *The Pied Piper* and *Parking* pertain to legends transmitted orally, and later written in verse, some thickening of characters and events is inevitable, but it is the nature of Demy's additions and transformations and how they serve his cinema that prove interesting for this study. The choice of genre requires him to locate his characters within strictly delimited spaces (a kingdom, a city-state, a classical region transformed into a modern metropolis and a hellish subterranean realm), surroundings that his characters are compelled to apprehend in certain ways.

Father–daughter desires and mother–daughter rivalries in *Peau d'âne*

Given that fairytales had always inspired Demy, it is unsurprising that he adapted one of them to the cinema screen. He chose *Peau d'âne*, among the least reproduced fairytales beyond France and given literary form in 1694 by Charles Perrault, most renowned for his *Histoires ou contes du temps passé, avec des moralités: Contes de ma mère l'Oye*, which included *Cinderella, Sleeping Beauty* and *Little Red Riding Hood*. The tale accords with Demy's aesthetic and thematic preoccupations. As Marina Warner reveals, Perrault exuded a 'tongue-in-cheek moralizing' and 'flippant irreverence' (1995: 325–6) and, though his original stories were intended for children, he also wrote them with an aristocratic adult readership in mind. As a child, Demy staged a puppet version of *Peau d'âne* for his friends. In the early 1960s, he sought to adapt the tale, but lacked access to the required resources.[1] *Peau d'âne* remains Demy's most popular production with French audiences and has endured as a staple of festive television entertainment in France.

Demy extends Perrault's satire by transforming the original text into a postmodern fairytale that, while paying homage to its source, also mocks it, hence its enduring appeal to adults and children. According to Fredric Jameson, the postmodern is expressed culturally via pastiche and parody. Both involve 'the mimicry of … the mannerisms and stylistic twitches of other styles' (1983: 113). Pastiche copies existing codes, but parody 'capitalizes on the uniqueness of … styles and seizes on their idiosyncrasies and eccentricities to produce an imitation which mocks the original' (1983: 113). Jameson's definition of parody pertains particularly well to *Peau d'âne* because it deliberately transgresses the divisions between present and past temporalities and defies received and purist interpretations of cultural taste and discernment. Moreover, consonant with Jameson's definition of postmodern parody, it reacts against 'the established forms of high modernism' and dismantles the distinction between 'high culture and the so-called mass or popular culture' (1983: 112).

For parody to function, it requires a serious issue at which it targets its irreverence. In *Peau d'âne*, this centres on bourgeois morality and values, which are challenged via its mocking of socio-economic privi-

---

1 Brigitte Bardot, who, in 1962, had agreed to star alongside Anthony Perkins, proved too costly (Taboulay, 1996: 99).

lege and dominant notions of good taste, and its narrative of incestuous desires about a king who wishes to marry his daughter. As Warner observes, the prohibition of incest 'holds universally in human society' (1995: 319). The Oedipal complex recounting the paternal interdiction of a son's sexual desires for his mother is commonly evoked in Western culture and mythology, but it is in fairytales that a father's sexual and romantic impulses towards his daughter make a 'strong showing' (1995: 320). Nevertheless, whereas the father's desires for his daughter are corrected at the end of Perrault's tale, the flames of incestuous passion appear to burn on in Demy's conclusion.

Peau d'âne opens on the King (Jean Marais) of the Blue Kingdom who, the voice-over narration recounts, was so loved by his people and respected by his neighbours that he was the happiest of all monarchs. Familial harmony and material affluence drive his felicity; he is in love with his beautiful Queen (Catherine Deneuve) and very proud of his talented and graceful daughter (also played by Deneuve). His financial fortitude is assured by his most valued possession, a donkey that defecates gold coins. However, his bliss is soon brutally ruptured by the Queen's sudden death. Before passing away, she beseeches the King to remarry only when he has found a woman more beautiful than she is, setting in train a brief quest that ends in the King seeking his daughter's hand in marriage. Upon the counsel of the Lilac Fairy (Delphine Seyrig), the Princess makes three seemingly impossible demands of her father. She insists that he has the royal costumiers fabricate three remarkable dresses, in the shades of the weather, the moon and the sun respectively. After he answers each of her requests, the Fairy advises the Princess to solicit the skin of his sacred donkey. Reluctantly, the King acquiesces and the Fairy forces the Princess to don the rancid hide and flee to a farm where she toils as a scullion, known as Peau d'âne. One day, the Prince-heir to the Red Kingdom (Jacques Perrin) stumbles across her in her log cabin and falls in love. When he requests that she bake him a cake, she drops her ring into the mixture. Upon finding it, he declares that he will marry the woman whose finger the ring fits. After it fails to fit any woman in the kingdom, the Prince calls for Peau d'âne and, as it slips easily onto her digit, she emerges from her donkey skin in her magnificent sun-gown. The Blue King and Lilac Fairy attend the wedding and, here, Demy inserts ambiguity. The Fairy announces her forthcoming wedding to the Blue King and urges the perplexed Princess to put on a good face. Seconds later, the Princess's expression turns to relief as her father embraces her and reassures her that they will never separate again.

This last exchange illustrates how Demy's version defies the fairytale's traditional function of guiding its readers along an accepted moral path. In his study of the meanings of fairytales, Bruno Bettelheim argues that they offer the boy-reader 'fantasy materials which suggest ... in symbolic form what the battle to achieve self-realization is all about, and it guarantees a happy ending' (1976: 39). This self-realisation and happiness derives from the successful resolution of the male child's Oedipal complex (1976: 39). Due to its focus on a father's desire for his daughter, such Oedipal concerns are less relevant in *Peau d'âne*. If any of the classical narratives that have informed (psychoanalytical) accounts of child development are pertinent, it is the Electra complex that seems most convincing, in which both mother (here symbolic in the Fairy) and daughter vie for the father's attentions. Although throughout the narrative the Fairy appears to function as the character through which society's repudiation of incest is articulated, her final line exposes her earlier diatribes as a means of eliminating the perceived threat of the Princess to her union with the Blue King.

Yet, *Peau d'âne* overtly disrupts such psychoanalytical prohibitions. Not only does incest remain unresolved, but also, unlike the classic fairytale heroine (and Perrault's protagonist), the Princess is denied recompense for her suffering. Earlier scenes suggest that the Princess begins to reciprocate her father's love; she rhetorically asks the Fairy why she would refuse his love and when she intones 'amour, amour je t'aime tant' ('my love, my love, I love you so'), images of her father materialise in her magic mirror. Moreover, it is the words of the biological mother (the Queen) that eventually orient the father's attentions towards his daughter (underlined visually in the casting of Deneuve as both Queen and Princess). The actions of the biological and symbolic mothers force the Princess to leave the space in which she is raised (and with which she is symbiotically aligned) to reside, first in a grubby wooden cabin on the edge of a farm and, second, in a castle that lacks the colours, fauna and live statues of her birthplace.

The incest plot allows Demy to further his apparent preference for passionate connections over romantic compromises. *Peau d'âne* suggests that the Princess marries to escape her wretched existence as a scullion. She, as well as the Fairy, colludes in luring the Red Prince. As he eats at the farm with his courtiers, he declares that fairies are an obscure force and compel people to act well or badly. Promptly, he walks into the forest and encounters a speaking rose that tells him to have faith in love and continue his path. Moments later, he stumbles upon Peau d'âne's cabin. Blocked by an invisible shield, he climbs onto the roof. As he looks down through the skylight, he is greeted with a Princess resplendent in her sun-gown who sings 'j'ai attendu que tu me portes ce bonheur depuis tant de temps' ('I have waited for you to bring me this happiness for such a long time'). When she tilts her hand mirror to see him spying on her, her agency in manipulating the situation is confirmed, prefigured in that she magically trans-forms herself into the Princess when she hears of his impending visit, and reinforced later in her act of slipping the ring into the cake. Given that the object of her affections appears to be her father, *Peau d'âne* depicts, as in *Les Parapluies de Cherbourg*, the thwarting of instinc-tive and visceral attraction by both external morality and a hegemonic value system, embodied by a manipulative mother figure, albeit for different motives. Yet, incest is a metaphor for non-normative desires more broadly. *Peau d'âne* playfully nods to a world in which unorth-odox urges and attractions cannot be easily curbed.

The undermining of patriarchy is reinforced by the film's critique of the woman's status as object and servant. In the Blue Kingdom, women are represented as status symbols. The Blue King falls in love with the Princess because of her beauty and his vanity, while his former Queen's dying wish heralds looks as the overriding crite-rion for her husband's remarriage. *Peau d'âne* thus represents not only the way women are objectified, but also how their acts can make them complicit in their own subordination. But such internalisa-tion of patriarchy is also mocked. Firstly, this takes form in the film's exaggeration of one of the key elements of fairytales about hetero-sexual romance: the Prince's quest to find the woman he encounters earlier in the narrative. The women of the Red Kingdom vainly try to alter the form of their fingers so that the ring will fit, but they then bitterly complain when their efforts cause them physical pain and disfigurement, while an older woman and a stable hand ridicule them. Secondly, parody of gender conventions is expressed through dialogues, which function reflexively to undermine the morality that maintains women in a position of objectification and servitude. For instance, Peau d'âne tells the old lady who spits frogs 'une souillon ne peut pas être propre ou bien ce n'est pas une souillon' ('a scullion cannot be clean or she is not a scullion'). Such a statement dilutes the subordination of women to a status as servant/slave by presenting this patriarchally ordained role as a self-conscious performance.

As in *Les Demoiselles de Rochefort*, then, ironic modes of spectator address invite the audience to participate in its satire of hegemony. Knowing nods recur, which literally pull the morality traditionally projected by fairytales apart from within. Again, engagement with this irony is not necessary in order to experience visual and narrative enjoyment; indeed, *Peau d'âne* has sparked the imaginary of generations of young girls, just as many have dreamed of being Solange and Delphine. And yet, irony runs throughout the film and aids in the film's framing of sexual politics and narrative pleasures.

Elsewhere, bourgeois materialism and privilege are derided in the donkey that defecates gold. The ass was an addition to Perrault's text, which, according to Warner, could be explained by the role of the jackass as the 'fall guy in the market economy of the fabulist's harsh world' (1995: 324). Furthermore, in 'medieval bestiary lore' the donkey suffers acute hardship and neglect and can never be delivered from these burdens (1995: 325). By contrast, in Greek mythology, the ass was a symbol of virility and became the sacrificial animal favoured by Priapus who coveted its large penis. *Peau d'âne* shifts the emphasis from the donkey's phallus to its anus and implicitly devalues material wealth as bestial waste. That the donkey belongs to the Blue Kingdom, the colour associated with ideological capitalism, symbolically connects greed with the proponents of right-wing politics. Conscience about the wellbeing of the people is aligned with the Red Kingdom; after apprising his mother (Micheline Presle) of the existence of scullions in the forest, the Red Prince complains that his father could improve matters in the kingdom.

The film's irreverence is reinforced by its use of temporal and cultural anachronisms. Much has been said of these in critical and academic texts, and it is thus necessary to discuss the principal examples here. It is difficult to pinpoint a timeframe in most fairytales because their morals are intended to transcend the ages, hence, the opacity of the classic opener 'once upon a time'. This line immediately locates the story in the indeterminate past, thus complying with the fairytale's emphasis on the present and future pertinence of completed events. Although Demy opens his story with the same words, he mixes his temporal and cultural referents and, in so doing, subverts the relation between past, present and future required for the fairytale's impact (on this see Hill 2005: 40–44). Deliberate solecisms allow Demy to alter the atmosphere of his adaptation and destabilise the tale's principal time-situating qualifier. As Berthomé has noted, the Blue King's costume evokes Henri II (1519–59), the beast's outfit in Cocteau's *La Belle et la bête* and late 1960s fashion in the glittery blue tones and shiny silver boots. The Princess's dresses are inspired by a Louis XV (1710–74) style, while moving images of clouds are projected onto her weather-dress (1996: 245).

Temporal and cultural distinctions are apposed and transcended via Legrand's score. At the 'Cat and Bird Ball', given by the Red Queen for her son to find a bride, music, dance and costume recall the French baroque style of Louis XIV. When the Blue King climbs the spiral stair-case to visit the wise man, a Disneyesque arrangement of ascending flute and clarinet notes is utilised. A percussive and symphonic theme accompanies Peau d'âne as she sings 'Recette pour un cake d'amour'. More obviously disruptive are the film's allusions to twentieth-century writers and modern gadgets. The Blue King marvels about tomor-row's poets and, in citing Cocteau, mentions a bar, telephones and gaslights, while the Fairy possesses a telephone and tells the Princess that her battery is running low. Yet more ostentatious, the Blue King and Fairy arrive at the Princess's wedding in a helicopter. Such anach-ronisms allow *Peau d'âne* to defy temporal plausibility and disregard history, one of the grounding principles of postmodernism. They also serve to reaffirm the parody of the fairytale and of the conventional morality it has traditionally been used to promote.

Postmodernism's function of reacting against modernism is served by the film's undermining of the canonical status of avant-garde art and derision of the elitism attached to it. Allusions to so-called 'legitimate' culture are apposed with references to suppos-edly 'lower' forms. Winks to classic fairytales and their screen adaptations are placed alongside nods to surrealism, pop art and modernism. The Blue King reads 'Les Muses' from Cocteau's *Ode à Picasso* (1919), with its references to Orpheus, and cites Guillaume Apollinaire's 'L'Amour' from *Le Guetteur mélancolique* (1952). The choice of authors is not fortuitous. Both are popularly associated with surrealism, even if, in the case of Cocteau, critics have questioned his links to the movement.[2] Surrealism produced abstruse artworks that favoured analogy, chaos and the logic of dreams. As Warner reveals, the 'extreme peculiarity' of *Peau d'âne* and its 'breaching of taboo' appealed to the surrealists (1995: 327).[3] However, in Cocteau in particular, Demy selects from an artist famous for having created one of the most recognisable images associated with surrealism. Cocteau's talking mouth, which appears in the protagonist's hand in *Le Sang d'un poète* (1932), is adapted in the speaking rose that the Prince encounters in the forest. A further layer of intertextuality enriches the referent as the rose also invokes the women-flowers in *Munchausen* (Josef von Báky, 1943). Some of the accessible aspects of surrealist art informed Demy's aesthetic choices. He had intended to work with Leonor Fini, whom he met in 1969; her work, in particular her lithograph *La Serrure* (1965), with its figure of a woman, her head framed with flowers, influenced the decors and the costumes created by Agostino Pace.

In interviews following the film's release, Demy recounts how, after having returned from two years in the United States, he wanted to rid himself of what he referred to as French good taste (in Langlois, 1970). He argued that in a country known for spearheading avant-garde art movements, a film such as *Trash* (Paul Morrissey, 1970), produced by Andy Warhol, would be impossible to make. He identified pop art, which Jameson includes in his list of postmodern cultural movements (1983: 111), as the principal aesthetic inspiration for his film. Pop art draws from advertising and other mainstream images; it both celebrates throwaway culture and illustrates how mass production and consumption have become idealised in the post-industrial Western world. The influences of pop art can be found in the paintings and stained glass windows in the blue castle, and fuses with allusions to surrealism, Disney, classic illustration and modernism. The open book that begins the film is an explicit nod to Disney's *Snow White and the Seven Dwarfs*, while the written words 'il était une fois' conjure the beginning of Cocteau's *La Belle et la Bête*.[4] The plant-adorned spiral

2 See www.passion-estampes.com/npe/newsletter28.html, accessed 22 April 2013.

3 The tale is mentioned in André Breton's *Manifeste du surréalisme* (1924).

4 Further references to *Snow White* include: the dwarfs, Peau d'âne's cabin, the glass coffin in the snow, the silhouette of the King kneeling and the *cake d'amour*; additional nods to *La Belle et la bête* include Marais, his costume, the Caryatid statues and the scene in which the Princess awaits in her chamber for the arrival of the King who brings the donkey skin (see Berthomé 1996: 242).

staircase that leads the Blue King to the wise man recalls the steps Snow White sweeps in her first scene, and those in front of the beast's castle in *La Belle et la bête*, replicas of Gustave Doré's ivy-covered steps in his illustration to accompany a nineteenth-century edition of *Peau d'âne*. The Princess first sings 'Amour, Amour' in front of a well that is bedecked with doves, reminiscent of the waterhole adorned with doves from which Snow White fetches water, while her courtier is bright blue, as are the living statues and dwarfs, recalling the incandescent colours favoured by pop and psychedelic art proponents.

Elsewhere, the modernist *nouveau cinéma* movement is embodied in Delphine Seyrig, famous for her roles in *L'Année dernière à Marienbad* (Alain Robbe-Grillet and Resnais, 1961) and *Muriel ou le temps d'un retour* (Resnais, 1963). The flat note chords of the Princess's organ-music recall aurally the disconcerting soundtracks of the new cinema, particularly *L'Année dernière à Marienbad*, written by Francis Seyrig, Delphine's brother. Yet, again, *Peau d'âne* recasts the referent by having Seyrig play the manipulative and capricious fairy, modelled on classic Hollywood actress Jean Harlow. Moreover, her status as an interfering and irritable time-traveller recalls Endora (Agnes Moorhead), the witch and meddling mother-in-law in *Bewitched*, the globally successful ABC television sitcom that aired from 1964 to 1972. The choice of artists and artefacts is seemingly not fortuitous; Apollinaire, Cocteau, Fini and Warhol are known for their free spirits and anti-establishment views and lifestyles. Cocteau's life and works resonate with queer meanings, as do those of Warhol, while Fini's art is known for having depicted strong, unapologetic women, of the type that recur in Demy's films; finally, *Bewitched* is camp reference *in extremis*.

Intertextuality also extends to Demy's own films. The casting of Jacques Perrin as the romantic Prince is reminiscent of his role as Maxence in *Les Demoiselles de Rochefort* and the dream sequence finally unites him on screen with Deneuve. When Peau d'âne searches for a recipe for the Prince, she stumbles across the King's Cake and instantly refuses to make it, parodying her diegetic predicament with the Blue King and Geneviève's acquiescence to Roland in *Les Parapluies de Cherbourg*. Moreover, the everyday and the fantastical intersect, as when the Fairy scolds her goddaughter for arriving before she is ready. Elsewhere, *Peau d'âne* is set in real locations in the Loire châteaux of Plessis-Bouré and Chambord, and the village of Gambais. Demy embellishes the interiors with the aid of decor designers Jim

Léon and Jacques Dugied, rendering the castle of the Blue Kingdom natural and that of the Red Kingdom man-made, with psychedelic and pop art uniting the two, as mentioned (Berthomé, 1996: 243–4). Ghislain Cloquet's cinematography and Anne-Marie Cotret's editing utilise familiar devices, including mobile camerawork, widescreen, bright colours (by Eastmancolor) and iris shots, rendered psychedelic by their respective fluorescent blue, red and green tones. *Peau d'âne* also pursues Demy's interests in representing subjective time. A surprising slow motion sequence shows the Princess, dressed in her donkey skin, running through the farmyard, the workers standing still as she leaps and dashes, with only the women's skirts and the animals' tails swaying in the wind. Peau d'âne's present advances at one speed while the workers' time is slowed, even frozen. Although seemingly a departure from his earlier work then, *Peau d'âne* bears many similarities to the rest of his output.

Peau d'âne was broadly well received by the critics as a good example of Christmas family entertainment (see Cervoni, 1970). Interestingly, for André Bessèges, instead of regretting the absence of cinematic revolutionaries in France, Demy should proudly affirm his status as a seller of dreams (1971). Such a comment overlooks the film's more political and philosophical comments on contemporary moralities and judgements. Demy would make his subsequent production in the UK, but he confounds expectations by accentuating a sense of authenticity in his representation of the society of the middle ages.

Politicising fable: *The Pied Piper*

Unlike *Peau d'âne*, *The Pied Piper* is fixed in time and place, and constitutes a detailed depiction of the corruption and immorality of the medieval society in which it is set. Research was undertaken into the socio-historical contexts of medieval times (Siclier, 1976) and these are portrayed in the situations and events that supplement the main narrative. *The Pied Piper* is brutal; the magical expected of a Demy film is minimised, embodied mainly by the peripheral musicians and the Piper, played by folk star Donovan, whose arrival in and departure from Hamelin open and close the film. It is a sumptuous production, its *mise en scène* strongly influenced by the rich compositions of Northern Renaissance paintings.

When Demy was invited to direct *The Pied Piper* by British producer David Putnam, Andrew Birkin had written the script and Donovan was cast in the central role and had composed the music. With the assistance of Mark Peploe, Demy embarked on modifications that imbue *The Pied Piper* with markers of his cinema. He retains the main events of Browning's tale, but makes additions and alterations to characters and atmosphere. Paradoxically given their obvious divergences in mood, *Les Demoiselles de Rochefort* can be interpreted as a direct antecedent of *The Pied Piper*, as Berthomé notes (1996: 264) and this is particularly evident in its structure and use of space. The narrative is condensed into a few days surrounding a unique event: the wedding of Franz (John Hurt), son of the Baron (Donald Pleasence), to Lisa (Cathryn Harrison), the daughter of Burgomaster Poppendick (Roy Kinnear). Moreover, the family troupe of nomadic mystery play performers led by Mattio (Keith Buckley), accompanied by English pilgrim Arthur Cecil (Peter Eyre) and the Pied Piper, recall Bill, Etienne and the fairground workers. Like these outsiders, Mattio, his family and the Piper are bystanders to the main events of the story.

However, fear of the ravages of medieval pestilence and intolerance supersede the exaltation that subsumes Rochefort. Where the links to the plague appear allegorical in the original fable, the pandemic is central to *The Pied Piper*, which, the intertitles inform us, begins at noon on Midsummer's Day in 1349, the 'year of the Black Death'. Gavin (Jack Wild), a young, wounded prodigy of the Jewish alchemist Melius (Michael Hordern), discovers a rat when visiting Lisa in her garden, although Arthur Cecil becomes the plague's first victim. Melius recognises the rodent as the black rat, which, as he confirms, was the main carrier according to papal physician Guy de Chauliac. Unconvinced by official and religiously motivated warnings that the plague is God's punishment, Melius vainly attempts to apprise the Burgomaster of the dangers. Maligned by the Bishop (Peter Vaughan) and his priests because he is Jewish, he is tried by an Inquisition and burned at the stake for heresy. The Piper leads the children out of town to a new world, free of the cruelty and corruption of the one they leave behind. Like Delphine in *Les Demoiselles de Rochefort*, Gavin joins the outsiders' convoy as it leaves for its destination of Flanders.

While the Charente River borders Rochefort, high walls separate

Hamelin[5] from the outside world, transforming the town into a fortress to which access is granted to a select few; the Piper is permitted to enter, accompanied by Mattio and his family, because his tune awakens Lisa from her sick slumber. *Intramuros* Hamelin is a sombre place, in which cupidity and exploitation are the defining traits of its governing class, and death and persecution hang as constant menaces over its more marginalised inhabitants. Where the colourful facades and bright sunlight reflect the ebullience of Rochefort's dwellers, the encumbered streets and lugubrious interiors intensify the sense of menace and oppression that dominates medieval Hamelin society. Director of photography Peter Suschitzky's highly mobile camera-work serves, paradoxically, to amplify the confinement of the town. Use of panning shots with a long focal length is recurrent, positioning us as distant observers, held back behind the many objects that clutter the image, including carts and the scaffolding for the new cathedral, as characters scurry between Melius's apothecary, the Baron's castle and the civic chambers. When Melius first visits Lisa in her sickbed, he traverses the main square, the camera filming him from behind pillars and bales of dried sticks, which serve as a gloomy portension of his execution. Similarly, when the warmongering Franz urges his father to conscript child soldiers to fight, the long focal distance shows both characters squeezed between two oversized pillars, the low ceilings and thick walls enhancing the sense of entrapment, further exacerbated by the low lighting and panoramic Cinemascope lens.

By explicitly setting *The Pied Piper* within the historical context of the plague, Demy amplifies the depiction of corruption and cruelty implied in the original fable. The plausibility of its reconstitution of medieval society is confirmed by the unambiguous resonances between its content and the historical transformations of the fourteenth century. As Berthomé reveals, the period heralded the transition between the 'old' ways of the middle ages and the 'new' emphasis on the arts, sciences, spirituality, politics and humanism ushered in by the Renaissance (1996: 266–7). After the failures of the Eighth Crusade to Tunis and the Ninth Crusade to Damascus in the thirteenth century, and the devastation engendered by the plague in the fourteenth century, the symbolic power of the aristocracy, State and Church was threatened. Demy portrays this through the Baron's

---

5 Because Hamelin had been bombed during the Second World War, the exterior scenes were shot in the Bavarian burg of Rothenburg ob der Tauber.

preoccupation with his legacy, the Burgomaster's fixation with status, the Bishop's resolve to have the cathedral completed (many were unfinished) and the Papal Nuncio's (Hamilton Dyce) insistence that the Baron contribute to a war against the Roman Emperor alongside Pope Clement VI. Merchants and artists were journeying south to Florence to gain knowledge of Renaissance art, and north to Flanders where Northern Renaissance painting was born. Such a moment of transition is emphasised in the opening encounter between Mattio, his family and Arthur, who is on a pilgrimage to the Holy City. Mattio's wagon is adorned with a large painting that obliquely nods to Giotto di Bondone's *Compianto sul Cristo morto* (1304–6) (*Lamentation: the Mourning of Christ*), while Arthur bears two religious relics, a sock said to have belonged to Thomas à Becket and a splinter supposed to have come from Jesus's cross, and which he believes will save him from the plague. By the end of the film, Mattio and his family survive the epidemic while, as mentioned, Arthur is Hamelin's first victim. Disenchanted, he insists that Mattio burn his amulets, which, he admits, were fakes.

Where Bondone's masterpiece represents woe at the loss of Christ, Mattio's fresco, which functions as a backdrop for his mystery plays, depicts the barbarity of orthodox medieval systems. A haloed figure is being burned at the stake, while a king looks on and a peasant fans the flames. Symbolically, it serves as a premonition of Melius's execution urged by the Bishop and clergy, authorised by the Baron and enacted by the Burgomaster's guards. Some have likened *The Pied Piper* to *Det sjunde inseglet* (*The Seventh Seal*, Ingmar Bergman, 1957) about a knight jaded with the crusades who returns to plague-torn Europe and plays a game with Death through which he ponders the existence of God, although for Berthomé, *The Pied Piper* is less allegorical than Bergman's film (1996: 266).

The work of a later Renaissance artist, this time from Flanders, Pieter Bruegel the Elder (1525–69), provides a fruitful comparison for interpreting the system of morals and values depicted in Hamelin. His *Nederlandse Spreekwoorden* (1559) (*Netherlandish Proverbs*) portrays the foolishness and malevolence of humankind in the mid-sixteenth century. Bruegel was influenced by Hieronymus Bosch, whose *Tuin der Lusten* (1480–1505) (*The Garden of Earthly Delights*) inspires Bernard and Jacques' conversation about lust in *La Luxure*. *Netherlandish Proverbs* depicts approximately one hundred aphorisms that bear a symbolic relation to the characters and events in *The Pied Piper*. The self-centred and preposterous leaders illustrate the dicta 'to catch fish without a net'; Franz tells his father 'your cathedral can be built for nothing, your masons don't have to be paid, they can be whipped' and the Bishops and clergy persuade the Baron to complete the cathedral through fear tactics. The Burgomaster and inhabitants depict the proverb 'a wall with cracks will soon collapse': in refusing to recompense the Piper, and in ignoring Melius's admonitions, they set in train the ultimate downfall of Hamelin society. The wedding exemplifies the aphorism 'love is on the side where the money bag hangs': the union between Franz and Lisa is intended to link standing (the Aristocracy) with political influence and prosperity (the State), while corroborating clerical authority (the Church). Franz is only interested in money whereas Lisa's affections centre on Gavin, the impossible love object, Demy thus inserting allusions to the narrative of condemned desires in *Les Parapluies de Cherbourg* (and replicated later in *Une chambre en ville*). One further renaissance artist provides the inspiration for the aesthetics that imbue some of the interior scenes: Johannes Vermeer. Light streams through and bounces off surfaces, while one of the maids that assist Frau Poppendick (Diana Dors) resembles the woman depicted in *Meisje met de parel* (1665–67) (*The Girl with the Pearl Earring*) with her headscarf. Elsewhere, the shots of Melius pouring over ledgers and concocting potions recall *De Astronoom* (1668) (*The Astronomer*) and *De Geograaf* (1668–69) (*The Geographer*).

According to Berthomé, *The Pied Piper* signals a departure from Demy's thematic interests in two ways: firstly, it shifts the focus to the father–son relationship and, secondly, it depicts a micro-cosmos in which free choice is stifled (1996: 276). The paternal figure is indeed often absent from Demy's early films or represented in typical ways as static and authoritarian, and exiled to the margins of the narrative. In *The Pied Piper*, fathers are more central and can be divided into benevolent and malevolent patriarchal figures: Mattio and most crucially Melius, Gavin's surrogate father, are exemplary in their altruism, bravery and foresight, whereas the Burgomaster and Baron are ineffectual and self-centred patriarchs. Unusually, women are marginal, defined by their relation to men, as in the case of Frau Poppendick and Lisa. Patriarchal omnipotence is further symbolised in the three institutions of the Aristocracy, State and Church, all of which are constructed as unequivocally unscrupulous, although the film reserves its strongest contempt for the clergy, visually distinguished by their scarlet robes, thus occasioning an extension of the agnostic cynicism evident in *Ars*. The symbolism is explicit when the rodents emerge from the wedding cake shaped in the form of the planned cathedral.

However, although Berthomé is correct in that the emphasis on chance and free will is less apparent in *The Pied Piper* precisely because of the weight of medieval malevolence, agency is still ascribed to its most oppressed characters. Melius, the film's central humanist, adopts the stance of resolve and optimism towards the alienating environment in which he lives. He instructs Gavin in the insights of the Greeks and importance of scientific facts over religious faith, rejecting the clerical scholar Papias the Elder for the historian Heroditus. As a Jew, he is unbound by the strictures of Catholicism, evinced when he dismisses the Bishop for reading the Last Sacrament to Lisa. Despite the Star of David emblazoned on the reverse of his tunic, Melius acts as if God is superfluous, incapable of safeguarding the people, unlike medical science, which may yield a cure for the plague.

Melius acts in the present and makes choices for the benefit of humankind. During the inquisition, he humbly declares 'I commend myself to your mercy in the hope that future generations may learn at least by your mistakes, if not by my discoveries'. Rather than capitulate, Melius utilises the Inquisition to plead for a fairer world, calling for future generations 'not only to tolerate each other's differences, but even to rejoice in them'. Faced with execution, Melius preserves his agency, telling Gavin that somebody will find a cure for the plague and insisting he leave for the Netherlands to study painting. Read through a Sartrean existentialist lens, at the moment of Melius's death, the essence of his life is confirmed in his integrity, courage and altruism.

The Pied Piper can be read as parodic. Costumes appear excessive, rendering the characters as grotesque caricatures. The Baron's conical hat is tall and crooked, and the Burgomaster's civic chain is gaudy and cumbersome. The bounding and ineffectual Burgomaster is often the source of visual comedy and the clergy's warnings are so bellowing and extreme that they seem absurd. Actors often typecast as baddies in commercial cinema and television play the three villainous leaders.[6]

6 Pleasence was James Bond's nemesis Blofeld in *You Only Live Twice* (Lewis Gilbert, 1967), Vaughan played evil Dr A. Jaeger in *The Avengers – My Wildest Dreams* (Robert Fuest, 1968) and Kinnear was cast as Veruca Salt's over-indulgent father in *Willy Wonka and the Chocolate Factory* (Mel Stuart, 1971).

Elsewhere, Demy makes an oblique nod to his use of anachronisms in *Peau d'âne*, constructing the Piper as a time-traveller like the Lilac Fairy. Donovan's songs, while inspired by medieval madrigals, reverberate with the idealism of early 1970's hippy folk music. He sings of 'riding homeward ... over the ocean', and is surrounded by children as if performing for a playgroup. His guitar, adorned with its psychedelic pattern, is a modern version of the more customary *guitarra latina*. Historical authenticity is thus partially undermined by the film's stylisation and objective of appealing to its target audience of children.

Yet, the potential of these elements to attenuate the film's starkness is mitigated by the unambiguous barbarity that frames the depiction of Hamelin society. Demy's Manichean division between a benign group of artists, a minstrel and an alchemist and the malignant governing institutions echoes and extends his counter-cultural positions with regards to the dominant classes. *The Pied Piper* is less the extension of the dreamlike *Peau d'âne* than a precursor of the politics mobilised within *Une chambre en ville*. While revealing the inequalities of medieval societies, it engages some of the concerns of the twentieth century. The text that concludes the film confirms the connection, suggested in the diegesis, between Melius's treatment by the clergy and Frantz, and the terrible plight of the Jews in the Holocaust: 'an estimated 75,000,000 died in the black death ... the persecution that followed was to remain without parallel until this century'. Moreover, *The Pied Piper* was made in the years leading up to the petrol crisis of 1973, which would herald the end of three decades of unprecedented growth in France and the West and bolster an increasing despondency with capitalism. The Aristocracy, the State and the Church of the mid-fourteenth century can be interpreted as surrogates of the regimes governing France (and the UK) at the beginning of the 1970s (fittingly, when the film was made, the 'aristocratic' Georges Pompidou and Edward Heath were French President and British Prime Minister respectively). Hence, the intolerance of difference and the disdain for the less privileged symbolises the perceived social complacency and bigotry at the time. The departure of the Piper, musicians and Gavin at the film's close can thus be read as optimistic, if not idealistic, implying the existence somewhere of a nirvana where fairness supersedes prejudice.

Elsewhere, the very same self-interest and self-preservation that lead the Burgomaster, Baron and Bishop to stifle new modes of thinking and being are redolent of what Demy saw as a resistance towards innovation within the French film industry. It will not be forgotten that he had spent nine years seeking funds to make *Peau d'âne*, that he was thwarted in his attempts to direct a musical in *Lola*, that the productions of *Une chambre en ville* and *Trois places pour le 26* were suspended and that a number of projects never materialised. British money enabled him to adapt *The Pied Piper*,[7] which was only screened in France some four years after it had been made, as part of an English-language section of the first Festival Cinématographique de Paris in 1975. It was declared a triumph, prompting a polemic among some critics surprised that it had not achieved a wider exhibition. A distributor was approached after it had been acclaimed in the UK and US, but it was viewed as not commercial enough (Remond, 1975). The reviewer from *Le Quotidien de Paris* complained 'qu'un pareil chef d'oeuvre ne soit encore diffusé montre à quel point il faut réviser les structures de notre cinéma de fond en comble' (Anon, 1975) ('that such a masterpiece has still not been distributed shows how we must revise the structures of our cinema completely'). A shift in interpretations of what is understood as French cinema appears to have occurred from a film culture that was perceived as supporting non-commercial projects to one that, from the early 1970s, is seen as turning its back on them. Yet, the problem – and it is an enduring one[8] – is more complex, since *The Pied Piper* can be deemed neither art-house nor mass entertainment cinema. It is this status, as a film located in the middle-ground between government-sponsored projects that emit an image of cultural sophistication, and mass appeal productions supported by commercial companies, that applies to Demy's work and partly explains his difficulty in financing his projects in France.

Re-modernising myth: *Parking*

Closer to its source than *La Baie des Anges*, *Parking* is a modern adaptation of the Greek myth about Orpheus's descent into the underworld to rescue Eurydice. *Parking* draws from and expands upon

7 Demy had wanted to make *The Pied Piper* since he was a child, when he saw the operetta by Louis Ganne, *Hans le joueur de flûte*, at Théâtre Graslin.
8 See Pascale Ferran (2007) 'Violence économique et cinéma français', *Le Monde*, 26 February 2007.

the original legend as it is transcribed in Robert Graves's definitive twentieth-century edition (1955: 111–14). Orpheus, son of the Thracian King Oeagrus and his muse Calliope, was the ancient world's most celebrated poet. His wife Eurydice receives a fatal viper bite on her heel when attempting to resist the advances of Aristaeus, at Tempe in the valley of the river Peneius. Distraught at her death, Orpheus charms the ferryman Charon with his music in order to enter the underworld at Aornum in Thesprotis. Orpheus's melody moves Hades, the indomitable king of the underworld, so much that he authorises him to escort Eurydice to the upper-world on condition that he refrains from glancing at her until they are both in the bright daylight. Nearing their destination, Orpheus perceives the light first and, anxious that Eurydice's strength is waning, turns to look at her, trailing in the darkness. When his gaze connects with her, Eurydice is returned to the underworld for perpetuity. Much later, Orpheus is savagely ripped apart by a group of Maenads, female warrior followers of the god Dionysus, at Apollo's temple in Deium.

Parking condenses the main events of the myth into the final thirty-two minutes of the narrative. Preceding this, it centres on Orphée's (Francis Huster) preparations for a concert at the Palais des Omnisports in Bercy in Paris, thus adapting the classic poet into a pop icon whose music impacts on his legions of adoring fans. Moreover, this section includes an initial descent into the underworld and its effects on Orphée. A voltage shock from an electric guitar sparks Orphée's descent, chauffeured by Caron (Hugues Quester). An underground multi-storey car park serves as the River Styx and one of its walls functions as the opening at Aornum. Informed by Hadès (Jean Marais) and Claude Perséphone (Marie-France Pisier) that his death is not programmed, Orphée is ordered to return to the upper-world. Hadès despatches Perséphone to follow Orphée to ensure his silence. Meanwhile, Dominique Daniel (Eva Darlan), head of the Club des Bacchantes, visits Eurydice (Keiko Itô) and leaves a sachet of heroin. When he discovers the narcotics, Orphée confronts Eurydice and a blazing argument ensues. Eurydice injects the drugs and dies of an overdose while Orphée celebrates his concert. Distraught, Orphée vainly attempts to save Eurydice by driving his motorcycle into the car park wall. Perséphone contacts Orphée to offer him a new contract, which he signs, therefore guaranteeing his passage to the underworld. As in the myth, he is allowed to transport Eurydice back, but just before they emerge from a road tunnel, Orphée, anxious that an uncontrolled car will hit them, glances at Eurydice. The film concludes with Orphée being assassinated by a member of his Bacchantes fan club after his concert. Bacchus was the Roman name for Dionysus, so Orphée's death at the hands of a Bacchante, the roman name for Maenads, re-inscribes the classic myth ending within modern narrative.

The inclusion of a first incursion into Hadès's austere realm is inspired by Cocteau's adaptation, *Orphée* (1950), in which Orphée is lured into the underworld after the death of a young poet, Jacques Cégestre (Edouard Dermithe). A producer from Gaumont, Denis Château, initially approached Demy to remake Cocteau's version, and several references to the earlier adaptation are included. *Parking* opens with the homage 'à Jean Cocteau qui aimait ces mots magiques "il était une fois ..."' ('for Jean Cocteau, who loved these magical words "once upon a time"'). It also casts Jean Marais, the erstwhile Orphée, as his nemesis, Hadès. The typography of the name Orphée written on the concert posters recalls the free handwriting style Cocteau preferred for some of his credits. The black Porsche is a modern version of the Rolls Royce driven by Heurtebise (François Périer), himself an adaptation of Caron, chauffeur to the Princess or Death (Maria Casarès), an amalgamation of Hades and Persephones. However, *Parking* is by no means a remake and Demy found his inspiration in the central theme of a passionate love affair in the source tale (Berthomé, 1996: 353).

Such an interest in the original myth is unsurprising given Demy's preoccupation with love, and, once again, he reconfigures classic morality to coincide with the ideology that transcends his oeuvre. Of all male heroes, Orpheus most obviously fits Demy's conviction in the requirement for courage to pursue and act upon instinctive passions. Although Orpheus's journey into a subterranean universe to save the woman he loves finds echoes in Roland's endeavours to provide stability for Lola, in Jean's efforts to save Jackie from her gambling addictions, and in George's attempt to rescue Lola, all three lack Orpheus's heroism. It is a cruel irony that after having finally adapted the myth to the cinema screen, the film would later cause embarrassment to Demy (Père and Colmant, 2010: 255). It had been expected at Cannes, but was preceded by bad press and was not presented. Its limitations are obvious. Huster is unconvincing, both as a leading rock star and mythical hero, lacking both charisma and strength.[9] Itô could not speak French and her hesitant pronunciation jars with the at times sophisticated language of her dialogues. Use of space seems absurd, particularly when Orphée begins his journey to return Eurydice to the upper-world; she complains of exhaustion and yet the ground they have covered seems very limited. However, despite its almost blanket rejection by critics, *Parking* nonetheless makes interesting and, for its time, original commentaries on the challenges and limitations of desire, love and identity, the implosion of a heterosexual couple, bisexuality, narcissism, the loss of affect in modernity and the blurring of the boundaries between the real and the imaginary.

In many ways, *Parking* complies with Rick Altman's definition of the backstage musical as 'primarily concerned with putting on a show' (1987: 200), evident in the scenes depicting rehearsals, concerts and deliberations about recordings and performances. The object, the classic legend of Orpheus, is perceived by Demy as invoking the modern mythologies associated with pop/rock stars. Demy saw Orpheus as a cross between Mick Jagger and John Lennon (in Schidlow, 1985). Demy's Orphée lives in a château in Sancerre built in the Loire style. Instead of a viper's venomous bite, it is another form of *piqûre* (prick or bite) that brings death to Eurydice: a lethal injection of heroin. Pop mythology is thus mobilised in this archetypal rock star death. Moreover, Orphée's assassination recalls Mark David Chapman's fatal shooting of John Lennon on 8 December 1980, the steps of Bercy replacing the entrance of the Dakota Building in New York. Aristaeus finds modern form in Aristée (Gérard Klein), Orphée's agent, and Calaïs (Laurent Malet) is transformed from an Argonaut into a sound engineer. In accordance with the backstage musical, Orphée's perceived virtuosity is reflected by two successful concerts, the emphatic crowd affirming his supposed talents.

The musical numbers serve as prognostications of the actions and events that unfold in the short- and medium-term future. 'Le Styx' presages an imminent future. Orphée suffers the electric shock during the rehearsal of this number and Caron materialises to escort him to the underworld. A short-term future is prefigured in the first

---

9 Demy imagined David Bowie as Orphée and approached Johnny Halliday, Bernard Lavilliers and Bernard Giraudeau, but they refused. Finally, he settled on Huster, a choice that he later saw as one of the film's biggest drawbacks (in Clech, Strauss and Toubiana, 1988: 61–2).

song we hear, 'Simplement'. Sung during the prologue, it anticipates the dispute that triggers Eurydice's suicide. Performed as Orphée and Eurydice relax in their living room adorned with beautiful classic and modern objects, and cast in various shades of white and cream, the scene initially implies romantic harmony. However, when Orphée declares that he loves Eurydice, she retorts that she does not believe him, which she echoes later in their menacing tirade. 'Entre vous deux', hints at emotions that are explained in the short-term future. It speaks of Orphée's love for two people, later confirmed as referring to Eurydice and Calaïs.

The stylisation of the songs also transcends temporal divides, allowing the past to coincide with the present. Orphée's opening tune seems aesthetically contemporary, with its minimalist instrumentals, but the subsequent song, a choral rendition of 'Bonheur de Vivre', appears anachronistic with its retro 1970s *jazz-variété* orchestration. This is then juxtaposed with the abstruse sounds of 'Le Styx', performed in a flat key with sudden shifts in rhythm and note length and a disharmonious saxophone arrangement. Such a lack of aesthetic coherence initially jars. Yet, by apposing different styles, *Parking*, in congruence with other Demy films, conflates temporal moments, triggering a sense of that which has already been lived within that which is currently being experienced. The recasting of Orpheus as a pop star is fundamental here, for, when we attend concerts, we expect to hear a past catalogue of the performer's music alongside their more recent releases. Moreover, the structure of a concert is such that chronology is not respected, with popularity of songs, irrespective of their era, dictating the order of play. The past thus interweaves with the present, but is also recast and weakened because, while songs trigger our memories of lived experiences, we can never relive the first time we heard them or saw the performance, and new arrangements of old hits accentuate this.

Parking juxtaposes the upper-world of Orphée's fantasy existence with Hadès's realm of purgatory. A transformation is effected, in which the dreamlike pertains to the territory of the living while the land of the dead constitutes a bleak reflection of the everyday. Orphée's seemingly magical lifestyle, at least in the first scenes, is evinced in his magnificent château with its expensive ornaments and furniture, classic motorcycle and the luxurious cars in which he is chauffeured, and via the adulation bestowed upon him by his adoring audiences.

Artists populate this living world, most obviously Orphée, but also Eurydice who is a sculptor, and are supported by their agents and fans. In the realm of the dead, blue and green filters bestow an ashen aesthetic, which symbolises the lack of vitality in our modern lives. At times, the tone is satirical. The recently deceased, from shipwrecks and wars, are processed at customs desks that double as versions of familiar civic counters.

Yet, such parody fails to undermine the starkness of *Parking*'s message about how, as individuals, we fail to act against the insidious ways in which hegemony affirms its control. The inhabitants of Hadès's realm are our avatars. Like humans trapped in bad faith, they wander aimlessly, functioning as automatons, their actions, behaviour, thoughts and feelings programmed by others. Hadès epitomises the human's need to seek a surrogate almighty figure. He tells Perséphone how he distrusts artists who think, dream and say whatever they wish. Interestingly, although Demy equates hegemony with bourgeois capitalism in many of his films, in Hadès's underworld it is broadened to encompass seemingly contrasting political systems. As Orphée leads Eurydice, they pass three outlets: a French tabacconist, a Russian cinema and an American motel. Traditional *petit commerçant* French culture is placed on the same level as communism and global consumerism, and perhaps even fascism, by association (the Cyrillic 'H' on the Russian cinema sign hangs precariously and is incorrectly placed in front of the Cyrillic 'N' or 'ï' that makes the cinema understandable also as a German *kino*).

By moulding its mephistophelian realm into a reflection of the everyday, *Parking* underlines how affect can become superfluous in modernity. It allows Demy to project, once again, his frustrations that, in our collective embrace of the new, we relegate love, passion and sentimentality to the past. For some, such a message is outmoded and idealistic, yet according to Demy 'il faut réinventer le romantisme, réapprendre à aimer. L'amour que la société moderne veut tuer, existe' (in Schidlow, 1985) ('we must reinvent romance. We have to learn to love again. The love that modern society wants to kill exists'). *Parking* achieves this reinvention of love in the relationships between Orphée and Eurydice and Orphée and Calaïs. More than any other Demy film, *Parking* depicts a configuration of love and desire that is neither monogamous nor exclusively heterosexual. Demy draws from Graves's anthology of Greek myths to bring out the classic poet's assumed bisexuality. Calaïs's love for Orphée is visually confirmed by the passionate kiss they share while celebrating the success of one of Orphée's performances. The images of the two men in deep embrace are disruptive because of the broader contexts of the period in which the film was released, when fears around AIDS were heightened. That their embrace does not elicit the shock of the crowd, despite their awareness of Orphée's marriage to Eurydice, disturbs hegemonic values since it suggests that difference in terms of sexuality can be accepted. Moreover, the lyrics of the song 'Entre vous deux' militate openly for bisexual desire, describing a love for a handsome blonde male and a brunette and ending rhetorically 'comment choisir? Pourquoi choisir?' ('how can I choose? Why should I choose?').

Elsewhere, *Parking* strongly implies a pre-existing lesbian relationship between Eurydice and Dominique, again visually, when Dominique attempts to caress Eurydice's hand. The effects of such a shift in values on the physical environment is figured in the transformation of the Café du Théâtre into a lesbian bar. Conventional heterosexual relationships are troubled or doomed, a prognostication already suggested in the incestuous couple Hadès–Persephone, the union of an uncle and his niece. A past homosexual relationship between Eurydice and Dominique indirectly brings about the ultimate implosion of her heterosexual romance with Orphée, which is prefigured in their excessively violent argument, and Eurydice's suicide roughly coincides with Orphée and Calaïs's kiss. Same-sex desire is lived out in the comparatively idealistic upper-world, while, as the ending suggests, heterosexual couplings are incarcerated within the hellish subterranean universe.

Parking ends on an ambiguous note. After his failed attempt at saving Eurydice from the underworld, Orphée, like his classic ancestor, laments his lost love as he walks through the gardens of his château. However, the sadness of which he sings is eclipsed by his joy at successfully recording his new song, aptly entitled 'Eurydice' and, later, at the euphoria following his final concert. His love for Eurydice is thus transformed into a resource for his continuing popularity and success. He sings 'Eurydice' at his concert, dressed in a white trouser suit, but opts for 'Bonheur de vivre' for his finale, declaring to his enraptured audience: 'je ne veux pas finir sur une note triste, parce qu'il faut croire dans la vie, croire au bonheur' ('I don't want to finish on a sad note, because you have to believe in life, believe in happiness'). Demy's familiar messages about faith in happiness are evident, but Orphée's ecstatic face implies that it is when he receives the adulation of his fans that he reaches the dizzying heights of elation. Orphée's elevation is figured literally; his devotees storm the stage and lift him above their heads before they lead him, jubilant, to the exit. Consequently, white, a familiar referent for sublime love in Demy's films is reconfigured to symbolise the euphoria of his success and the impression of self-affirmation that this engenders. Orphée's is not a joy arising from a reciprocal exchange, but the deriving of intense pleasure from a narcissistic interpretation of his own appeal. When Orphée is ultimately transported back to Eurydice's arms in the underworld, his facial expression is tense, frozen in a characteristic iris shot, hinting at his anxiety at a perpetuity of reciprocity (love of the other) rather than narcissism (love of the self).

As in his musicals, Demy's fairytale, fable and myth fail to end happily. Peau d'âne's bemusement at her father's forthcoming wedding and Orphée's anxiety as he embraces Eurydice show the compromises that both have been forced to make. Some optimism emerges at the end of *The Pied Piper* in the form of Gavin, but at a price, in that his mentor is executed and he must flee his hometown. Peau d'âne and Gavin are forced to escape their space against their will. As for Orphée, he is transferred to a dour elsewhere seemingly as punishment for his narcissism. This tension between narcissism and altruism, individualism and reciprocity, seen in *Parking*, informs many of the representations of romance in Demy's cinema, as will be explored in the next chapter.

References

Altman, Rick (1987) *The American Film Musical*, Bloomington IN, Indiana University Press.

Anon. (1975) 'L'Enchanteur *Joueur de Flûte* de Jacques Demy', *Le Quotidien de Paris*, 22 November.

Berthomé, Jean-Pierre (1996) *Jacques Demy et les racines du rêve*, 2nd Edition, Nantes, L'Atalante.

Bessèges, André (1971) '*Peau d'âne*', *La France catholique*, 1 February.

Bettelheim, Bruno (1976) *The Uses of Enchantment*, London and New York, Penguin.

Browning, Robert (1888) *The Pied Piper of Hamelin*, London, Frederick Warne and Co.

Cervoni, Albert (1970) 'Le Familier et le merveilleux: *Peau d'âne* de Jacques Demy', *L'Humanité*, 16 December.

Clech, Thierry, Strauss, Frédéric and Toubiana, Serge (1988) 'D'un port à l'autre: Entretien avec Jacques Demy', *Cahiers du Cinéma*, 414, December: 10–11, 57–62.

Graves, Robert (1955) *The Greek Myths*, London, Penguin.

Hill, Rodney (2005) 'Peau d'âne', *Film Quarterly*, Vol. 59, No. 2

Jameson, Fredric (1983) 'Postmodernism and Consumer Society', in Hal Foster (ed.), *The Anti-Aesthetic*, Port Townsend WA, The Bay Press, republished as *Postmodern Culture*, London, Pluto Press, 1985.

Langlois, Gérard (1970) 'Jacques Demy, *Peau d'âne*: La féerire existe-t-elle?', *Les Lettres françaises*, 23 December.

Mairet, Philippe transl. (1948) *Existentialism is a Humanism*, London, Methuen.

Orr, Christopher (1984) 'The Discourse on Adaptation', *Wide Angle*, 6 (2): 72–6.

Père, Olivier and Colmant, Marie (2010) *Jacques Demy*, Paris, Éditions de la Martinière.

Perrault, Charles (1695) *Peau d'âne* in *Histoires ou contes du temps passé or Les Contes de ma Mère l'Oye*, Paris, Claude Barbin, 1697.

Remond, Alain (1975) '*Le Joueur de flûte:* La terrible candeur des enfants', *Télérama*, 31 December: 73.

Sartre, Jean-Paul (1946) *L'Existentialisme est un humanisme*, Paris, Nagel, transl. Philippe Mairet, *Existentialism is a Humanism*, London, Methuen, 1948.

Schidlow, Joshka (1985) '*Orphée* tournage', *Télérama*, 13 March.

Siclier, Jacques (1976) 'Le *Joueur de Flûte de Hamelin* de Jacques Demy', *Le Monde*, 6 June.

Warner, Marina (1995) *From the Beast to the Blond: On Fairytales and their Tellers*, London, Vintage.

1 Woman in love? C (Jeanne Allard) following her gigolo lover Emile (Angelo Bellini) around their studio apartment in *Le Bel Indifférent* (1957).

2 Absent lover? Lola (Anouk Aimée) still dreams of Michel (Jacques Harden) in *Lola* (1960).

3 A plan in the making: Madame Emery (Anne Vernon) delivers an engagement ring sent by Roland (Marc Michel) to her daughter Geneviève (Catherine Deneuve) in *Les Parapluies de Cherbourg* (1963).

4 Euphoria in excess: Delphine and Solange Garnier (Catherine Deneuve and Françoise Dorléac) decide on dance routines for the town fair with fairground workers Bill (Grover Dale) and Etienne (George Chakiris) in *Les Demoiselles de Rochefort* (1966).

5 Lola in LA: Anouk Aimée walks the boulevards, with Jacques Demy and Agnès Varda in pursuit during filming of *Model Shop* (1968).

6 Fatherly intentions? The Blue King (Jean Marais) impresses his daughter the Princess (Catherine Deneuve) with talk of the poets of tomorrow in *Peau d'âne* (1970).

7 Gender trouble: a seemingly pregnant Marco Mazetti (Marcello Mastroianni) and his wife Irène de Fontenoy (Catherine Deneuve) in *L'Evénement le plus important depuis que l'homme a marché sur la lune* (1973).

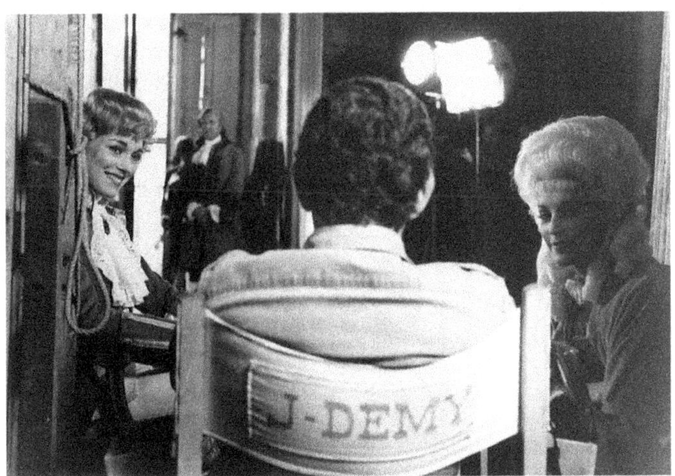

8 Artists at work: Jacques Demy enjoying a chat with Catriona MacColl and Christine Böhm while filming *Lady Oscar* (1978).

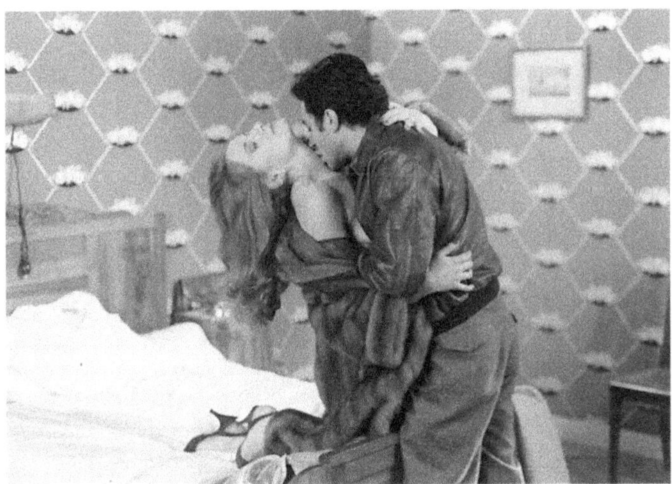

9 Doomed passions: Edith Leroyer (Dominique Sanda) in passionate embrace with François Guilbaud (Richard Berry) in *Une chambre en ville* (1982).

10 Embedding the Demy myth: sailors dance in *Trois places pour le 26* (1988).

11 Mythical places: diaphanous light streams through the glass ceiling in the Passage Pommeraye.

12 The Katorza cinema that Demy frequented as a child and which Roland (Marc Michel) visits in *Lola* (1960).

13 Demy iconography: the Pont Transbordeur (Transporter Bridge) that brings the fair into town in *Les Demoiselles de Rochefort* (1966)

14 The making of a myth: the famous 'Brasserie des Demoiselles' is firmly on the tourist circuit in the central Place Colbert in Rochefort.

4

Gender and sexuality in the *Demy-monde*

Demy began his filmmaking career when, as Geneviève Sellier recalls, surveys into the attitudes of young people in France revealed significant distinctions between the aspirations of men and women (2005: 6). In 1958, journalist Françoise Giroud, credited with having coined the term 'nouvelle vague', published a book, *La Nouvelle Vague, portraits de la jeunesse*', based on a sample of 15,000 letters sent to *L'Express* magazine and concluded that young women felt determined by their 'condition' as woman (Giroud, 201 in Sellier, 2005: 11–12). Although modernity heralded greater freedoms for middle-class men, heterosexual women noted the near insurmountable challenge of reconciling society's expectations of virtue before marriage and motherhood with their own desires for an education and independent career. For Sellier, Nouvelle Vague films exemplify the prevailing gender-based hypocrisies by privileging a 'masculine-singular' perspective on the world (2005: 6). Sellier interprets *Lola* and *La Baie des Anges* in this light and argues that Lola and Jackie form the objects of Jean and Roland's displacements of their non-resolved Oedipal desires for their mother/the ideal woman (2005: 105–7).

However, gender in Demy's cinema is complex since, although he portrays some women as objects of consumption and exchange within a patriarchal economy, he also highlights the gender inequalities and injustices that persist as post-war modernity sets in. Moreover, rather than always positioning women as victims, his films reveal the actions some take to claim agency within patriarchy. Furthermore, the blurring of the boundaries between theatricality and authenticity serves to render obvious the performative and constructed dimension of gender roles, particularly femininity.

This chapter explores the representations of gender in relation to four films: *Le Bel Indifférent*, *La Naissance du jour*, *L'Evénement...* and *Lady Oscar*; it also provides an overview of Demy's heroes and heroines more generally. Simone de Beauvoir's *Le Deuxième Sexe* (1949) will inform the discussion, since her emphasis on choice and agency chimes with Demy's interest in free will. Moreover, her studies of the 'woman in love' and the 'narcissist' in her second volume of *Le Deuxième Sexe* relate closely to his depictions of self–other relations within the romantic encounter. Such a return to Beauvoir contributes to a recent reappraisal of the importance of her work for understanding representations of gender in film (Boulé and Tidd, 2012), although the focus on Demy situates the analysis in the pre-contemporary period. The final section examines how Demy's films mobilise queer modes of affect, desire, identity, aesthetics, space and time. It does not seek to claim Demy as a queer filmmaker, but the resonance of his films for non-straight audiences (Colomb, 1998: 39; Renouard, 2003: 151) is a vital and often overlooked aspect within existing criticisms of his work, and has been a pivotal factor in assuring his lasting legacy as a key player in French cinema history.

'Woman' in love: *Le Bel Indifférent*

Beauvoir offered a polemical insight into the situation of women in romantic relationships that can be applied to Demy's adaptation of Cocteau's *Le Bel Indifférent*. Owing her philosophical grounding in part to Hegel, Nietzsche and Sartre, Beauvoir reads heterosexual romance in existentialist terms and argues that for woman 'l'amour est une totale démission au profit d'un maître' (1949: 540 (vol. 2)).[1] Patriarchy works to maintain woman within a domain of dependency and immanence labelled feminine (1949: 117 (vol. 1)), and this is partly achieved by enslaving her to her reproductive function. Yet, as Boulé and Tidd note, for Beauvoir, somewhat controversially, 'both men and women perpetuate patriarchy' (2012: 5). As a bearer of consciousness, woman is inhabited by transcendence, but she has 'internalised and

---

1 'Love ... is a total abdication for the benefit of a master.' (Borde and Malovany-Chevallier, 2009: 699) Beauvoir acquires this term 'maître' from her re-reading of Hegel's master–servant dialectic in which woman constitutes a dependant consciousness like that of an animal (1949: 116 (vol. 1)).

adapted to [her] oppressed state' (2012: 5). The woman in love seeks to justify her oppression to herself via gendered forms of bad faith. Beauvoir conceptualises ideal love as egalitarian, but she emphasises the necessity for each lover to recognise the agency of the other: 'l'amour authentique devrait être fondé sur la reconnaissance réciproque de deux libertés; ... aucun n'abdiquerait sa transcendance' (1949: 571 (vol. 2)).[2]

The notion that the female partner justifies her situation as immanent other to her male master is dramatically portrayed in *Le Bel Indifférent*. Cocteau wrote the original play ten years before Beauvoir published her volumes; although probably autobiographical in part, he had his close friend Edith Piaf and her lover Paul Meurisse in mind, and both singer and actor played themselves in its first staged versions in 1940. In 1953, when Piaf's fame had increased, Cocteau removed all references to the couple. When Demy adapted the play in 1957, Pathé had wanted Piaf to play the main role, but she was committed to a year-long tour. Demy lacked the confidence to approach Maria Casares or Jeanne Moreau as the protagonist C and Jean Marais as her *bel indifférent* Emile (Berthomé, 1996: 73). Jacqueline Moreau and Evein introduced him to theatre actress Jeanne Allard. They wanted Emile to be played by an unknown who they spotted at the Café Bonaparte and re-baptised as Angelo Bellini for the film's credits. Cocteau was involved in post-synchronisation and, although critical of both versions, preferred Demy's to his own (Boulangé, 2013: 30).

Demy's *Le Bel Indifférent* retains Cocteau's minimalist narrative structure consisting of C's monologue about her vain attempts to cling to her indifferent lover Emile. Her discourse is preceded, as in Cocteau's script, by two brief telephone conversations that reveal her paranoid state. She begins when Emile returns from an undisclosed engagement and ends when he leaves. Her litany is punctured by two moments of hysteria: the first when she rushes to the window claiming that she will jump, in an echo of the penultimate scene of Ophüls's *Le Plaisir*, and the second when she strives to prevent Emile from leaving her. Demy adapts Cocteau's script by modifying and inserting features that bolster the film's melodramatic resonance, opting for stylisation over realism, emphasised by Evein's decor,

2 'Authentic love must be founded upon reciprocal recognition of two freedoms; ... neither [lover] would abdicate his [*sic*] transcendence.' (Borde and Malovany-Chevallier, 2009: 723)

Moreau's costumes and Marcel Fradetal's cinematography. He labels his protagonist C, but alters the first caller's name from the exotic M. Totor to the more banal M. Raymond. He also adds off-screen sounds that emphasise C's state of anxiety and isolation, as he had done in *Les Horizon morts*, including two lovers talking in the hallway, footsteps on the stairs, knocks on a door, slamming doors, a woman's laughter and the noise of an ascending lift (taken from Cocteau's script).

It is through this adapted *mise en scène* that Demy stages the position of the female lover as doomed and/or devoted (vouée) to immanence (Beauvoir 1949: 540 (vol. 2)). The entire film is set in one room, painted in a deep scarlet that re-casts it as an infernal, hellish cell. Camera movement intensifies the sense of imprisonment; characteristic forward and sideways tracking shots, and pans, are deployed, but, rather than relaying ground coverage, they emphasise the characters' – and our – entrapment. The starkness of C's monologue and impression of suffocation exuded by the decor, reinforced by the large, cumbersome dark wood furniture, are patent. Both the monologue and environment deny the audience any respite from her situation that may otherwise be gained from the dramatisation of the *mise en scène* and distancing effects of the slow Latin musical arrangement.

Cocteau's play lacks mirrors, forcing the characters to confront each other. By contrast, Demy uses mirrors prominently, thus multiplying the reflections of Emile's indifference and C's self-denial, and duplicating the oppressive walls and furniture. As we saw in chapter 2, for Barthes, displays of extreme distress at a lover's distance constitute a form of sentimental obscenity (1977: 210). Via the combination of short focal length and confined, encumbered space, we are forced to confront C's 'unseemly' breakdown. The moving camera strays temporarily from the protagonist and her lover, thus mirroring our impulse to seek a distraction or escape, but Demy returns us to C as her depressing litany verbalises her wretched existence.

Demy refrains from aligning us with C's gaze, but his colour scheme indexes her emotional state. The scarlet walls serve phenomenologically as a spatial extension of her feelings, ranging through frustration, anger and despair. Her dark hair, sombre make-up and black velvet dressing gown are external markers of her melancholia. Although Emile is often framed in the bright light of the bathroom, and his white vest and the white sheet illuminate his face, C is almost always positioned against the tenebrous wallpaper. Even when she walks towards the bathroom, Demy has the camera cross diagonally, and gets the character to move towards the lens so that she is largely maintained within her red outer and black inner chromatic frames. Her impotence is accentuated via her movements. She retraces her steps, walking around the room as if unable to forge new trajectories and break the closed circle of her existence, emphasised by the repetition of the same line 'où étais-tu?' ('Where have you been?').

C is unwilling to conceive of any existence for herself other than that of Emile's lover. Emile dominates her thoughts, even when he is absent. We see her check whether the alarm clock is broken, its enhanced ticking a further indication of her anguish in isolation and abandonment. She lies on the bed and stares at the room, suspended in a state of inert attendance. Knocks on a door and footsteps cause her body to jolt upwards, her face turned slightly sideways to decipher any noise potentially announcing Emile's imminent entrance. She listens attentively to an off-screen conversation consisting of two lovers whispering tentative arrangements for a future encounter, the medium close-up shot scale highlighting her mounting neurotic agitation. She stands and presses the side of her head against the door. Demy extends the representations of her psychosis through two telephone conversations in which she claims to M. Raymond that Emile is perfect for her and never leaves her side, and invents a dialogue with Emile while on the phone to his sister Simone.

Paralysed by her situation, C seeks sanctuary in Emile as a surrogate metaphysical presence; she tells M. Raymond that Emile is an angel, thereby conforming to Beauvoir's complicit female lover for whom love becomes a religion (Beauvoir, 1949: 540 (vol. 2)). She transfers responsibility for her state onto Emile, accusing him of shackling her in chains and abandoning her in an oubliette. And yet her flat and empty vocal delivery belies her awareness of the falseness of her allegations. She feigns indifference to Emile's behaviour, but accuses him of being a liar. Yet, the liar is C because of her incessant campaign of self-delusion. She turns her head away from her reflection in the mirror as if unable to avow to herself the self-denial she enacts.

For Beauvoir, 'dans l'amant, [l'amoureuse] s'enivre de rencontrer un témoin' (1949: 545 (vol. 2)) ('She is exhilarated at finding a witness in her lover') (Borde and Malovany-Chevallier, 2009: 703). Yet, through his indifference, Emile avoids bearing witness to C's devotion, his silence pivotal in denying her solace from her anguish. Demy transposes Emile's detached apathy from Cocteau's script, only very occasionally allowing him to glance at C, for instance when she wakes him, his gaze visibly unfocused, and when he is about to go out. The newspaper Emile reads serves as an additional marker of his disinterest. C vainly attempts to convince herself that he remains attentive, but no sign of interest or empathy is apparent. At each turn, her attempts to convince herself that Emile treats her with affection are disavowed. When Emile does not reply to her calls that his 'mistress' is on the telephone, she misinterprets his silence as a mark of respect and promptly apologises for her behaviour, but then discovers that he was merely sleeping. She recounts how she used to resent Emile when he slept, jealous of the people he would dream about. For Beauvoir, in sleep, the male affirms the contingency of the female's existence: 'le dieu, le maître, ne doit pas s'abandonner au repos de l'immanence; c'est d'un regard hostile que la femme contemple cette transcendance foudroyée' (1949: 558 (vol. 2)).[3] Now, though, C uses Emile's slumber as a means of continuing her self-delusion.

Costume and character placement enhance C's ghostly immateriality for Emile. In three key shots, she stands or moves in profile while Emile lies on the bed, the first two taken from its foot as he reads the newspaper, and the second from the side, the camera tracking the length of the bed from Emile to C. For Jean-Luc Godard, her profile is reminiscent of Piero della Francesca's early renaissance paintings, whose profile of Sigismondo Pandolfo Malatesta (c. 1450) with his dark, straight hair closely crowning his head is the most appropriate, as well as Picasso, whose *Mujer que Llora* (1937) (*Weeping Woman*) with her long face and strong features is recalled in C's tortured features, and Racine's *Bérénice* (1958). In all three shots, C's figure assumes a foreboding quality reminiscent of the grim reaper of medieval folklore. The second shot recalls Cocteau's *Orphée* when the Princess or Death (Maria Casarès) stands at Orphée's bed watching him sleep. Yet, it is her own symbolic death that C heralds. Unable to draw any justification for her situation from Emile, she becomes ever more desperate, avowing her jealousy, ineffectually declaring her dependence and threatening murder and suicide. Again, her threats

3 'The god, the master, should not give himself up to the repose of immanence; it is with a hostile look that the woman contemplates this destroyed transcendence' (Borde and Malovany-Chevallier, 2009: 713).

reinforce her impotence. Emile goes to the bathroom when she runs to the window and simply moves past her when she returns.

C's bad faith and self-subordination reach a predictable climax before Emile's exit: 'tu rentres, c'est que tu tiens à moi ... tu me tromperas avec qui tu veux ... tu peux mentir ... me faire attendre ... autant que tu voudras'.[4] Much like Bergman's medieval knight Antonius Block (Max von Sydow), who vainly prays for reassurance to a silent God as Death appears to take him to the dark world at the end of *The Seventh Seal*, C's pleas fall upon deaf ears. Yet, C can also be interpreted as a version of Block's cynical squire Jöns (Gunnar Björnstrand), her awareness that her actions are futile conveyed through her hollow voice, and her incessant need to pose the same questions and cyclical movements. In ignoring her pleas for a false sanctuary in the state of immanent female lover to a transcendent male master, Emile cruelly denies C's existence any meaning. And here is the tragedy, for C is unable to take that crucial step to become a subject herself. The film leaves her stripped of any security and willingly powerless to assume her own agency.

Le Bel Indifférent can be read as misogynist by representing the female lover as pitiful and subjugated. Nevertheless, Demy – building on Cocteau's script – brings into sharp relief the tensions and contradictions characterising the situation of women at the time, ambiguously positioned within a patriarchal society embracing modernity with increasing fervour. As mentioned, while urban, educated young white men enjoyed access to new freedoms, women continued to be constrained by traditional morality and obligations. When Cocteau wrote the play, women were still denied the vote and full citizenship, the contraceptive pill was unavailable and abortion was a crime. Moreover, Demy implies that immanence can apply to Emile. While Emile may be indifferent to C, he is preoccupied with his own physicality. He scrutinises himself in the mirror, contorting his face and inspecting his chin and eyes. For Beauvoir 'le narcissisme est un processus d'aliénation bien défini: le moi est posé comme une fin absolue et le sujet se fuit en lui' (1949: 519 (vol. 2)).[5] Beauvoir sees

---

4 'You come home, that means that you still care for me ... you can betray me with whoever you want ... you can lie ... make me wait ... as much as you want.'

5 'Narcissism is a well-defined process of alienation: the self is posited as an absolute end and the subject escapes itself in it.' (Borde and Malovany-Chevallier, 2009: 683)

narcissism as another means through which woman justifies her internalisation of patriarchal power structures and shows that transcendence cannot be gained from a narcissistic apprehension of the self as object: 'il n'est pas possible d'être *pour soi* positivement *autre, et de se saisir dans la lumière de la conscience comme objet*' (1949: 520 (vol. 2)).[6] Just as in the original Greek myth in which Artemis engineers Narcissus's death by having him stab himself through frustration at not being able to consummate his auto-erotic desires (Graves, 2011: 287–8), narcissism incurs a form of self-annihilation. In *Le Bel Indifférent* this is in process; Emile is constructed in Cocteau's script as a magnificent gigolo whose looks are about to fade ([1939] 1989: 85). As his subjectivity is only worth his value as an object of desire, his fading looks threaten the imminent loss of that identity. His encounters with women perpetuate his dependency on his status as an *homme-objet* and, since he does not recognise and act upon the warning signs that his erotic appeal is slipping, they are also examples of his self-denial.

'Woman' out of love: *La Naissance du jour*

If C strives to cling to her position as Emile's subordinate lover, Colette (Danièle Delorme), at the age of fifty-four, decides to relinquish the ambition to love again and assume what she perceives as a more serene and independent existence. *La Naissance du jour* initially appears anomalous in relation to Demy's other films. Not only is it a faithful adaptation of Colette's text, written in 1927, and produced for television, but also its narrative, about a woman's decision to no longer love, clearly departs from Demy's staple characters, defined by their romantic relationships and aspirations. Moreover, while, as argued in chapter 1, Demy's cinema celebrates intuitiveness over cogitation, Colette's text is ostensibly a reflective piece in which she makes a pact with her past male lovers: 'il n'est de si bonne compagnie qui ne se quitte; mais je m'engage ici à prendre courtoisement mon congé' ('there is no better company than those who don't leave each other; but I undertake here to courteously take my leave'). Passionate

---

6 'It is not possible to be *for self* positively Other and to grasp oneself as object in the light of consciousness.' (Borde and Malovany-Chevallier, 2009: 684; emphasis in original)

love, often celebrated by Demy, is denied or dismissed, and melancholy sustained from a broken heart is trivialised as inconsequential.

However, interestingly, Colette began a passionate affair with Maurice Goudeket as she wrote *La Naissance du jour*. She married Goudeket in 1935 and remained with him until her death on 3 August 1954. Hence, *La Naissance du jour* can be seen less as an authentic final farewell to love than a reflection on romantic encounters and relationships. Demy's proximity to the text and Colette is illustrated by his casting of Delorme who, as Varda notes in her commentary, not only knew the author, but also bears a close resemblance to her.[7] Demy also shot the entire film in Colette's house, La Treille Muscate, near St Tropez, but redecorated its interior so it bore the hallmarks of his decors; the walls are adorned with striped wallpapers composed of contrasting colours, such as dark blue and pink.

While it may be poignant and nostalgic, *La Naissance du jour* is far from tragic. Melancholy is conveyed in various scenes, such as when Colette ponders about the empty place setting opposite her at lunch. Yet, as in Colette's work in general, in which, according to Diana Holmes 'love represents a distraction from more vital experience' (1991: 125), her closing off of this aspect of her life is depicted as productive for her. A crucial component of vital experience for Colette is a sensorial engagement with her natural environment. Jean Larnac notes that 'on ne lit pas Colette; on voit ce qu'elle voit. On respire ce qu'elle respire; on touche ce qu'elle touche' (1927: 213) ('one does not read Colette; one sees what she sees. One breathes what she breathes; one touches what she touches'). Such an emphasis on the sensual world as it is experienced through the ocular, haptic and olfactory presents a challenge to a director commissioned to adapt Colette's text for a limited budget and for television in the late 1970s. Demy responds in traditional ways, via a combination of first-person voice-over and close-ups of wild flowers and animals that punctuate each section. Two such shots are utilised to identify Colette early on, as the image track cuts from her manuscript of *La Naissance du jour* to a poppy in a field and then a cat – flowers and felines being familiar signifiers of the author.

From the beginning, sound emphasises Colette's sensual connection with the natural world depicted in the image. As she walks from

7 La Naissance du Jour vu *par Agnès Varda* (Thomas Benigni and Valentin Vignet, 2008).

the beach to her garden in the opening sequence, the noise of the waves lapping against the sand and the breeze ruffling the trees are superseded by birdsong, the cry of a cockerel and bark of a dog. Demy also uses sound to blur the distinction between exterior and interior. As Colette writes and strolls around her home at night, we hear croaking toads and howling winds while, in the daytime, the grinding of cicadas provides much of the ambient noise. Many scenes unfold in a halfway space between inside and outside, on the terrace and in the courtyard, where the noises of the wind, insects and animals intensify.

Colette's embodied experience of the fauna surrounding her house is highlighted in a sequence in which she walks in the tall wild grasses and flowers of the coastal meadows. The tracking shots follow Colette, slowing and pausing as she touches and collects flowers and leaves. When her descriptions of the plants and their effects become precise, the camera maintains Colette in medium shot. As she picks myrtle and tastes it, the voice-over describes in detail its colour, flavour and side effects, which can provoke nausea or ecstasy. Monologue and image invite an embodied response in the audience, as if we too were walking in the fields and tasting the bitter plants. The lens remains at eye-level as Colette, now seen in long shot, is completely framed by short and tall grasses and wildflowers, literally swamped by this place, which, as stated in the voice-over, abounds with life. Colette walks towards the camera and lies on her side in the grass close to the lens, blurring the boundaries between human corporeality and natural vegetation. This vital experience is set in juxtaposition with her former life via a combination of image and dialogue. Colette abruptly shifts topic from her natural surroundings in the voice-over to a question in direct speech, seemingly in response to an imagined criticism, either from an acquaintance or herself: 'grandir? Pour qui? Oser? Qu'oserai-je donc de plus?' ('Grow up? For who? Dare? How much more daring will I be?'). The image track then cuts in close-up to the heads of two marigolds, one with a ladybird crawling on its underside.

It would be misguided to identify Colette's environment as feminine. As Holmes observes 'Colette's texts reverse, redistribute and assign new meanings to familiar physical signifiers of masculinity and femininity' (1991: 91). Colette is the narrative subject and Vial (Jean Sorel) becomes her object. We see him walking around dressed in tight beige shorts, his defined torso exposed to Colette. He lies on her bench, his arm holding his head as he looks up at the sky. For Colette, Vial constitutes nothing more than an object to contemplate. Hence, whenever he shows his emotions, she complains via voice-over: 'le moindre désordre sentimental dérange les traits de Vial' ('the slightest emotional disorder disrupts Vial's traits') which are normally 'réguliers, assez beaux' ('normal, quite handsome'). Colette's thoughts betray her gender-based chauvinism. When he lies face down on a beach towel, she muses 'je l'aime toujours mieux quand il cache son visage' ('I always prefer it when he hides his face'), adding 'je lui ai même affirmé un jour qu'on pourrait le guillotiner, sans que personne ne s'en aperçoive' ('I even told him one day that he could be guillotined, without anyone noticing'). Colette derives pleasure when a male abandons himself to the immanence of rest because she can contemplate him as a pure object whose subjectivity is, momentarily, silenced. This displays Colette's limited passion for Vial whose personality is experienced as a nuisance, an irony given that he was inspired by her future husband, whose age of 38 was only marginally older than her male character's 35 years. Demy transmits the futility of Vial's attempts at imposing his authority in the voice-over. In the scene where Colette is shown digging the garden, he scolds her for transcending the boundaries of the feminine domain, in which she would amuse herself with collecting flowers and walking along the sea's edge. Yet, the voice-over immediately reaffirms Colette's superiority; she dismisses Vial's comments as the remarks of an ordinary man.

Faced with Colette's indifference, Vial declares his love for her in a long scene in the lounge, kitchen and study. True to form, Demy uses colour to signify sublime adulation; Vial is dressed from head to foot in white, with only a blue scarf breaking the monotony of his costume. As Colette turns the conversation to a banal description of the weather, Demy superimposes her thoughts, drowning out direct speech and maintaining the focus on Vial's corporeal qualities: 'pendant que je parlais, il rapetissait ses yeux et refermait tout son visage' ('while I was speaking, his eyes got smaller and his face shut back up'). When she asks about his life when she is absent, he replies that he lives from little and from her. Here, then, Vial recalls C's dependency upon the object of her devotion, unable to assume a liberated existence, and resigned to his state as distant, unrequited admirer. He attempts a new strategy, decrying Colette for trying to manipulate a union between him and Hélène Clément (Dominique Sanda), and for projecting the younger woman as a rival for his attentions. Colette, though, recognises his strategy of reverse psychology and refuses to allow it to push her off course: 'Vial attendait tout de sa passivité. Ce n'est pas une tactique étrangère à l'homme, au contraire' ('Vial expected everything from his passivity. It's not a tactic that is foreign to men, on the contrary'). She reaffirms her decision to be alone and sits behind her desk in a gesture for him to take his leave.

However, *La Naisssance du jour* shows how Colette's yearning for serenity and simplicity becomes her own narcissistic project. Her ploy to match-make Vial with Hélène is self-serving because, should it succeed, it would demonstrate her omnipotence by confirming her foresight and wisdom. When Hélène first visits the house, Colette is placed at a distance, positioned in the middle of her guests at the end of the table, sat back from them and contemplating their behaviour. Her thoughts focus on Hélène and imply a sarcastic resentment for so-called independent women of her type who, rather than embroider, lather coconut oil on their bodies and sunbathe on the beach.

La Naissance du jour shows a Colette who believes that she is emancipated, but her decision to no longer love again is an inauthentic act. She recognises the impossibility of separating cerebral will and corporeal desires when she acknowledges how much her body yearns for a male partner to lie beside her: 'si la tête est sauve, le reste se débat, son salut n'est pas sûr' ('if the head is saved, the rest battles on, its withdrawal is not sure'). Her intentional retreat from romantic relationships is also motivated by concerns around ageing and its consequences for her own self-image. She imagines that a future lover would see emerging from her naked body an older woman. Later, when she inadvertently touches Vial's naked torso, her mind focuses on the juxtaposition between his relatively young skin and her ageing hand, marred by scars, blemishes and dirty fingernails. She is proud of her hands, she claims, but they nonetheless visually symbolise her age difference from Vial and, perhaps, feed her anxiety about a future as an older lover of a younger male partner. Her mask is seen to slip momentarily during the central exchange with Vial. After he admonishes her for promising to help Hélène seduce him, he asks whether their age difference was a motivator. His question prompts her to think condescendingly 'pauvre Vial ... il y pensait donc à notre différence d'âge?' (poor Vial ... he was thinking about it then, our age difference'), but she contradicts her thoughts by declaring falsely 'je n'y songe jamais à la différence d'âge' ('I never think about that, our age difference') and asks 'tu t'es attaché à moi, malgré, comme tu dis, la différence des âges?' ('you've grown attached to me, despite, as you put it, our age difference?') Although Emile's narcissistic project is threatened because of the ageing process, Colette's fantasised retirement from the amorous and erotic is not hopeless. Yet, the above instances imply her difficulty in overriding physical desire and emotions with will, which, for both Demy and Colette (given her actual affair with Goudeket at the time) is a form of self-delusion.

From the complicit to the empowered: women, mothers, men and fathers in the *Demy-monde*

C and Colette can be placed towards either end of a scale encompassing Demy's female characters. Towards the C end, Geneviève in *Les Parapluies de Cherbourg* fails to affirm any meaningful subjectivity beyond her externally imposed status as pretty daughter, girlfriend, wife and mother. From the moment she enters Dubourg's jewellers, her future is – metaphorically and literally – set in stone. Roland's precious gems are mapped onto her as if she were nothing more than a prized jewel to be admired and acquired by wealthy men. Her off-white coat and white jumper reflect the box containing the diamond ring, with Geneviève herself, with her pale skin and blonde, straight hair, corporeally emulating the surfaces of the precious gem.

Even the more apparently independent characters 'abdicate their transcendence', to adopt Beauvoir's terms, as a result of their romantic union with men. Eurydice abandons her autonomy to become Orphée's muse and devotes her artistic talents as a sculptor to reflecting her devotion to him. That she takes her own life implies, as in C, that she cannot conceive of an existence independent of her attachment to Orphée. Edith in *Une Chambre en ville* escapes a life as Edmond's trophy wife; yet, her implied prostitution and public displays of nudity are attempts at rebellion rather than acts of independent choice. Moreover while François dies from his battle wounds, beyond their relationship there is nothing for Edith, hence her suicide.

The women in both *Les Demoiselles de Rochefort* and *Peau d'âne* relinquish their agency by identifying with their objectified image and/or assuming their allotted role in the heterosexual romantic encounter. When she first sees Maxence's portrait of his 'ideal female in all her simplicity' and recognises her likeness to the woman depicted, Delphine declares 'comme ce type doit m'aimer puisqu'il m'a inventée' ('how this guy must love me since he invented me'). In projecting herself into this image, she transfers her subjectivity to its unknown creator and complies with Beauvoir's female lover who 'demeure engloutie dans cette amante que l'homme a non seulement révélée mais créée' (1949: 572 (vol. 2)) ('she remains engulfed in this loving woman whom man has not only revealed, but created') (Borde and Malovay-Chevallier, 2009: 724). Despite being a gifted composer, Solange succumbs to Andy, taking up her prescribed position in their choreographed seduction. Similarly, while Yvonne manages a cafe, she occupies her place in the hold traditionally reserved for women as she dances a reunion waltz with Simon.

In the *cake d'amour* scene, Demy shows Peau d'âne, dressed in her ass's hide, reading aloud the recipe to her clone dressed as the Princess, who undertakes the physical tasks. Psychological fantasy and narrative reality converge in that a lowly servant girl identifies with a sublimated image of a Princess and vice-versa. And yet, in assuming this exalted status as the perfect Princess, Peau d'âne's ability to achieve her objectives is constrained. To escape her father she is forced to live a debased existence in exile, which she can flee only by marrying the Red Prince. The colour of the kingdom may have changed, Peau d'âne's status has not. Elsewhere, rather than use her unearthly powers and forge a new trajectory, the Lilac Fairy channels her energies into securing the Blue King for herself. She shifts from ultimate agency, able to transcend time, to a fixed future as spouse. Her smugness to the Princess is telling, for, like the narcissist, she requires external acknowledgement of her victory. In all these cases, then, Beauvoir's authentic love based on a meeting between two free subjects fails.

However, as mentioned, Demy deploys formal strategies to highlight gender inequality rather than reinforce it. His use of the face-to-face encounter in *Les Parapluies de Cherbourg*, combined with the colours, alert the spectator to Geneviève's aversion to Roland and, thus, the extreme emotional and material challenges of her predicament. Such an approach had already been adopted in the encounter between the mother and father in *La Luxure*. Elsewhere, the parodic mode of address in *Les Demoiselles de Rochefort* and *Peau d'âne* targets and undermines patriarchal ideologies that require women to accept their status as object and servant.

Towards the other end of the continuum, both Lola and Jackie can be interpreted as more emancipated, to differing degrees. Rather than surrogate mothers for Roland and Jean, their strength and dynamism serve to highlight the weakness and dependence of their male admirers. Despite her status as single mother, and her abandonment by Michel, Lola achieves some autonomy. Moreover, she combines the traditionally opposing poles of sexuality and maternity. Both her affair with Frankie and her separation from her son are the products of her job, but Lola claims that she slept with Frankie because he reminded her of Michel, and she judges herself to be a good mother. While she likes to attract the gaze of the (male) other, she does not allow her occupation as an erotic dancer to define her subjectivity. She maintains her freedom to determine her own life path, telling Roland that she will consider his offer during her temporary transfer to Marseilles and, in *Model Shop*, refusing George's pleas for her to love him as if he were her child. Jackie appears more successful than Colette in choosing an authentic existence outside of love. She enters a male world independently and plays among them. She is nomadic, unconfined by geographical location, and does not seek affirmation through men. Yet, again, Demy sets Jackie's life within the context of early 1960's France and shows that her freedom is circumvented; she must depend financially on others, including punters, Jean and her best friend.

As shown, for Demy, theatricality and authenticity are integral parts of everyday experience. Such a worldview also frames his depictions of femininity. Lola, Jackie, Yvonne, Delphine, Solange, Peau d'âne and the Lilac Fairy all display, to various degrees of knowingness, patriarchal femininity as a performance rather than an innate essence. In this, then, they present early examples of Judith Butler's conceptualisation of gender as performative, repeated through strategies of imitation and citation rather than 'naturally' assumed at birth (1993: 313). Hence, when Lola tells Roland she has got lipstick on his cheek, when Solange casts a fleeting look at the camera at the moment of her *enamoration*, and when Peau d'âne states that a scullion must be dirty to qualify as a scullion, Demy is reminding the audience, through humour, that all of these feminine types that have frequently appeared in cultural representations – the flighty young woman, the romantic heroine and the subordinated slave – are nothing more than constructs. The women thus become parodies of archetypes and it is through this that Demy undermines the ideology that perpetuates such myths and the power imbalance on which that ideology is based. And, as we have seen, if we doubted his motives, his recurring representations of the material constraints that dictate women's lives make his gender politics clear. If women are excessive in the Demy monde, it is not only because their gender is theatricalised, but also because their desires, aspirations and behaviour exceed the patriarchal regulations in force, which are thus revealed to be antiquated and ineffectual. This undermining of patriarchy, this revelation of gender roles as constructs, extends to heterosexuality, as will be seen in the final section of this chapter.

A prominent feature of Demy's depictions of the 'condition' of woman is the mother–daughter dyad. Married to Varda since 1962, and having adopted her daughter Rosalie, Demy enjoyed first-hand access to this relationship. Rapports between mothers and their daughters trigger tensions, according to Beauvoir, because the mother can project onto her daughter 'toute l'ambiguité de son rapport à soi; et quand s'affirme l'altérité de cet *alter ego*, elle se sent trahie' (1949: 374 (vol. 2)) ('all the ambiguity of her relationship with her self; and when the alterity of this alter ego affirms itself, she feels betrayed') (Borde and Malovany-Chevallier, 2009: 575; emphasis in original). Mothers satisfied with their lives admire their daughters' independence. This is how Beauvoir views the relationship between Colette and Sidonie (1949: 374 (vol. 2)), hence in *La Naissance du jour* Sidonie's complaints that Colette's second husband will distract her from her writing. Desnoyer in *Lola* seems anxious to provide Cécile with opportunities not available to herself. Less sympathetic mothers can experience jealousy of their daughter's greater freedoms (1949: 376 (vol. 2)). In preventing Geneviève from choosing her destiny, Emery in *Les Parapluies de Cherbourg* is the archetypal Machiavellian maternal figure and who enjoys, as Beauvoir describes, 'l'amer plaisir de se retrouver en une autre victime' (1949: 374–5 (vol. 2)) ('the bitter pleasure of finding another victim') (Borde and Malovany-Chevallier, 2009: 576). Had Geneviève succeeded in living happily with Guy, she would have reflected Emery's lack of courage in choosing her own existence. Similar resentment fuels the acerbic exchanges between

Langlois and Edith in *Une chambre en ville*. Having spent a lifetime with a husband she neither desired nor loved, Langlois dismisses her daughter's complaints about her marriage to Edmond and blames his impotence on Edith's inability to satisfy his desires. By contrast, Violette's mother supports her daughter's choices by abnegating her own existence, declaring that she has already lived her life while Violette has hers in front of her.

The father–daughter bond is an obvious motor for some mothers' jealousy towards their daughters. This, as mentioned, underpins the narrative of *Peau d'âne*. As will be seen, it also emerges in *Trois places pour le 26*, studied in the final chapter. This film brings together elements from Demy's main full-length features and, accordingly, the relationship between Mylène de Lambert (Françoise Fabian) and Marion (Mathilda May) contains many of the characteristics of gender representations in his cinema. Like the Lilac Fairy, Mylène sees her daughter as a rival for Montand's affections. Like Yvonne, she behaves more like a sister than a mother, comparing diets for instance. Like Langlois, she has been disappointed by an earlier marriage. Like Emery, she discourages her daughter from determining her own life path by warning her against leaving her job for a stage career.

While Demy's depictions of his women point to their ambivalence in patriarchy, his men broadly conform to one broad type: the forlorn and feckless male struggling to claim his freedom, cast in the light, perhaps, of an erstwhile Baptiste from *Les Enfants du paradis*. Vial is subordinated by his devotion to Colette; Roland is sublimated by his love for Lola; Jean gambles because of his infatuation with Jackie; and George requires Lola's wisdom and determination to break free from his inertia and despondency. While Michel has achieved success and freedom, he becomes seduced into gambling. Orphée's status as a pop star confuses self with image, hence his constant need for affirmation from those around him, and Emile is preoccupied with his looks. All of the main adult male characters in *The Pied Piper* bar Melius, Mattio and the Piper, are foolish and unscrupulous. In Simon, Barthes's depiction of the abandoned lover as female is reversed; Andy talks of his regrets at having chosen his career over love; Maxence's obsession with finding his ideal woman restricts his future happiness to the romantic encounter; and the Blue King is the Lilac Fairy's puppet. Again, these masculine types in *Les Demoiselles de Rochefort* and *Peau d'âne* serve to intensify these films' parody of dominant gender roles.

Attempts at affirming paternal authority also fail, as evidenced in Roland's boss and Jean's father. As will be seen, Oscar's father, the Général de Jarjayes (Mark Kingston) in *Lady Oscar* is the exaggeration of this inability of the patriarch to assert his paternalistic power. Demy's men, then, tend not to live up to their expected status as transcendent beings and are often disempowered. By contrast, Marco Mazetti (Marcello Mastroianni) in *L'Evénement...* manages to maintain his virility despite being diagnosed with pregnancy, but, as the next section will reveal, Demy utilises this as a means of underlining the implicitly feminist slant of his earlier work.

Challenging sexism through male pregnancy: *L'Evénement le plus important depuis que l'homme a marché sur la lune*

Demy's interest in fatherhood heightened predictably when Varda was carrying her second and his first biological child, Mathieu, in 1972. Initially, he viewed Varda's pregnancy with sexism, telling her that if he were carrying a child, he would not speak about it as much, and this exchange inspired his idea for a screwball comedy about a man who falls pregnant.[8] Demy decided that a comic film would allow him to reach broad audiences and give him license to approach such absurd themes. Despite being dismissed as a failure, *L'Evénement...* serves as a precursor of the groundbreaking and lucrative comedies of the following decades in which the 'crisis of masculinity' becomes a preoccupation, of which Coline Serreau's *Trois hommes et un couffin* (1985) is the most famous example.

L'Evénement... has a simple and chronological narrative structure. It follows driving instructor Marco's diagnosis of pregnancy and the reactions of his partner, Irène de Fontenoy (Catherine Deneuve), their friends and colleagues. Typically, Demy extends this local curiosity into a broader critique of the insidious ways in which ordinary people are exploited by bourgeois and consumerist cultures. Marco's case serves to boost the prestige of gynaecologist Professor Gérard Chaumont de Latour (Raymond Gérôme); newspaper headlines and television

8 Deneuve and Mastroianni spent a week with Demy and Varda at Noirmoutier, while Varda was still pregnant, and the ideas for the film were germinating. Deneuve was heavily pregnant with her daughter, Chiara Mastroianni, when the film was being shot (from *L'Univers de Jacques Demy* (Agnès Varda, 1993/95)).

debating programmes sensationalise his experiences; and a company specialising in maternity-wear exploits him for his novelty value. Chaumont's dubious medical findings are utilised by politicians to project the apparent superiority of French medical research against its German, British and American counterparts. The global reach of Marco's condition is depicted, as men are seen suffering from similar symptoms from Moscow to Sydney. Consumerism is held responsible for this astounding physiological development; Chaumont preposterously claims that male pregnancy has evolved due to modern methods of food production, such as battery farming.

However, the film's potential to challenge patriarchal power, privilege and prejudice is undermined by its ending. Chaumont reveals that Marco's diagnosis was erroneous, dismissing the other cases as a collective psychosis; Irène declares that she is pregnant and the couple marry.[9] Such a dilution of its political potency is critiqued by Le Gras, for whom *L'Evénement...* frames its preoccupations with derision, subjects serious feminist concerns to a farce and ends with a traditional dénouement (2010: 136). Yet, as Marie Colmant observes, beyond the film's slapstick tone and reductive ending, a more militant feminist discourse can be identified.[10] *L'Evénement...* directly challenges heterosexual male complacency by considering how men would react should they fall pregnant. More importantly, it explicitly advocates the campaign, led by Beauvoir, to legalise abortion.[11] Such political contexts are explicitly woven into the dialogues when female hairdressers and clients imagine life were men able to bear children: 'la pilule sera en vente partout' ('the pill will be sold everywhere') predicts one, 'et ils avorteront quand ils voudront' ('they will abort when they want') portends another, 'oui, je ne vois pas le PDG abandonnant son usine pour huit mois hein, il sera avorté'

---

9   Demy was forced to cut an alternative ending showing Marco giving birth. His frustrations are portrayed in the final shot showing a copy of the *Le Parisien* being swept away by a road cleaner, its headline declaring that the story of the pregnant man was phoney (see Taboulay 1996: 40).

10 From L'Evénement le plus important depuis que l'homme a marché sur la lune *par Marie Colmant* (Thomas Benigni and Valentin Vignet, 2008).

11 Deneuve, Varda and Seyrig added their names to Beauvoir's *Manifeste des 343*, published in the *Nouvel Observateur* magazine on 5 April 1971, admitting that its 343 female signatories had undergone an abortion. Such activism pressurised the Giscard government to respond and the Simone Veil law decriminalising abortions was ratified in January 1975.

('yes, I can't see the Chief Executive abandoning his factory for eight months, eh? It would be aborted'), foresees Irène, which prompts her customer Madame Corfa (Micheline Dax) to augur 'et il n'ira pas en prison pour autant' ('and he won't go to prison because of it').

However, *L'Evénement...* maintains rather than undermines patriarchal gender roles as they are culturally constituted. The comic device of inversion is deployed, but is mainly restricted to the early scenes. Medical complaints and corporeal evolutions are the first indications of Marco's pregnancy. He experiences a headache, dizziness, faintness, an aching stomach and lower back pain, and is advised to avoid salt, alcohol, tobacco and extreme sports. After his diagnosis, he notices his growing abdomen in a mirror adorning a shop facade, purchases a medical dictionary and strawberries – Irène's craving when pregnant with Lucas (Benjamin Legrand). The stereotype of blushing female and confident male that typifies depictions of the conventional proposal scene is overturned when Marco declares to Irène 'maintenant que je suis ... dans cet état-là, il faudra que tu te décides ... à m'épouser' ('now that I'm in this state ... you will have to decide ... to marry me') to which Irène replies 'ben oui, moi je veux bien, ça ne me gêne pas, si t'y tiens' ('alright yes, I don't mind, it doesn't bother me, if you insist').

Beyond these playful examples of gender insubordination, Marco's masculinity is uncompromised. He remains gruff and macho. He chides his elderly female student Mademoiselle Janvier (Madeleine Barbulée) for her incompetence, refers to Irène as his 'little hen' and pulls her into his lap after hinting that she should marry him. Medical expertise is used to confirm his normative masculinity. Chaumont reassures Irène that her husband is 'perfectly constituted' and describes Marco's case more as a 'transfer' than an 'inversion'. In *L'Evénement...*, a male may thus conceive a child without danger of emasculation. Meanwhile, Irène reflects Marco's transcendent masculinity. Her occupation as a hairdresser pertains to the realm of the feminine, concerned with appearance rather than the acquisition of skills as in Marco's work. She is temperamental, crying when she imagines he is seriously ill, and declaring, much like C in *Le Bel Indifférent*: 'lutter seule, vivre seule, je ne pourrais pas, j'ouvrirais le gaz ou j'irais me jeter par la fenêtre' ('I could never live alone, fight alone, I would turn the gas on or throw myself through the window').

Nevertheless, by maintaining Marco's external virility, Demy not only maximises the comic potential of his film, but also shows how sexism and homophobia are perpetuated and trivialised in everyday discourse. Before knowing his diagnosis, Irène mocks Marco for gaining weight and later predicts that he will be enormous by the end of his pregnancy. His friends joke about his possible homosexuality; Lucien Soumain (Claude Melki) asks if he has been penetrated and when Leboeuf (Jacques Legras) accuses Soumain of sodomising him, the latter replies to the enjoyment of the crowd that he refused. Dr Delavigne (Micheline Presle) attempts to reassure Irène that her partner is not homosexual, which Chaumont quickly dismisses, expressing what would become a familiar homophobic diatribe: 'vous savez bien que les homosexuels n'auront jamais d'enfants; seuls un homme et une femme peuvent faire un enfant' ('you know full well that homosexuals cannot have children; only a man and a woman can create a child').

As mentioned, the real target of the film's satire and disdain are the people with power who seek to profit from the experiences of the ordinary citizen. Chaumont is depicted as condescending and exploitative, convincing Marco to appear alongside him during his speech at the international medical conference in Paris, as if a freak specimen. Director of *La Société Prénatale* Scipion Lemeu (André Falcon) uses the novelty of Marco's case as a resource for promoting his maternity wear company. He urges his all-male team of designers and marketing managers to create and promote a selection of seasonal outfits for the pregnant man. Pregnant women are conspicuously absent from the negotiations and women in general are subordinated or superfluous to proceedings, bar Irène who tentatively demands paid holidays in addition to the offer of a salary of 10,000 Francs per month. Consequently, these scenes depict the absurdity of a sector that denies women a voice even though their physiological transformations in pregnancy is its *raison d'être*. And this, it seems, is the film's point: the persistence of misogyny in the modern world. Such a concern with endemic sexism as a product of traditional power hierarchies is also central to *Lady Oscar*, as will be seen.

Challenging sexism through gender insubordination: *Lady Oscar*

Lady Oscar is Demy's lavish adaptation of Japanese author Riyoko Ikeda's manga entitled *Rose of Versailles*. Ikeda studied History in Paris and cultivated a fascination for the pre-Revolution period. Over twelve million copies of her manga were published in Japan. Producer Mataichiro Yamamoto bought the rights and, eventually, asked Demy to make the film. Yamamoto secured some financing from cosmetics manufacturer Shiseido, whose target clientele were young women attracted by French beauty products and couture. Conscious of the exotic appeal of Ikeda's manga, Yamamoto decided to make the film in France. The result is a truly transnational production – originating in and financed by Japan and based on a story penned by a Japanese author adapted by Demy and American screenplay writer Patricia Knopp, unfolding within the most iconic moment of French history, shot in France, administered by Varda's film company, Ciné-Tamaris, and featuring a cast of mainly British actors. *Lady Oscar* attracted two million spectators within eight weeks of its Japanese release and made eight million dollars at the Japanese box office, but it was only seen twice in France, as part of the *Cahiers du Cinéma* week in April 1980 and during a section of the Angers film festival dedicated to Demy in 1981. Demy is mainly faithful to the manga. He transposes its emphatic stylisation via expressive acting, concise and simplistic dialogues and Legrand's sentimental score.

Lady Oscar furnishes a complex web of main and subsidiary stories. Oscar-François de Jarjayes (Catriona MacColl) is born a girl but declared a boy by her father the Général de Jarjayes, frustrated at having already fathered five daughters. The film traces her attempts to reconcile herself with her sex and depicts her eventual emancipation from her father's control, thus recasting a typical Oedipal narrative within a discourse of free will. André (Barry Stokes), Oscar's childhood friend and her father's stable-worker, declares his love for her, but is tragically shot dead by a soldier's bullet during the storming of the Bastille, constituting yet another allusion to *Les Enfants du paradis*. The affair of the Queen's necklace, famously embellished in Alexandre Dumas's *Le Collier de la Reine* (1849–50), provides a sub-narrative that highlights the obsession with wealth and power at the time. Jeanne Vallois (Anouska Hempel) flees her poor dwelling and convinces the Marquise de Boulainvilliers (Rosemary Dunham) to adopt her. After marrying Nicolas de la Motte (Mike Marshall), she exploits the gullible Cardinal Louis de Rohan-Guéménée (Gregory Floy) for money. With her lover Marc Rétaux de Villette (actor unknown), she forges Marie-Antoinette's (Christine Böhm) signature on letters, promising the Cardinal an audience in return for money. Jeanne secures a deposit on an expensive necklace already refused by Marie-Antoinette because it had been created for Louis XV as a gift to Madame Barry. Eventually, she is exposed and punished, branded with a 'v' for 'voleuse' or thief. Meanwhile, her sister Rosalie (Shelagh McLeod) seeks revenge against the Comtesse Gabrielle de Polignac (Sue Lloyd) for having fatally wounded her mother in a driving accident, assaults her at court and becomes an activist in the revolutionary struggle.

As a faithful adaptation of a romantic manga targeted at adolescent girls in Japan, *Lady Oscar*'s scope for questioning biologically deterministic gender identities is limited. Rather than an overt tale about a biological female's inability to learn and assume her femininity, it is mainly concerned with Oscar's reconciliation of her gender with her biological sex. Demy utilises cultural and corporeal markers of femininity to constantly remind his audience of Oscar's femaleness. She speaks in a high voice, her facial features are refined, she has long blonde hair and wears make-up. Marie-Antoinette, André and Nanny (Constance Chapman) constantly refer to her as a woman. Oscar is depicted as enduring a crisis of gender. She asks André why she cannot kill 'like a man', inspects her breasts in a mirror and covers them with her arms as if ashamed of her female physique.

Yet, despite its apparent reinforcement of the established gender binary, *Lady Oscar* gestures to the problems of a society in which sexual differentiation is so obviously marked, and traces this constraining system to the very moment of its primary declaration. In her most famous assertion, Beauvoir affirms 'on ne naît pas femme, on le devient' (1949: 13 (vol. 2)) ('one is not born, but rather becomes, woman') (Borde and Malovany-Chevallier, 2009: 293). For Beauvoir 'c'est l'ensemble de la civilisation qui élabore ce produit intermédiaire entre le mâle et le castrat qu'on qualifie de féminin' (1949: 13 (vol. 2)) ('it is civilization as a whole that elaborates this intermediary product between the male and the eunuch that is called feminine') (Borde and Malovany-Chevallier, 2009: 29). The film's prologue illustrates the constructionist thinking behind Beauvoir's point. In long shot,

Jarjayes paces past his five daughters as he awaits the birth of his latest child. An off-screen cry followed by a crying baby is then heard as Jarjayes declares 'a son at last'. When Nanny informs him that his wife, who died in childbirth, bore him yet another daughter, he declares 'the child you hold is Oscar François de Jarjayes, heir to my commission as commander of the Royal Guards'. Jarjayes exercises his patriarchal power to realign his child's gender and set it on a predetermined and circumscribed trajectory.

As in *L'Evénement...*, the target of the film's critique is not gender roles, but institutionalised sexism. Jarjayes embodies the distillation of the inequalities and misogyny of the French monarchical system within a nobleman's family.[12] He is depicted as stern and domineering, indifferent to the feelings of the women of his household. In the prologue, his daughters sit in silent attendance, arranged from oldest to youngest and dressed in yellow and white dresses and blouses, with flowers pinned to their chests. Clearly within their earshot and directed at their Nanny, Jarjayes states 'my wife would not give her life for so lowly a contribution as another daughter' and orders 'you will bring your orphaned grandson into our home, Nanny. In this house of lace and silence, my son will need a male companion'.

With André's encouragement, Oscar defies patriarchy. The catalyst of her rebellion is her father's order that she marries the Conte de Girodet (Martin Potter) and become a Countess, a role defined by marital association with a male. Here, then, the agency hitherto enjoyed by Oscar is revealed as superficial, susceptible to removal at any point because she is biologically female. As a pseudo-male, she remains subject to her father's will. Her biological sex constrains her to a position of contingency. Afraid of the abyss of radical freedom, Oscar claims to André that she lacks the power to withstand her father. André vociferously reminds her that she can still act and transcend her predetermined existence. As a result, Oscar refuses Girodet's offer. She attends the black ball which is intended to announce their engagement in a white officer's costume and kisses a *courtisane* (Consuelo de Haviland) who refers to her as 'sir'. Her rebuff of Girodet triggers the final duel, first verbal and then with swords, with her father, which she wins with André's help.

12 The House of Bourbon prohibited female succession for fear of producing a foreign heir. When Marie-Antoinette gives birth to a daughter in a later scene, the King tells his physicians that they will only receive a quarter of their fees.

This rapport between transcendence and immanence, between agency and passivity, extends to social class and status. Jarjayes's reluctance to embrace change is diametrically opposed to Rosalie and André's determination to see the installation of a new egalitarian society. Through a combination of scenes depicting misery and revolutionary militancy, and André's statements, critique of class privilege is transmitted. While Oscar is held within a position of passivity, André, although a biological male, is constrained by the monarchical system because of his status as a servant. When Jarjayes tells Oscar that she is being dispatched to serve at the Court and that André will work in the stables, he declares 'you will each assume responsibility for your separate stations in life'. Later, through André, Demy articulates his admiration for American liberalism in contrast to French parochialism. André informs Oscar 'equality exists in America ... a man can love whoever he wants in America' and declares 'I would gladly give my life for the future equality of France', a somewhat tragic portension given the ending, but one that, prospectively, undercuts its melancholy. In what is almost an echo of Melius's speech to the Inquisition in *The Pied Piper*, André imagines 'I would have everything, through my death, my life would have great meaning'.

Despite seemingly 'playing God' by altering his child's gender as he sees fit, Jarjayes's plans for a son are eventually derailed by Girodet's desire to marry Oscar. Money and status are the motors in this unequal and egotistical society. Individual choice is directly linked to the ignorance of the aristocracy towards the misery and suffering of the people. Early on, when Rosalie tells Oscar that the people are starving, she angrily asks André why he had not informed her, to which he responds: 'why didn't you look, why didn't you see? We've travelled these streets a thousand times, hunger isn't hiding, it's everywhere'. Wilful blindness is depicted to excess in Marie-Antoinette who refuses to listen to the Chancellor's pleas to curb her spending, urges him to raise taxes and insists on having a theatre constructed to keep her amused. Elsewhere, despite her first-hand knowledge of poverty, Jeanne rejects her past life, telling her husband to evict Rosalie when she comes to tell her of their mother's death. Both Queen and fraudster are punished, the latter within the narrative, the former in its historical dénouement. *Lady Oscar* thus imbricates both gender and class within the same struggle to achieve a radical freedom in which its proponents can acquire the right to determine their own existence.

The film illustrates how sexual and social subordination are a consequence of aristocratic and bourgeois patriarchal control, which, as has been argued, recurs throughout Demy's cinema.

The queerness of the *Demy-monde*

As seen, queerness maintains a constant, if implied, presence in Demy's cinema. Object choices frequently defy heteronormative ideals, as shown in the incest narrative that serves as an allegory for the complexities of actual desires, and some of the messages contained within the dialogues chime with aspects of the fight for lesbian and gay emancipation, as in Melius's call for tolerance in *The Pied Piper* and André's ode to American liberalism (see Duggan, 2013: 129). Moreover, queerly marked individuals are often seen in the periphery of shots, from the loiterer who leers at Cécile in *Lola* to the sailors that hang out in the streets. In *La Naissance du jour*, Colette and her friends observe two men dancing together in a club. When asked why, they reply that women cannot dance well, but the camera reveals two women waltzing around the floor, thus confirming that the men dance together through choice. The whispering voices C hears in *Le Bel Indifférent* of lovers arranging a future encounter in the hallway sound masculine, and Langlois's dead son in *Une chambre en ville* was apparently originally intended to have committed suicide because he was gay (Lefèvre, 2013: 76). The locations of gay male cruising also figure, as in the multi-storey car park in *Parking* that Demy is said to have wanted to portray as a place of illicit sexual encounters (Boulangé, 2013: 32).

Often, queer characters can be signified via their clothes, gesturality and behaviour. In *L'Evénement...* one of Irène's clients, Clarisse de Saint-Clair (Andrée Tainsy) wears a black beret and coat, has short, dark hair, smokes a cigar and speaks in a low voice, while another (Janine Souchon), who also has short, dark hair, sports a suit jacket, a white shirt and a checked tie. Elsewhere, Ramona Martinez (Alice Sapritch) wears a trilby hat and beige trench coat, smokes cigars and speaks in low tones – her appearance and behaviour evoking an erstwhile Jean Gabin – and fine arts student Rodolphe (François Wimille) is dressed exuberantly in a red velvet jacket with gold motif, yellow patterned shirt and neckerchief. When Irène observes that, in fact, his real dream is to change his sex, he replies 'à chacun sa petite

fantaisie, non?' ('each to his or her own fantasy, don't you think?').
Such gender troubling is a central concern of queer theory which, as
Jean-Yves le Talec summarises in his book on camp in France, 'inter-
roge la notion de frontière, ou de limite, entre le corps qui serait un
support neutre et malléable préexistant à toute signification sexuelle,
et l'esprit, qui concentrerait et exprimerait toute la charge et le sens
d'une identité de sexe ou de genre' (2008: 133).[13] Even the apparently
straight male characters adopt feminising poses in recline, as in
Emile in *Le Bel Indifférent* and Vial in *La Naissance du jour*.

Girodet in *Lady Oscar* disrupts this notion of a fixed frontier between
body and mind, masculinity and femininity. His potency as a destabi-
lising force is constituted in his fusion of physical and behavioural
characteristics ascribed to both men and women. Moreover, he is
sexually attracted to men, women and – it is comically inferred –
animals. After negotiating his forthcoming marriage to Oscar, he
stumbles across André in the hallway and reassures him that he may
continue seeing Oscar, adding 'after all, you're nearly as pretty as she
is'. Girodet is an overtly erotic agent. After Oscar's entrance at the ball,
he tells her 'I don't return goods I've paid a high price for, I study
them closely, I feel them, I smell them, I peel away the layers until I
have learned how they are constructed'. Oscar is thus positioned as his
plaything, the object of future desires that straddle the cerebral, the
sensual and the sexual. As a lecherous aristocrat who utilises his privilege to exploit men and women beneath him, Girodet stands outside of
Demy's class ethics. And yet, he elicits a queer pleasure. Coming well
over a decade before the inception of the New Queer Cinema coined
by B. Ruby Rich (1992), Girodet epitomises that movement's defiance
of what Michele Aaron summarises as the 'tasteful and tolerated'
gay culture co-opted by the mainstream (2004: 7–9). He is playfully
depraved and a welcome antidote to Oscar and André's worthiness.[14]

By locating his narratives in port and coastal cities and towns,
Demy's films unfold within a liminal space through which visitors
pass, and brief dalliances are commonplace. His characters frequent

13 'questions the idea of boundaries, or limits, between the body which can be
   a neutral and malleable entity that pre-exists all sexual significations, and the
   mind, which concentrates and expresses all the means and meanings of a sexual
   or gendered identity.'
14 Elsewhere Marie-Antoinette refers to Polignac as 'my love' and their affair is
   discussed at court.

establishments in which so-called dubious morals are practiced, sometimes as a means of escaping the prevailing bourgeois morality that governs their hometown: the Eldorado Cabaret in *Lola*, the casinos in *La Baie des Anges*, the peep show in *Model Shop*, the tango club transformed into brothel in *Les Parapluies de Cherbourg*, the hotel room in *Une chambre en ville* and so on. Furthermore, Demy often dresses his provincial townscapes and interiors in new clothes, modifying infrastructure so that it masquerades in its new drag gear. *Les Parapluies de Cherbourg*, *Les Demoiselles de Rochefort* and *Peau d'âne* all exude a queer camp aesthetic centred in the decors. Elsewhere, as seen, America is heralded as a nirvana of emancipation for some of the French characters who inhabit these places, as is boldly articulated in André's monologue to Oscar cited above. Yet, Demy's cinema also reveals the equivocation of the US as both the site of liberalism and origins of a nefarious consumerist culture. Demy thus establishes an ambivalent cultural space in which some characters look to America as an inspiration for freedom, while they and others are victims of the cultural homogenisation wrought by consumerism.

For some, the queer sensibility of Demy's cinema emanates from the perceived similarities between its narratives and the experiences of non-straight spectators. Colomb distinguishes *Les Parapluies de Cherbourg* from *Les Demoiselles de Rochefort*, arguing that the former's queer resonances emerge, not from its aesthetics, but from its tale of a doomed romance, which, in his view, symbolises the moral history of closeted homosexuality (1998: 39–43). However, although his films end unhappily, they nonetheless nod to a conceptualisation of existence and futurity in which structures can be modified to accommodate difference. As argued, music and colour alert the spectator to these alternatives and allow Demy to shine a spotlight on the tragic implications of not pursuing a possible future that withstands the constraining values of the present. In this, his films may be said to allude to an alternative – or queer – 'utopia' by not representing it explicitly.

For José Esteban Muñoz, queerness represents an 'ideality' that has not-yet-been-lived (2009: 1). Muñoz views the 'here and now' as a 'prison house' and urges us to 'strive, in the face of here and now's totalizing rendering of reality, to think and feel a *then and there* ... we must dream and enact new and better pleasures, other ways of being in the world, and ultimately new worlds' (2009: 1; emphasis in original). Demy's cinema is interested in positing the possibility of a reconfigured 'here and now'. Thus, when Geneviève and Guy discuss their plans for their future family after their evening at the opera and tango club, while their words construct a normative ideal, they are conjuring, within the constraints of their particular 'here and now', a future that they believe will transpire, one that will transcend class distinctions and bourgeois morality and in which they will be able to live their desires freely. Though not seen literally, the 'what-could-have-been' bears a presence throughout the narrative, it is frustratingly near, imminent, located, perhaps, in the mind of the spectator. Hence, although Demy's films often end with the camera remaining static as characters walk off into the distance (see Lalanne, 2013: 229), it is the nearness of this more pluralistic and accepting sphere to the world that his audience experiences, that contains the optimism conveyed by his cinema.

Demy's films underline the imminence of this different mode of being by portraying the alternative ways in which his characters apprehend the world in which they live. His cinema often rejects what Halberstam terms as the 'middle-class logic of reproductive temporality' (2005: 4). By compressing his narratives within a delimited period, Demy highlights the divergence between normative, objective temporality and time as it unfolds within consciousness, ungoverned by external morality. Conventional temporality is guarded by patriarchal figures, such as the company director in *Lola* who berates Roland for his tardiness, or Jean's father in *La Baie des Anges* whose job is a clock and watch repairer, gatekeeper, then, of objective, chronological time. Freer characters are unconfined by such temporality, as in Lola in Nantes who constantly has to rush off because she has lost track of the time.

Elsewhere, by blurring the distinction between reality and theatricality, Demy depicts the stance with regards to the world often associated with those positioned at a slant from hegemonic culture, such as queer individuals and communities. A slippage arises between narrative events and dialogues, and their delivery and/or contexts. A parodic knowingness is marshalled between film (and director) and spectator that allows the audience, should they wish, to take distance from the hegemonic values seemingly espoused in the actions and words, as seen in the mobilisation of camp parody in *Les Demoiselles de Rochefort* and *Peau d'âne*. A good – and somewhat prognosticative example – is Chaumont's comment in *L'Evénement...* that 'homosexuals will never have children'. It is not homosexual parenting that is ridiculed, but rather heteronormative and homophobic logic. The politics of such a comment assume greater political resonance with the burgeoning lesbian and gay rights movements of the 1980s and 1990s and, particularly, with the anti-gay activism triggered by the adoption of gay marriage in France in 2013. As seen, later, Demy would be more explicitly political, in Orphée's overt questions about why he cannot love both a man and a woman in *Parking*.

Heteronormativity tends not to succeed in Demy's cinema. The choice of genre in fairytales and musicals helps in rendering this failure absolutely explicit. Both are concerned with projecting hetero-sexuality as an ideal and, accordingly, end with the construction of the perfect heterosexual couple. In her chapter on myths, Beauvoir explains the importance of such stories for the perpetuation of hegemonic masculinity and femininity, arguing that chivalrous tales such as *Sleeping Beauty* and *Peau d'âne* flatter the man as much as the woman, since he requires someone upon whom to lavish his wealth, otherwise it remains abstract (1949: 301 (vol. 1)). This salvation narra-tive recurrently runs aground in Demy's films. The myth – or what Beauvoir calls the Cinderella myth – founders in each case and, as a result, so does the heterosexual morality it has been used to promul-gate. Here, then, Demy's precise preoccupation with the Orpheus story can be seen in a different light. Although Orpheus is portrayed as heroic, he is unable to save Eurydice. The original Greek myth thus recounts the failure of the heterosexual ideal, which Demy appropri-ates and develops in many of his films. Consequently, in his manipu-lation of the heterosexual couple, physical appearance and behaviour, the environment, temporality and modes of social interaction, Demy points to the contingency of dominant notions of the real, in spatial, temporal, social and sexual terms.

While it may be a grandiose overstatement to label a male director a 'women's filmmaker', as if the experiences of women could be so neatly homogenised and articulated through the voice of a man, Demy's cinema implies an awareness of the ambiguities framing the status, existences, expectations and representations of women in society. Moreover, his films reveal how gender and class subordina-tion are interrelated. Such an apparent familiarity with alterity and the disempowered could be deterministically linked to his own self-projection as an outsider, announced in his early short *Les Horizons morts*, and his reported bisexuality. For some, this alignment with alternative points-of-view, this ability to mobilise modalities of interpolation and affect that speak to nonconformist audiences, is the very motor of the myth that has outlived his physical life, as will be seen in the next chapter.

References

Aaron, Michelle (2004) 'New Queer Cinema: an Introduction', in M. Aaron (ed.), (2004) *New Queer Cinema: a Critical Reader*, New Brunswick and Edinburgh: Rutgers University Press: 3–22.

Barthes, Roland (1977) *Fragments d'un discours amoureux*, Paris, Seuil.

Beauvoir, Simone de (1949) *Le Deuxième Sexe 1 et 2*, Paris, Gallimard, transl. Constance Borde and Sheila Malovany-Chevallier, *The Second Sex 1 and 2: a New Translation* ([2009] 2011), London, Vintage.

Berthomé, Jean-Pierre (1996) *Jacques Demy et les racines du rêve*, 2nd Edition, Nantes, L'Atalante.

Borde, Constance and Malovany-Chevallier, Sheila transl. ([2009] 2011) *The Second Sex 1 and 2: a New Translation*, London, Vintage.

Boulangé, Guillaume (2013) 'Quand Jacques Demy croise Jean Cocteau', in Anon. (eds), *Le Monde enchanté de Jacques Demy*, Paris, Skira Flammarion, La Cinémathèque Française and Ciné-Tamaris: 28–32.

Boulé, Jean-Pierre and Tidd, Ursula (2012) *Existentialism and Contemporary Cinema: a Beauvoirian Perspective*, New York and Oxford, Berghahn.

Butler, Judith (1993) 'Imitation and Gender Insubordination', in Henry Abelove, Michèle Aina Barale and David M. Halperin (eds), *The Lesbian and Gay Studies Reader*, New York and London, Routledge: 307–20.

Cocteau, Jean (1989) *Théâtre de poche*, Monaco, Edition du Rocher.

Colomb, Philippe (1998) 'L'Étrange Demy-monde', in Marie-Hélène Bourcier (ed.), *Q comme Queer*, Paris: Cahiers Gay, Kitsch, Camp: 39–47.

Duggan, Anne E (2013) *Queer Enchantments: Gender, Sexuality and Class in the Fairy-Tale Cinema of Jacques Demy*, Detroit: Wayne State University Press.

Giroud, Françoise (1958) *La Nouvelle Vague, portraits de la jeunesse'*, Paris, Galimard.

Godard, Jean-Luc (1958) *Le Bel Indifférent*, *Arts*, 10 December.

Graves, Robert (1955) *The Greek Myths: the Complete and Definitive Edition*, London and New York, Penguin.

Halberstam, Judith (2005) *In a Queer Time and Place: Transgender Bodies, Subcultural Lives*, New York and London, New York University Press.

Holmes, Diana (1991) *Colette* (Women Writers), Basingstoke and London, Palgrave MacMillan.

Lalanne, Jean-Marc (2013) 'Pièges de cristal', in Anon. (eds), *Le Monde enchanté de Jacques Demy*, Paris, Skira Flammarion, La Cinémathèque Française and Ciné-Tamaris: 226–9.

Larnac, Jean (1927) *Colette, sa vie, son oeuvre*, Paris, Éditions Krâ.

Lefèvre, Raphaël (2013) *Une chambre en ville*, Crisnée, Belgium, Editions Yellow Now.

Le Gras, Gwenaëlle (2010) *Le Mythe Deneuve: Une 'star' française entre classicisme et modernité*, Paris, Broché.

Le Talec, Jean-Yves (2008) *Folles de France: Repenser l'homosexualité masculine*, Paris, La Découverte.

Muñoz, José Esteban (2009), *Cruising Utopia: the Then and There of Queer*, New York, New York University Press.

Renouard, Jean-Philippe (2003) 'Demy, Jacques', in Eribon, Didier (ed.), Dictionnaire des cultures gays et lesbiennes, Paris, Larousse: 151.

Rich, B. Ruby (1992) 'The New Queer Cinema', in H. Benshoff and S. Griffin (eds), (2004) *Queer Cinema: The Film Reader*, Oxford and New York: Routledge: 53–9.

Sellier, Geneviève (2005) *La Nouvelle Vague: Un cinéma au masculin singulier*, Paris, CNRS Editions.

5

Mythologising Demy

Since his death in 1990, Jacques Demy has assumed mythical status among many admirers in France and beyond. According to Jean-Marc Lalanne, few oeuvres have permeated the memories of successive generations of French movie watchers as much as that of Demy (1995: 6). References to the affective impact of his work can be found in unexpected places, including: Pascale Ferran's *L'Age des possibles* (1995), in which two of the characters sing 'Rêves secrets d'un Prince et d'une Princesse' from *Peau d'âne* and Alexandra Leclère's *Les Soeurs fachées* (2004) in which the two protagonists recall singing and dancing to 'La Chanson des Jumelles'.[1] They can arise allegorically, as in the scene in *Holy Motors* (Léos Carax, 2012) in which Denis Lavant and Kylie Minogue, dressed to resemble Patricia (Jean Seberg) from *A bout de souffle*, wander around a disaffected La Samaritaine department store in Paris, thus subtly recalling an erstwhile Lola and Roland in the Passage Pomeraye, while Kylie's spontaneous burst into song supplements these visual nods to Demy with clear references to the Hollywood musical number. Evocations of Demy's cinema also transcend medium; an anodyne dialogue is expressed through song in a television advertisement campaign directed by Etienne Chatiliez in 1987 for *Le Trêfle*'s scented toilet paper range. This particular advertisement plays on the common, somewhat dismissive, perception of Demy's peculiar way of theatricalising the everyday through song as absurd, often referred to as 'passe-moi le sel' ('pass me the salt').

1 Further allusions include Nicolas Engel's short *Les Voiliers du Luxembourg* (2005) with its central single-mother protagonist Edith from Nantes (Juliette Laurent), dialogues entirely expressed through song, and narrative about love and chance encounters.

More pointedly, Agnès Varda has been pivotal in assuring recognition of her husband's significance, most prominently in the three films she has devoted to his life and cinema, *Jacquot de Nantes* (1990), *Les Demoiselles ont eu 25 ans* (1992) and *L'Univers de Jacques Demy* (1995), as well as the references to him in *Les Plages d'Agnès* (2008). Moreover, Berthomé and Taboulay's monographs have reinforced this mythologisation within critical, cinephile and academic circles, as have Père and Colmant's beautifully illustrated hardback, the anthology of essays edited by Casas and Iriarte to coincide with their retrospective in San Sebastián in September 2011, many excellent scholarly articles and chapters, and, perhaps, this book. Elsewhere, since the mid-1990s, filmmakers have extended beyond the odd nod and wink and recalled the significance of Demy's work, not only as oases of charm and poignancy within an otherwise esoteric cinematographic landscape, but also as commentaries on identity, self–other relations, memory and time. The major exhibition devoted to him at the Cinémathèque de Paris in 2013 confirmed his accession to the status of legend.

The myth, as Barthes notes, 'est une parole choisie par l'histoire: il ne saurait surgir de la "nature" des choses' (1957: 194) ('is a type of speech chosen by history: it cannot possibly evolve from the "nature" of things') (Lavers, 1991: 108). Myths constitute a meta-language that deforms an object from its original meaning, endowing a certain signification, influenced but not dictated by its source. Yet, as Barthes notes, 'la parole mythique est formée d'une matière *déjà* travaillée en vue d'une communication appropriée' (1957: 195; emphasis in original) ('mythical speech is made of a material which has *already* been worked on so as to make it suitable for communication') (Lavers, 1991: 108). The preceding chapters have revealed the primary materials of Demy's oeuvre that have compelled his transition to mythical status. Demy explicitly lays the foundations for his myth in *Trois places pour le 26*, an amalgamation of all the distinctive markers of the director's cinema. Such alacrity to highlight the merits of his craft is unambiguously self-celebratory, its audacity amplified in that it is ventured through a biopic about a performer/movie star assumed to have acceded to legendary status himself.

Embedding the Demy myth: *Trois places pour le 26*

On the surface, *Trois places pour le 26* celebrates the singing and acting star Yves Montand.[2] It depicts his return to Marseilles, after a twenty-year absence, to perform in a show about his life. In honouring an existing star through his material body and past memories, *Trois places pour le 26* fuses the biopic and backstage musical. It complies with Altman's definition of biopics, which bend 'a biographical account to dual-focus presentation' (1987: 104) in that Montand's past is altered to recount a story of a heterosexual romance. Moreover, it adheres to the conventions of the backstage musical, which constructs its 'plot around the creation of a show ... with the making of a romantic couple both symbolically and causally related to the success of the show' (1987: 200). However, Demy transforms both sub-genres by recasting the heterosexual romance in order to address one of his primary preoccupations: incest.

When rehearsing for his musical at the Opéra Municipal de Marseille, Montand recalls his first love, a young woman from Brittany called Mylène le Goff, whom he met at Le Paradis bar where she worked as a hostess known as Maria. Mylène/Maria's daughter, Marion, aspires to become a stage performer under the name of Roxanne and secures the role of Maria in the show, replacing Betty Miller (Catriona MacColl). Characteristic of Demy's predilection for missed connections, Marion is unaware that she plays her mother, and Montand is unaware that he is performing alongside his daughter. Marion is instantly attracted to Montand; the couple have sex and afterwards discover their biological link. The film concludes with Marion reuniting Montand with Mylène, and this unorthodox family leaves for Paris, father and daughter unperturbed by their sexual encounter. Montand's recollections are thus eclipsed by his fictional affair with Marion, transferring us from the star's experiences to the director's concerns. Montand's autobiography and Demy's fabricated tale coincide in such a way as to disturb the distinction between reality and fiction, a point inadvertently underlined in stories in the media at the time about the fact that a young woman was pregnant with Montand's child. And yet, it is through the act of storytelling, within

---

2 Demy penned the script in February 1975; it was initially entitled *Les Folies bourgeoises* and then *Dancing*. Isabelle Adjani was intended to play Marion, while Delphine Seyrig was to incarnate her mother, Marie-Hélène.

which Montand becomes the main protagonist, that Demy elevates his own myth over that of Montand.

In an interview Demy recalls his initial reticence when approached by producer Claude Berri,[3] referring to the project as outdated, but then asserts what he perceives as his foresight and providence in taking on this modern musical: 'je suis toujours persuadé d'avoir dix ans d'avance sur l'ensemble de la société cinématographique' (in Clech, Strauss and Toubiana, 1988: 10) ('I've always been convinced that I am ten years ahead of the whole of film society'). In this, he echoes the plot of the most obvious Hollywood antecedent of *Trois places pour le 26*, *The Band Wagon* (Vincente Minnelli, 1953). Music hall star Tony Hunter (Fred Astaire) is out of step with the times; his friends, Lily and Lester Marton (Nanette Fabray and Oscar Levant), call him to New York to perform in a show directed by British stage actor Jeffrey Cordova (Jack Buchanan). Cordova insists on directing a modernist version of *Faust* (Johann Wolfgang von Goethe) and casts ballerina Gabrielle Gerrard (Cyd Charisse) as Tony's love interest. The show flops after its first night. Undeterred, Tony reworks it into a conventional musical and reverses its fortunes. *The Band Wagon* thus rehabilitates time-honoured entertainment against modern transformations. Rather than fossilised and vacuous, the musical is upheld as pertinent precisely because it is entertaining. A similar effect is achieved by *Trois places pour le 26*, which, as reviewer Iannis Katsahnnias observes, brings storytelling back to French cinema (1988: 60).

Montand insisted on evoking Hollywood musicals in the numbers performed on stage. Such allusions bear historical authenticity – Montand was cast alongside American stars, most famously Marilyn Monroe in *Let's Make Love* (George Cukor, 1960) with whom he had an affair. Yet, *Trois places pour le 26* extends the links, not only to reinforce Montand's celestial status, but also to elevate Demy's films to the ranks of the most legendary musicals. This is asserted in the prominent number 'Ciné qui chante'. The costumes and choreography (top hats, tails, sequinned dresses and jazz tap dance) are unmistakably Hollywood. The lyrics proclaim the appeal of the musical as timeless: 'ciné qui danse, Ciné qui chante, Cinéma ta bonne humeur m'enchante, Ciné rieur, Ciné bonheur ... Moi ce que

3 Demy was given complete freedom and it was the first time Montand had ever sung and danced in a movie. However, only 295,017 spectators went to see the film.

je préfère, C'est le musical'.[4] Montand's quotations from iconic Holly-wood numbers, including 'Cheek-to-Cheek' and 'Singin' in the Rain', and the interjection of a female performer dressed as Marilyn Monroe who intones 'I Wanna be Loved by You', serve as reminders of the abiding pleasures of the genre. The existing mythical object is then recast so that it expresses and transmits the quality and innovation of Demy's cinema, and actuates a promulgation of his myth; Montand concludes his medley by singing the main line from 'Le Thème des amants' from *Les Parapluies de Cherbourg*.

Characteristically, Demy combines self-reverence with self-parody. Marion falsely informs her mother that she is going to see an 'old musical' at the cinema with a friend. Similarly, after Betty quits the show, Montand barks at his production team 'c'est quand même léger, non? Mais de quoi on a l'air?' ('well, it's a bit farcical, isn't it? What do we look like?'). Yet, where in his earlier films such comments project Demy's playful self-mockery, here they function as a means of self-promotion. They elicit acclaim that affirms his value as a director over Montand's virtues as a performer. When Marion reviews Montand's performance after the first rehearsal, her words echo the terms recurrently associated with Demy's cinema, 'ce que j'aime dans ce que vous faites, c'est le passage de l'émotion et la légèreté' ('what I like in what you do is the transition from emotions to lightness'). Her praise of the performer-star is comparatively less articulate, as Marion continues 'et puis votre voix et l'accent, c'est, c'est très bien' ('and your voice and accent, it's, it's very good').

Memories and the cultivation and rekindling of passions are the main themes of *Trois places pour le 26*, but the title of the internal show, 'souvenirs de Montand', can be reworded and used as a subtitle of the film itself, as 'souvenirs de Demy' – or even 'souvenirs du public de Demy' since many of its pleasures derive from his knowing audience's recollections of his films. As mentioned in the introduction and chapter 2, in her analysis of Demy's musicals, Herzog invokes Bergson's theories of perception and memory, which pertain particularly well to *Trois places pour le 26*. As we saw, spontaneous memories arise within the 'temporal delay' between perceived object and the perceiver. The object, *Trois places pour le 26*, elicits the informed audience's recollections of Demy's earlier films, via its

---

4 'Cinema that dances, Cinema that sings, Cinema your good mood enchants me, Laughing cinema, Happy cinema ... What I prefer is the musical.'

narrative, mood, characterisation, dialogues and musical numbers. Within the present, the knowing audience engages with and responds to the dialogues and action as they unfold in front of them, but the exchanges and *mise en scène* simultaneously activate recollections of situations and characters from Demy's previous films.

In their first scene, Mylène and Marion quarrel over Marion's ambition to become a performer and their precarious situation; Mylène's husband, the Baron de Lambert, is serving a five-year prison sentence for fraud. Mylène thus shares with Desnoyer and Langlois financial difficulties and shame caused by an absent male partner. Moreover, like Geneviève and Edith, Mylène married for material security rather than love. Yet, Mylène's former occupation recalls Lola's status as a dancer, as do her admission that she has always loved Montand, and her departure with him and her daughter at the end of the film, while her gravelly voice and steely resolve nod to Jackie. Although Marion's appearance evokes Cécile with her dark, straight hair and flowing dresses, she also boasts the talents of Solange and Delphine: she has studied piano and dance for seven years and, incidentally, was born a Gemini, just like Demy. Elsewhere, her disobedience recalls Geneviève, her aforementioned lie conjuring Geneviève's lie to Emery that she is going to the theatre with Cécile.

The film's tightly limited narrative, which begins and ends with the arrival and departure of an outsider, marks *Trois places pour le 26* as a Demy production. The title informs us that the plot progresses towards a concluding date – the 26th. Key markers of objective time are verbalised: a journalist for the one o'clock news interviews Montand as he arrives in Marseilles; the stage director orders the actors and extras to rehearse at 9 p.m.; Mylène tells Montand she will meet him at 3 p.m. in Le Paradis bar; and Montand asks Marion to join him at the station at 2 p.m. Failed encounters also punctuate the fictional narrative: Montand and Marion narrowly miss each other in the street twice; Montand arrives too late to see Mylène as she visits his hotel; Montand fails to recognise Mylène from her married name and title inscribed on her calling card; Montand and Marion do not realise their biological links. Such obviously contrived sequencing evokes the connivances between director and audience in both *Lola* and *Les Demoiselles de Rochefort*.

Key scenes and iconic shots from Demy's films are replicated. Montand's visit to the bookshop in Marseilles conjures Desnoyer,

Cécile and Roland when they first meet in *Lola*. When Montand asks whether the bookseller (Dominique Varda) knows the whereabouts of his friend Marius Ceredo (Pierre Maguelon), she informs her assistant that he is the brother-in-law of M. Favigny, the shoe shop owner – the same name and profession of the contact Claire gives to Roland for the job of taking the briefcase to Johannesburg, in *Lola*. Moreover, after Montand signs their book, he enquires whether they know Mylène, opening his question with a line almost identical to that of Desnoyer when Roland offers to give Cécile his dictionary 'je ne voudrais pas abuser de votre gentillesse' ('I would not like to disrespect your kindness'). Montand appears as a ghost in the beauty shop where Marion works, recalling Peau d'âne's spiritual appearance in the Red Prince's dreams. Elsewhere, an aerial shot, taken from above the Place de l'Opéra, conjures the opening credit sequence of *Les Parapluies de Cherbourg*. Montand is seen walking with manager Max Leehman (Paul Guers); a father and his son pass through; three drunken sailors cross to chat up a prostitute; and Marion enters with Toni Fontaine (Patrick Fierry).

Decors and costumes visually reinforce these intertextual associations. The deep blue, baby blue, violet and ochre walls of Mylène and Marion's apartment jar with Mylène's emerald skirt suit and Marion's pink dress, and transport us to Emery and Geneviève in their umbrella shop, and Langlois and Edith in Nantes. The neo-classical style of the municipal opera building closely approximates that of the Théâtre Graslin in Nantes. Within the show, a transporter bridge is lowered onto the stage, alongside key Demy icons, including a cinema, a hairdresser's, a sailor and a prostitute. Later, Montand sings 'L'Esprit frappeur' against the mock backdrop of a large liner in a dry dock, and he visits a real dry dock in Marseilles. While these environmental markers are representations of the sites and landmarks of Montand's youth, they suffuse our present perception of his biography with the past memories of Demy's films and life. Lola's comment that she knows Marseilles without even having been there appears visually evinced in that our actual view of the Mediterranean city is partly shaped by our recollections of Demy's representations of the Atlantic port.

And yet, as always with Demy, this invocation of the past within the present is actuated in order to throw into question the dependability of memory and recognition. The characters we see, although bearing close similarities to earlier protagonists, are other, their experiences, while analogous, are distinct. Hence, as in Roland's conjuration of the Passage Pommeraye in *Les Parapluies de Cherbourg* and the exchanges at Yvonne's dinner party in *Les Demoiselles de Rochefort*, the present image closely resembles but is never exactly the same as the past memory. Furthermore, *Trois places pour le 26* reveals that the experiences of the individual are always unique, that the already lived can never be repeated. Hence, Lola's prediction is proved wrong since *Trois places pour le 26* demonstrates that it is not possible to know with any degree of confidence exactly what Marseilles is like without having experienced it.

Centring the narrative on a real-life familiar figure highlights the unreliability of memory and perception, for it stymies our ability to have faith in the psychological connections we make as we watch the film. The incest subplot usefully illustrates how Demy continues this within the narrative itself. Memories of earlier depictions of incest are prompted, but *Trois places pour le 26* offers a more explicit commentary on intra-familial desire, which is both enacted and avowed. Where the mirror implies Peau d'âne's burgeoning attraction for her father in her log cabin, the bathroom mirror reflects Marion's realisation that she has just had sex with her father. Typical of Demy's de-drama-tising approach, Marion shrugs off their act and engineers Montand's reunion with Mylène.[5]

By its very nature as a popular genre, the musical divests Demy of the requirement of offering an explanation for his characters' motives and the impact of their actions.[6] In not addressing social attitudes, Demy highlights the emphasis that abounds in his oeuvre on instinc-tive desires over external morality. Such a concern is furthermore articulated through the dialogues; Montand tells Marion not to worry about forgetting her lines, and that only inner feelings and instinct matter. However, Demy's audacity is somewhat attenuated in another line from Montand to Marion, which confirms that the incestuous

---

5 An alternative ending was considered, in which the familial reunion would have been revealed as the conclusion of the stage show, but Demy insisted on keeping the sexual encounter between Montand and Marion within the actual life of the characters.

6 A parody of the intergenerational dimension of Hollywood romances between an experienced male star and his female prodigy is evident here (for example, *A Star is Born* (George Cukor, 1954), *Easter Parade* (Charles Walters, 1948), *The Band Wagon, Singin' in the Rain, Funny Face* (Stanley Donen, 1957), and *My Fair Lady* (George Cukor, 1964)).

narrative is fictional 'tout ce qu'on voit sur scène c'est vrai, c'est ma vie, c'est tout ce qui est autour qui est du cinéma' ('everything that you see on stage is real, it's my life. Everything else is cinema'). Yet, while mitigating any negative impact of the incest sub-plot for Montand's image, his comment undermines the dependability of the present image. Consequently, *Trois places pour le 26* explicitly questions the authenticity of what we see *and* the reliability of what we recall, therefore blurring the distinction between diegetic reality and fantasy.

Such deliberate falsification dominates the diegesis, in which all the characters portray themselves differently from their actual identities. Montand and Marion adopt stage names. As mentioned, Maria is Mylène's escort pseudonym, and Montand's show depicts her assuming the names of at least two husbands, while off-stage she becomes the Baronne de Lambert through marriage. Both Montand and Mylène lie to each other, pretending that they are happy. When Mylène reveals the truth that Montand is her daughter's father, she falsely tells him that she is in Italy, thereby paving the way for the incest subplot. More disruptive still is the inscription of this deception within the film's production. The age difference between Montand and Fabian – Montand was sixty-six while Fabian was fifty-five – undermines the plausibility of the narrative, the premise of which hinges on the fact that they were young lovers and last saw each other twenty years before Montand's return to Marseilles. *Trois places pour le 26* thus reaffirms Demy's perceived adeptness at prompting serious philosophical questions around authenticity and existence within a seemingly light film.

Circumscribing the Demy myth: Agnès Varda's homages to her husband

Through the films she made following his death, Varda constructs her husband's cinema as constituting a universe of significations and sensibilities, and upholds Demy as the original creator of that universe. Though broader than the usual spatial term deployed to describe Demy's cinema – the *Demy-monde* – Varda's *univers* is a clearly demarcated entity, with its specified constellations of meanings and influence, enclosed within a clearly delineated value system. The primary materials of this universe are, of course, his films, but Varda traces their inspiration and interprets their meanings by deploying the family as her most recurrent motif, thus shifting metaphors from the hyper-global to the domestic. The family as it emerges from Varda's work is conventional. She constructs his birth family as idyllic, and portrays his relationship with her and his children as harmonious. She also extends this family motif to the people who worked on his productions and to those who claim to have been affected by them.

Each one of Varda's Demy films is a poignant testimony of her love for him and of the lasting quality and significance of his work, and a moving act of mourning. Nowhere is this more affecting that in *Les Plages d'Agnès*. She breaks down at her exhibition of photographic portraits of deceased friends and artists and qualifies Demy as the most cherished of the dead. She inserts family photographs featuring Demy and stills from some of his shoots. She likens their relationship to Magritte's *Les Amants* (*The Lovers* (1928)), and a sequence shows a heterosexual couple naked, the male visibly aroused, walking backwards in space – and symbolically retreating into the past of her memories – their heads covered in a tight white shroud indexing their love as blind, suffocating and sublime. She observes 'c'est quand-même mieux de vieillir à deux, c'était notre projet et encore plus depuis qu'on s'était retrouvé' ('it's actually better to grow old together, that was our plan, even more so since we got back together'), thus obliquely referring to her reported two-year separation from Demy in the late 1970s. By giving such prominence to her late husband within her own career, Varda bolsters her endeavours to keep both him and their love alive within the imaginary of her audience.[7]

Her description of their time together, travelling and visiting museums, and her heartrending testimonies of their love, prefigure her acknowledgement of Demy's death as a result of AIDS, the first public confirmation that he had been suffering from the condition. Varda recalls 'Jacques ... savait que le sida était insoignable ... nous le savions tous. Personne n'en parlait. C'était une sorte de silence affectueux et parfaitement respectueux de Jacques qui n'en parlait pas'.[8]

---

7 She extends this to other supports, including the book by Père and Colmant, at the back of which, in a plastic envelope, are inserted four postcards, all addressed to Demy, dated between March and June 2010.

8 'Jacques ... knew that AIDS could not be cured ... We all knew it. Nobody spoke about it. It was a kind of affectionate silence, perfectly respectful of Jacques who never spoke about it.'

His silence attests to the broader fears around AIDS and can be read as an attempt to safeguard his legacy, which may now seem misguided, but AIDS denied Demy such hindsight. The significance of Varda's avowal of the cause of Demy's passing cannot be overemphasised, and the personal impact upon her of their life together and his death are rendered patently and movingly evident.

Varda's first Demy film, *Jacquot de Nantes*[9] focuses on his life with his biological family from the ages of ten to nineteen (Demy is played by Philippe Maron, Edouard Joubeaud and Laurent Monnier), with the addendum of his host parents, the clog-maker and his wife (Henri Janin and Marie-Anne Héry), with whom he and his brother Yvon (Clément Delaroche and then Rody Averty) stayed during the Occupation. As Kristi McKim aptly notes, *Jacquot* idealises Demy's childhood by presenting 'the fantasy of a narratively unified subject, who is unabashedly creative, adventuresome, curious and generous' (2008: 213). Such nostalgic embellishment of everyday life is a legacy of Demy's cinema as it spills into Varda's biopic, and it is endorsed by Demy's authentication of the representations when compared with his recollections.[10] By projecting Demy's artistic and directorial significance, *Jacquot* endeavours to ensure his legacy well beyond his physical death.

Past, present and future intersect, as evidenced in the flashbacks and flash-forwards between Demy as a youth, filmed in black-and-white, and as a middle-aged man, shot in colour. As Demy recounts his memories, his voice-over occasionally transgresses temporal distinctions between past biography/docu-fiction and present footage, in which Varda films him through a combination of proximity and respectful distance. She affirms that she wanted to stay within the present, to accompany Demy during his suffering and thus to film him as a living person, an experience which for her fused feelings of both joy and pain.[11] Medium long shots show Demy sitting or lying on the beach at Noirmoutier, and vertical and horizontal tracking shots in extreme close-up (filmed by Agnès Godard's 35mm camera) trace the contours and blemishes of his ageing skin, greying hair, stubble, his

9 While ill at home, Demy started writing his childhood memoirs and showed them to Varda, who decided that they would make a beautiful film, but Demy urged her to direct it because he was too weak.

10 Confirmed in *Les Plages d'Agnès* (2008).

11 In Jacquot de Nantes *vu par Agnès Varda* (Dominique Rabourdin, 2011).

eye and the intricate weave of his cardigan. A haptic quality inheres in these shots, the proximity of the lens to Demy's skin, hair and clothes creating the impression that we can actually touch him.

Within her fictional reconstitution of his childhood, Varda inserts colour shots to identify and isolate key moments, such as when he sees his aunt from Rio (Christine Renaudin), the performer in La Cigale restaurant (Véronique Rodriguez) and the establishment's interiors, puppet shows, the bright wallpaper of his grandmother's interior and the juxtaposition between his neighbour's dark blue and yellow patterned dressing gown and her red patterned carpet as she lies dead on the floor. Via these images, specific aspects of his childhood are marked as prescient and revelatory, conveying not only his astonishment at what he sees, but also his ability to project this internal amazement outwards. Through these colour additions, Demy's skill in elevating the monochromatic everyday into polychromatic fantasy is framed as innate and unique.

Jacquot de Nantes connects Demy's films to these past moments by inserting carefully chosen extracts, often indicated by a hand pointing forward or backward in time and space, modelled on a sign in the Demy garage. Moreover, inspiration for his characters is sourced in his childhood. The blond evacuee is called Geneviève (Fanny Lebreton) and his father's (Daniel Dublet) garage technician is named Guy (Jean-Charles Hernot). In an early exchange between Raymond Demy and a client, *Jacquot de Nantes* literally cites, in normal dialogue, the first line of *Les Parapluies de Cherbourg* and then transports us to the corresponding sequence in the film. Elsewhere, his aunt from Rio tells Jacquot that she has put lipstick on his face, citing (or prefiguring) Lola's question to Roland, and declares her love of casinos, which cues a cut to Jackie playing roulette in *La Baie des Anges*. Reine, his pregnant teenage neighbour (Marie-Sidonie Benoist), declares she hates carnivals, just like Geneviève, and we learn that Jacquot's father used to lodge with a Colonel's widow who was an alcoholic, the image-track cutting to Langlois and François in *Une chambre en ville*.

For the knowing spectator, these intertextual allusions are not flash-forwards, but flashbacks, triggering our memories of Demy's films. Informed by Vivian Sobchacks' point that 'the spectator is an active agent in constituting what counts as memory, fiction, or document' (1999: 253), McKim argues 'we ascertain our proximity (to *Jacquot*) based on the degree to which we empathize with or resist its attempts to make meaningful its memorial and cinephilic evocation' (2008: 225). It is this process (just as Demy had done in *Trois places pour le 26*) that aims to ensure his legacy. 'The conservation of faith and hope' constitutes the dream that informs *Jacquot*, according to McKim (2008: 225), thus rekindling the message that underlies many of Demy's films. In the face of death, Demy opts to search back into his repertoire of experiences for happy moments, to seek joy at the precise point when all hope appears to have been lost.[12]

In Varda's film of the celebrations for the twenty-fifth anniversary of the making of *Les Demoiselles de Rochefort*, the family is broadened to encompass the people involved in the production and the inhabitants of Rochefort. *Les Demoiselles ont eu 25 ans* combines footage of the celebrations and interviews with extras, filmmakers and fans, with black-and-white film from the period by other directors, including André Delvaux, and Varda's film chronicle of the shoot. It portrays the claims made on *Les Demoiselles de Rochefort* by Rochefort inhabitants and their descendants. Primary school teacher Marc Le Gouard shifts ownership from director and actors to Rochefort residents: 'c'est le film des Rochefortais comme un immense et gigantesque film de famille' ('it's the people of Rochefort's film like an immense and gigantic family film'). *Les Demoiselles de Rochefort* is held responsible for the creation of new families and the perpetuation of fraternal harmony within existing ones. Joël and Dominique Berton, extras who played a mother greeting her son outside Boubou's school, reveal that they later fell in love and married. Didier and Alain Quella-Guyot, both cast as young boys in street scenes with Kelly, proudly show their sailor hats and exchange extracts from their diaries. *Les Demoiselles de Rochefort* is firmly inscribed in the town's cultural heritage. The Mayor attributes the town's regeneration to the film; footage shows him officiating at ceremonies in which the road leading to the transporter bridge is renamed 'avenue Jacques Demy', and the square in

---

12 *Jacquot de Nantes* was selected for the Cannes Film Festival in 1991, but Demy's family requested that it be seen outside of the competition. Sailors replaced the Republican Guard, and the theme from *Les Parapluies de Cherbourg* played as Varda, Rosalie and Mathieu walked up the steps to the screening. A large photograph of Demy was projected and actors who had appeared in his films read lines from their scripts. *Jacquot* was used by the French Department of Education as one of the prescribed films for their programme 'École et Cinéma' for over ten years and the city of Nantes screened the film for children at a reduced rate of half price (Rabourdin, 2010c: 64–5).

front of the railway station is re-baptised 'place Françoise Dorléac'.[13]

The affective impact of *Les Demoiselles de Rochefort* for its audience is projected via occasional fan testimonies. For instance, Anne Goscinny states that it forms part of a collection of works 'qui comptent pour moi, qui font partie de moi … c'est ma vie' ('that matter to me, that are part of me … it's my life'). Moreover, Le Gouard recounts how his material experience of the town was mediated by his recollections of the film. The legend of *Les Demoiselles de Rochefort* thus superimposes the Demy myth, but Varda's commentary and the selection and sequencing of images remind us that her late husband is the architect of this reshaping of the real town into a magical space. She films him much like a love-struck admirer and awestruck fan, and transforms Delphine's song into an ode to her husband, thus projecting him as the masculine ideal of the original lyrics. Adulation also emerges from Jacques Perrin's testimony. He declares 'je pense que des fois à travers des oeuvres des gens on connaît assez bien les gens alors … je crois que je connais un peu Jacques' ('I think that sometimes through people's work we can know enough about people … I think I know Jacques a little'). Perrin implies that he is particularly interested in Demy himself. Here, then, he evokes Barthes's point in *Plaisir du texte* that, although 'comme institution, l'auteur est mort … j'ai besoin de sa figure (qui n'est ni sa représentation, ni sa projection), comme il a besoin de la mienne' (1973: 45–6).[14]

Varda projects pseudo divine status onto her husband in her third homage to him, aptly entitled *L'Univers de Jacques Demy*, intended as an extension of and response to *Jacquot de Nantes*. *L'Univers de Jacques Demy* brings together extracts from all of his films (apart from some of his shorts), separated in segments structured non-chronologically, with testimonies from his most faithful collaborators, including his actors, fellow filmmakers and fans, and interviews with the director. Again, Varda's commentary serves as an interpretative guide that unifies this broad group of interlocutors as an extended family of privileged insiders and carefully selected admirers of Demy and his myth. For Barthes, 'le mythe a un caractère impératif, interpellatoire:

13 Visitors can tour the film's locations using a colourful map accompanied with explanations provided by the tourist office and the central Place Colbert boasts a 'Brasserie/Restaurant Les Demoiselles'.

14 'as an institution, the author is dead … I need his/her figure (which is neither its representation nor its projection) as he [*sic*] needs mine.' (Miller, 1975: 27)

... c'est *moi* qu'il vient chercher: il est tourné vers moi, je subis sa force intentionnelle, il me somme de recevoir son ambiguïté expansive' (1957: 210; original emphasis).[15]

Yet, it is not simply whether or not we notice the object that gives rise to the mythical discourse that matters, but precisely how we apprehend it – that is, how it is brought to bear on our personal lives and experience of the world around us. In her phenomenologically informed account of queer affect, Sara Ahmed informs us that emotionality is oriented, directed towards the object we encounter (2006: 2–3). If we apprehend an object as fearsome, we turn away from it whereas, when we view it as attractive we orient ourselves towards it. When we apprehend an object as enlightening, we allude to its potential to influence our opinions and beliefs. Accordingly, many of Demy's admirers reveal that his cinema suddenly not only commanded their attention, but was also brought to exert a formative impact upon how they understood themselves and their lives.

Such adulation is illustrated in Camille Taboulay's fan letter, which she reads to open and close the film. Taboulay had written to Demy in the summer of 1990, but failed to post her letter before his death. Although sections uphold his talents as a 'cinéaste réellement original et neuf' ('a really original and innovative director'), she explicitly articulates his edifying effect on her: 'vos films m'ont tant appris ... j'ai aimé la vie grâce à vos films parce qu'elle y est à la fois exaltée et bercée à jour, cruelle et enchantée. Vos films nous donnent le goût du bonheur, le plaisir d'attendre, la force d'attendre en étant attentif à tout'.[16] Taboulay's eulogy exemplifies how the committed specta tor's pleasure in watching films derives partly from their fantasies about the *auteur*'s motivations and convictions. Demy is neither an actual representation nor projection, but the combination of various assumptions made by Taboulay based on his films and through which he is moulded into a kind of mentor.

Some contributors locate the exact moment when this determinative encounter occurred in their childhood. Fan Martine Jouando

15 'Myth has an imperative, buttonholing character: ... it is *I* whom it has come to seek. It is turned towards me, I am subjected to its intentional force, it summons me to receive its expansive ambiguity.' (Lavers, 1991: 123)

16 '... your films taught me so much ... I have loved life thanks to your films because it is depicted as both exalted and everyday, cruel and enchanted. Your films give us a taste for happiness, the pleasure of waiting, the strength to wait while being attentive to everything'.

recalls how she totally identified with Cécile and that she was an emblematic image of her life. Another adept, Marine Landrot, declares that, after having watched *Les Parapluies de Cherbourg* for the first time when eight years old, her life completely changed. By contrast, Caroline Bongrand, asserts that, in addition to assisting children and adolescents as they cope with the transition into adulthood, Demy also allows adults to mentally return to the magic of their childhood, and thus momentarily escape the irreversible progression of objective time. According to these admirers, Demy is able to trigger recollections of realised events, sensual memories and forgotten aspirations. For Anne-Marie Rassam, his ability to lead us to entrancing realms is reminiscent of the legendary Pied Piper: 'il peut emmener n'importe qui hors de la ville ... C'est ce qu'un enfant veut. Si j'étais un enfant, je voudrais avoir Jacques Demy comme père' ('he can take anyone out of the city ... That's what a child wants, if I were a child, I'd love to have Jacques Demy as my father').

This exaltation of Demy, not only as an ideal paternal figure, but also as a kind of deity, is transmitted by the testimonies of his actors. Both Anouk Aimée and Jacques Perrin convey a belief in the convergence of themselves with the characters they played. Aimée refers to her casting as Lola as a magnificent gift and adds 'elle est tellement avec moi que je ne sais plus où elle finit en moi' ('she is with me so much that I don't know where she finishes in me'). Perrin wonders what it could have been within him that made Demy think that he was his 'masculine ideal', thus conveying what he interprets as the director's ability to discover hidden qualities within his actors and then reveal them through their roles. Although Catherine Deneuve is cautious to frame this discovery story in professional terms, she nonetheless commends his input in moulding her as an actor.[17]

In addition to its creative and protective qualities, the traditional patriarchal and godlike figure is authoritarian. Such decisiveness is attributed to Demy via the comments of Richard Berry and Jean-François Stévenin. For Berry, Demy was 'complètement intraitable

---

17 In a later interview for the special edition of *Les Inrockuptibles* to coincide with the Demy exhibition, Deneuve echoes Perrin's sentiments by implying that he had seen something special in her that she did not yet recognise (in Lalanne, 2013: 52). Marc Michel similarly claims that Roland is an unfinished part of him (in Blondeau, 2013: 57), while Richard Berry recalls that he grew up watching Demy's films (in Barnett, 2013: 56).

… tu ne pouvais absolument pas négocier … avec lui' ('he couldn't be swayed … you absolutely couldn't negotiate … with him'), while Stévenin recalls that he had 'une épée à l'intérieur' ('a sword inside his body'). Rather than tarnishing his myth, these comments transmit Demy's perceived clarity of vision and ability to discern quality, reinforcing the construction of the director as a film *auteur*.

However, such circumscription of the *Demy-univers* in Varda's Demy films elides crucial aspects of the director's cinema, its pleasures and meanings for some audiences. For instance, by containing the Demy myth within a discourse of familial cohesion, *Jacquot de Nantes* fails to reveal the reasons why he was so interested in portraying fractured and fragmented family relations in his films. Elsewhere, while *Les Demoiselles de Rochefort* is reclaimed as belonging to the people of Rochefort, and its hyper-feminine female characters are upheld as icons for young girls, its meanings and pleasures for other – namely queer – audiences are unacknowledged.[18] Even the sailors walk around with purpose, rather than loitering on street corners or in cafes. Moreover, the testimonies engage with Demy's work on its literal level and are framed as sincere reflections of his lasting impact and legacy; the ironic and disruptive are underplayed or absent. For Adrian Danks, Varda's Demy films lack consideration of her husband's sexuality 'partly as a result of his own reticence on the matter but also due to Varda's subsequent unwillingness to work such a discussion into … the series of interconnected films she has made about his work' (2010: 161). Danks warns against deterministic claims that source Demy's thematic preoccupations and aesthetic proclivities to his apparent sexuality. Yet, elision of any understanding of the queer resonances of Demy's films inaccurately reflects the meanings of his cinema and the pleasures it offers for all his audiences, as well as his significance for subsequent generations of filmmakers.

The ending of *Jacquot de Nantes* implies, only obliquely, the existence of alternative narratives and resonances within Demy's cinema.

18 At a press conference coinciding with the opening of the exhibition devoted to Demy on 8 April 2013, Varda qualifies the approach to her late husband's work through the angle of its 'gay sensibility' as unusual. In her opinion, such a sensibility constitutes a 'stream' compared with the 'river' represented by his background and the class struggle that flows through his films (http://yagg.com/2013/04/09/agnes-varda-repond-a-yagg-sur-la-sensibilite-homosexuelle-des-films-de-jacques-demy/, accessed 29 April 2013).

As Varda shoots Demy on the beach at Noirmoutier – her voiceover recounting Prévert's poem *Sables mouvants* with its analogies about love as something that we can neither control nor escape – her husband smiles partially at the camera and then turns to face the ocean. For Varda, such a shift in his gaze symbolises his acknowledgement of his impending death. Yet, the object of his look appears to be the Atlantic Ocean, which stretches to America, the country that has pivotal meaning within Demy's films as a site of difference and freedom of expression. This attraction for alterity and freedom is a component of Demy's myth that is invoked and pursued further in the many films by directors beyond his wife.

Reconfiguring the Demy-myth: intertextual tributes and revisions

According to Rosalie Varda-Demy, a number of established directors – including John Woo, Hou Hsiao Hsien, Benoît Jacquot and André Téchiné – have affirmed their admiration for her father's cinema, while others describe themselves as Demy's children, including Olivier Ducastel, Jacques Martineau and Christophe Honoré (in Rabourdin, 2010a: 71). In an article initially conceived to examine the affinities and influences between Demy's work and that of filmmakers in the 1990s and beyond, Jérôme Baron declares by contrast that 'aucun des films rencontrés ne suscite à mes yeux, même a minima, autant d'intérêt que le cinéma de Demy lui-même' ('none of the films discovered elicits in my eyes, even in the slightest, as much interest as Demy's own cinema' (2011: 34)). In glossing over a lineage of Demy's legacy, Baron misses the opportunity to reveal how the principal aesthetic and ethical concerns raised by Demy's cinema are developed within the output of later filmmakers.

Due to the limited scope of this book, and by way of providing fruitful counterpoints of both Baron's article and Varda's films, this discussion will examine the work of François Ozon, Ducastel and Martineau, Honoré, as well as Mathieu Demy's *Americano* (2012). Allusions to Demy in Ozon's cinema often surface in the form of thematic or formal *clins d'oeil*. Incest is depicted in *Sitcom* (1998) and toyed with provocatively in *8 femmes* (2002) and *Potiche* (2010). The most obvious visible manifestation of Demy's legacy in Ozon's films is the casting of Deneuve in *8 femmes* and *Potiche*. As Gaby in *8 femmes*, Deneuve plays

Darrieux's daughter, thus prompting recollections of *Les Demoiselles de Rochefort*. Slightly stronger are the connections between *Potiche* and *Les Parapluies de Cherbourg*. Deneuve plays Suzanne Pujol – whose husband Robert (Fabrice Luchini) is the manager of an umbrella factory – and who rekindles her affair with union leader Maurice Babin (Gérard Depardieu).[19] The time lapse between the end of *Les Parapluies de Cherbourg* and *Potiche*, which is set in 1978, renders Ozon's film a plausible continuation of Geneviève's story; indeed, the title translates as 'trophy wife'. Yet, this is not a sequel; Emery sold her umbrella shop while Robert inherits his father-in-law's umbrella factory, and Robert is far more assertive than the forlorn Roland.

The filial associations between Demy and Ducastel and Martineau appear more explicit, heralded by their first full-length feature *Jeanne et le garçon formidable* (1998; hereafter *Jeanne...*).[20] The most obvious connection is in the casting of Demy's son Mathieu in the central role. In an interview I conducted with the filmmakers on 11 November 2011, Ducastel and Martineau explained their trepidation with regards to casting Mathieu Demy as a young man who dies of AIDS, given the circumstances of his father's death, and were unsure about what he knew about his illness. Mathieu convinced them to give him the role, reassuring them that he could cope emotionally. For Ducastel, it was his affective connection to the story that allowed him to invest his performance with such determination, overcoming his limited dancing skills to perform with the rest of the cast. Yet, although AIDS links the fictional character Olivier with actual director Demy, the similarities stop there. While Demy responded to his illness and impending death by remaining by the side of all his loved ones and collaborating in a film about his life, Olivier discharges himself from hospital and leaves Jeanne to spend his final months in his parents' care.

Martineau admits to having written the script of *Jeanne* 'en utilisant les schémas narratifs de Demy sans aucune pudeur' ('by using Demy's

---

19 We recall also that Demy had wanted Deneuve and Depardieu to play Edith and François in *Une chambre en ville*.

20 Such admiration for Demy in his work was already evident in Ducastel's short *Le Goût de plaire* (1989), which combines the recitative of *Les Parapluies de Cherbourg* and *Une chambre en ville* with the joyful numbers and choreography of *Les Demoiselles de Rochefort*. Further nods include the score, which uniquely comprises jazz-based scores, and the brightly coloured costumes of the two main female protagonists (Anne Alvaro and Christine Millet) who sing about being two seductresses in an update of 'La Chanson des Jumelles'.

narrative formulas without any shame'). Ducastel and Martineau set personal stories about love, illness, death and the quest for identity within a broader political context that includes, as mentioned, living with HIV and AIDS, race discrimination and gay rights. *Jeanne...* is a musical about the doomed love affair between Olivier and Jeanne (Virginie Ledoyen), which is brutally curtailed by Olivier's death from AIDS. Their second feature, *Drôle de Félix* (2000) follows Félix (Sami Bouajila), a young, HIV-positive gay man of part North African descent who crosses France in search of his biological father. Chance encounters and missed recognitions move the narratives into new areas. Jeanne meets Olivier by literally falling into his lap as a Métro train screeches to a halt. Félix constructs a family from the people he encounters, some of whom recall familiar tropes; Mathilde (Patachou) married a man she never loved, while Isabelle (Ariane Ascaride) is a single mother with three sons from different fathers.

As with Demy, bright colours recast the grey realities of the everyday in an uplifting topcoat. *Jeanne...* is saturated in a pastel palette, while *Drôle de Félix* drips with summery hues in many of its scenes. Complex and sophisticated wallpapers are also in evidence, particularly in *Jeanne...* and also in their television film *Juste la fin du monde de Jean-Luc Lagarce* (2010). Techniques also recall Demy's cinematography, as in the sequence-shot of the birthday party scene in *Jeanne....* A slow 180-degrees pan shows the table during dinner, the kitchen where the candles on the cake are lit and the lounge where the family play charades. Objective and subjective time are thus differentiated since the jovial spirit of the family party continues irrespective of the forward movement of chronological temporality. In *Jeanne...,* Martineau uses a familiar linguistic register, similar to *Une chambre en ville* and, to a degree, *Les Demoiselles de Rochefort* that ironically blurs the distinction between natural dialogue and song. The reductive image of Demy's musicals is parodied in the breakfast scene, in which Jeanne literally sings the words 'passe-moi le sucre' ('pass me the sugar') when she complains that her coffee is too bitter. Moreover, the ubiquitous bookshop scene surfaces once again, as Olivier looks for a gift for Jeanne and flirts with the shop assistant.

Yet, according to Ducastel and Martineau, their work differs from Demy in the unambiguous modernity of their themes. Demy's gaze, they argue, turned away from the contemporary in his final productions, either by revisiting history (*Une chambre en ville*) or nostalgically celebrating a seemingly outdated form (*Trois places pour le 26*).[21] Of *Jeanne...* they identify the film's explicit politics as that which distinguishes their work, in terms of tone and themes, from that of Demy: 'le film parle très frontalement du sida enfin [c'était] un film très moderne à l'époque' ('the film speaks openly about AIDS, well, that it was a very modern film for its period'). Elsewhere, Ducastel claims that they use colour more intuitively than Demy, that the particular hues of their films were not chosen to project a symbolic meaning beyond perhaps the obvious (such as the orange and yellow tones at the ending of *Crustacés et coquillages* (2006) that add to the scene's utopian summery warmth). Moreover, they claim that the colourful wallpapers that appear in their films were found by chance in the houses in which they located their films. While shots may at times recall Demy's cinematography, this is also, they affirm, a product of coincidence, as in the sequence-shot of the birthday party scene in *Jeanne...*.

Nevertheless, Ducastel and Martineau develop some of Demy's philosophical concerns. Their characters determine to be happy, despite the challenges of their lives. Félix refuses to allow his HIV, ethnic and unemployed status to deter him from his quest for contentment. While *Jeanne...* is more morose, Ducastel and Martineau insert splashes of optimism. Following Olivier's discharge from hospital, Jeanne does not implode or fall into the arms of an unwanted husband, unlike Geneviève. Although naive and blinkered, her ebullience reassures the audience that she, like Lola, will never relinquish her hope to find happiness.

Such re-examinations of the messages transmitted by Demy's films are pursued more intensely in Honoré's cinema. Honoré's first film unequivocally evokes Demy's cinema in its title, which brings together the original first name of his heroine in *Lola*, as well as that of Desnoyer's daughter, with the surname of Roland: *17 fois Cécile Cassard* (2002). References to Demy's cinema recur in Honoré's two musicals *Les Chansons d'amour* (2007) and *Les Bien-Aimés* (2011). Both feature surface nods that thinly shroud their more reflective engagements with his ethical messages. *Les Chansons d'amour* depicts the tragedy of a lover's death and follows Ismaël Bénoliel's (Louis Garrel) painful transition from bereavement to acceptance and deliverance. Julie Pommeraye (Ludivigne Sagnier), his aptly named girlfriend, dies unexpectedly from a blood clot in her heart outside a club where they

---

21 Ducastel had worked as assistant director on *Trois places pour le 26*.

had been watching a gig. Initially, Demy's signature lyricism appears absent. The film is set in the tenth arrondissement of Paris in the winter of 2006/7. The decors are dour and trees bare; the sky, heavy and overcast, is reflected in the wet pavements, and Alex Beaupain's poignant compositions amplify the melancholy atmosphere.

Yet, amidst this decidedly un-Demy landscape appears a seemingly familiar figure, shot from behind as she walks through the Paris streets towards a cinema, her long, straight, blond hair spilling over onto her vintage white, woollen coat. Geneviève is thus recalled, but a reverse shot reveals that it is Julie. The narrative is structured around the same three sections that form the basis of *Les Parapluies de Cherbourg*: 'le départ', 'l'absence' and 'le retour', and iconic shots from the film are recycled – Julie is transported backwards into the Parisian streetscape in a direct reference to the tracking shot of Geneviève and Guy after they learn of his conscription.

Crucially, these self-conscious allusions to Demy's films do not simply serve as reminders of his work, but also revisit and pursue his questioning of the dependability of memory. What the informed spectator is currently watching is troubled by what they recall. *17 fois Cécile Cassard* disrupts fictional history in that Cécile Cassard would have been Lola's married name had she wed Roland and not embarked on a dancing career, which therefore would have prevented Roland from marrying Geneviève. The disparity between recollections and present images serves as a reminder of the impossibility of duplicating the already lived. The grey Parisian streetscape of *Les Chansons d'amour* signifies that this is not Demy's universe, while Julie's determined walk counters memories of Geneviève's trepidation. Thus, the spectator may be momentarily duped into believing that they have already witnessed what they are watching somewhere before, but the distinctions are rendered manifest, producing a *déjà vu* that has never actually been seen.

The divergence between the work of Demy and *Les Chansons d'amour* is strengthened by the films' obviously queer twists. Where Demy may have been timid, *Les Chansons d'amour* is bold. Like Simon Dame in *Les Demoiselles de Rochefort*, it is a male, Ismaël, who must endure the absence of his lover. However, even when alive, Julie is not completely present, preferring to share him with his female colleague Alice (Clotilde Hesme). Moreover, the familiar scenario in which the apparently tragic protagonist determines to find contentment obtains a queer slant. Another male embodies Ismaël's 'ray of light', Erwann (Grégoire Leprince-Ringuet), who conjures Maxence's idealism through his determination to seduce Ismaël. His buoyancy rubs off on Ismaël who, finally, comes to terms with Julie's death and visits her grave, fittingly in the Montparnasse Cemetery where Demy is buried. These twists may be seen as extensions of Demy's own endeavours to modernise romance as he had claimed with regards to *Parking*. Nevertheless, unlike Calaïs who remains powerless against Orphée's narcissism, Erwann and Ismaël's burgeoning relationship is more reciprocal. While Erwann finally enchants his ideal male, Ismaël convinces him of the merits of a durable love over temporary gratification.

Les Chansons d'amour also probes the relationship between objective and subjective temporalities, a concern which, as seen, consistently and recurrently arises in Demy's cinema. Subjective and objective time is juxtaposed when Ismaël returns to his area, clutching a bag containing Julie's belongings. The soundtrack and images temporally locate us in the morning immediately following Julie's death. The lyrics recall the moment when Ismaël learns indirectly of her death via the policeman who transmits the code DCD (décédée or deceased) on his CB radio. We see him walk along the street in freezing rain and make a telephone call, and are then transported to Julie's parents' (Brigitte Rouan and Jean-Marie Winling) bedroom, in which we observe her father's reaction to the news. The first of five black-and-white stills are inserted, showing Julie's sister Jeanne's (Chiara Mastroianni) tear-stained cheek. A cut then projects us forward to the morgue and a second black-and-white still depicting Ismaël and her parents standing over Julie's open coffin. We then see Ismaël in the street again, hesitant to return to his apartment, before we are projected once again into the near future at the funeral, the sunlight conveying the difference in objective time. Julie's younger sister Jasmine (Alice Butaud) gasps that she cannot find her book, which Jeanne retrieves from the car. Three black-and-white stills show Jeanne handing the book to Jasmine, its text speaking of a soul leaving a body. Once again, we return to Ismaël in the street, struggling to stand up. A cut transports us to Alice in the back of a car, tears streaming down her cheeks, before another takes us to Ismaël as he leaves a synagogue. Affective time is imprinted over objective temporality. For Ismaël and Julie's family, normal chronology is disrupted, the distinctions between the immediate past, actual present and near future blurred and obscured by grief. While the flow of objective time is depicted in the moving colour images, the black-and-white stills bear a dual signification as both markers of the indeterminate future and of the most affecting moments of the family's bereavement.

Les Bien-aimés pursues this re-examination of the moral and philosophical significations of Demy's cinema. Visual markers are, once again, evident. The film is set over a thirty-five year period, between 1964 and 2009. The first section, located in Reims, conjures the bright pastel aesthetics of *Les Demoiselles de Rochefort*. Shoe-seller Madeleine (Ludivine Sagnier) steals a pair of designer slippers and works as a part-time prostitute. She has a child with Jaromil (Radivoje Bukvić) and moves to Prague, but returns to Paris because of the Soviet invasion and marries gendarme François Gouriot (Michel Delpech), with whom she raises Véra (Clara Couste). *Les Bien-aimés* revisits Demy's cherished theme of fidelity. Two love triangles are formed, the first between Madeleine, Jaromil and François, the second between an adult Véra (Chiara Mastroianni), Henderson (Paul Schneider) – an HIV-positive gay man with whom she falls in love – and Clément (Louis Garrel). Fidelity of the heart is distinguished from sexual fidelity. Just as Lola's love for Michel remains intact and uncompromised by her affairs, Jaromil's fling with a young woman in Prague fails to prevent Madeleine from loving him and Véra has sex with other men despite her emotional connection to Henderson.

As implied in the title, the film asks a rhetorical question, voiced through Madeleine (now played by Deneuve) to Clément towards the ending: 'est-ce qu'il vaut mieux être à la place de celui qui est aimé ou celui qui aime?' ('is it better to be in the place of the one who loves or is loved?'). Unsurprisingly, her interlocutor replies that he would have given anything to be Henderson and Madeleine agrees. The common figure that spans Demy's oeuvre of the unrequited lover since *Les Horizons morts* is thus re-appropriated by Honoré and embodied by François and Clément. François accepts his situation, allowing Madeleine to continue her affair with Jaromil provided that they stay together. Yet, he is eventually discarded as she walks off with Clément after Jaromil's death, thus reflecting back to him his lack of power and agency. By choosing to stay with a woman who does not love him, he has always lived in bad faith, much like Roland.

Madeleine's question is revealed as somewhat redundant, however. For, even though she rejects François, and Véra dismisses Clément, both women are also constrained by their love for another, Jaromil and Henderson. While, later in life, Jaromil (now played by Miloš Forman) returns Madeleine's love, Henderson is more effusive. When Véra asks him to give her a child, he refuses. She tells him 'for four years your eyes have been my life, your smile my joy … In four years, I never once had the idea … so vital to me that you loved me … What can I do? Live without your love? I can't'. After sex with Henderson and his young admirer Mathieu (Dustin Segura-Suarez), she steals his medication and swallows it, dying of an overdose in the hotel bar. Just like Edith and Eurydice, Véra is unable to accept a life without Henderson and chooses death. The characters thus seem trapped within a (deadly) cycle, unable or unwilling to gain mastery over their situations, a gradual awareness of which is portrayed through Madeleine.

The shift from a younger to a more mature Madeleine, figured visually in the transition of actresses, recalls the change in Lola from her life in Nantes to that in Los Angeles. The young Madeleine is happy and carefree, but as she ages, she begins to complain of the 'kilograms of sentiments' she carries with her. The tenor of Madeleine's first song changes when sung later. In the early scenes, she sings to a young Jaromil 'je peux vivre sans toi, tu sais? Le seul problème, mon amour, c'est que je ne peux pas vivre sans t'aimer' ('I can live without you, you know? The only problem, my love, is that I cannot live without loving you'). In the closing scenes, after Jaromil and Véra's respective deaths, she transforms the lyrics slightly by singing 'je peux vivre sans toi, oui, mais ce qui me tue mon amour, c'est que je ne peux vivre sans t'aimer' ('I can live without you, yes, but what's killing me, my love, is that I cannot live without loving you'). Clear resonances with Geneviève's comment to Guy – 'je ne pourrais jamais vivre sans toi' ('I could never live without you) – abound, although Honoré updates the referent; Madeleine can live without her love, but not without loving him. To love outlives material presence, but what was once a difficulty is now characterised as life threatening because of the weight of her emotional baggage. Yet, beyond tragedy and deception lies a muted happiness. Madeleine tells Clément 'le bonheur je n'y pense plus depuis très longtemps. Ça ne m'empêche pas d'être heureuse. J'ai confiance dans la vie, mais je n'ai pas confiance dans le bonheur'.[22]

22 'I haven't thought about happiness for a very long time. That does not stop me from being happy. I have confidence in life, but I don't have confidence in happiness.'

Where Demy appeared to believe that to want happiness is to taste it, Madeleine articulates a more mature, muted apprehension of happiness, redolent, perhaps, of Lola and George at the end of *Model Shop*.

Mathieu Demy's *Americano* revisits themes and aspects from Demy's cinema. Martin (Mathieu Demy) discovers that his mother, who was living in Los Angeles, has died, and he immediately leaves to manage her affairs. When staying at her house in the Venice neighbourhood, where he had lived as a young boy, he discovers that she had become close to a young Mexican immigrant named Lola. Having learned that his mother wanted Lola to inherit her house, he journeys to Tijuana to meet her. He stumbles across a woman who claims to be Lola (Salma Hayek), unsurprisingly, a pole dancer and escort/prostitute. After having initially spurned him, 'Lola' accepts his offer of help, but Martin later discovers that the 'true' Lola has died. Nevertheless, he decides to give the young woman, named Rosita, the house when he returns to France.

The ambience of *Americano* is a far cry from the light and lyrical atmosphere of *Lola*. Martin never smiles, the aesthetics are dark and the Mexican town in which he stays is violent. *Americano* is thus a stark and morose exploration of a son's relationship with his deceased mother that partially develops the Lola–Yvon story. Like Yvon, Martin was sent to France, although to live with his biological father. Martin declares 'my mother ... wasn't happy, I was just part of her story', nodding to Lola in Los Angeles, who has lost her spark and returns to Paris to be with Yvon. Frustration towards his mother is eventually superseded by anger at his father for not having assisted her when she needed help. *Americano*'s other main point of reference, Varda's *Documenteur* (1981), also shot in Venice, Los Angeles, aids the sense of reconciliation between son and mother. Extracts from Varda's film puncture the image-track as unannounced flashbacks from Martin's childhood, the differences in screen format and aesthetics the only indicators that the scenes depict Martin's recollections.

Yet, familiar aspects emerge. Misrecognitions are prominent. Martin takes Rosita for Lola, and his mother is an imbrication of Lola, his mother in *Documenteur* Emilie Cooper (Sabine Mamou) and Varda herself, since she was also a French woman in Los Angeles with a young son, Mathieu, who played Martin in her film. Like his father, Mathieu disturbs truth and authenticity, perception and memory. As in *Trois places pour le 26*, the fictional and the factual are merged so as to blur the distinction between fable and (auto)biography, fantasy and reality.

In an interview published twenty years after Demy's death, Mathieu Demy recalls how his father brought him up with his films, requiring that he watch them (in Rabourdin, 2010b: 73). That Demy insisted on his son knowing his work echoes the self-confidence about its value that he displayed most explicitly in *Trois places pour le 26*. Similar nurturing influences emerge in the responses of some of Demy's fans and actors. The 'master' film poet, it seems, is invoked in the recollections of the formative processes and moments of his biological and adopted offspring, whose awareness of the world is, they claim, partly shaped by his work. If these witnesses attempt (somewhat paradoxically) to affirm the assimilation of the consciousness of the other (Demy) within the consciousness of the self (his admirers) and/or vice versa, then the work of his 'cinephilic progeny' (Ozon, Ducastel and Martineau, and Honoré) attests to the plurality of interpretations – perceptions – of the same object. Demy's cinema escapes fixed definition and categorisation. Far from being exclusive, Demy represents a myriad of significations and resonances, which continually exceed and bifurcate from each other in the recounted imaginaries of his audience, a process of revisiting and revising that continues the director's own play with cinephilic memory.

Bernard Toublanc-Michel recalls that, during his final visit to Demy, the director wondered whether people would continue watching his films after his death (in Orléan, 2011, reprinted 2013: 41). The answer is a resounding yes, as the many examples and quotations above illustrate, and as the exhibition devoted to him at the Cinémathèque in Paris in 2013 confirms. This major cultural event, which ran for four months from 10 April to 4 August, transformed the world of Demy into a three-dimensional experience. Configured as a series of six spaces that focused on various aspects of the filmmaker's life and oeuvre, from his youth in Nantes through his most famous and successful musicals and time in Los Angeles to his last productions, the exhibition became a walk in time and space through Demy's cinema. Each section opened up onto the next, allowing the visitor a visual glimpse or aural suggestion of what was to come, but never opening out onto the beyond-the-Demy-world. This was a world that was conceptualised to project a sense of plenitude and satisfaction, as if to suggest that everything the visitor could need or desire could be found within its temporary walls – and thus that everything the viewer could need or desire could be found within Demy's films.

However, although intensely pleasurable for the Demy connoisseur, the exhibition became troubling when the visitor reached the final destination: the shop. A confectionary store of colourful paraphernalia, including replicas of Delphine and Solange's broad-rimmed yellow and pink hats, framed prints of various film stills and cardboard cut outs of sets, it transformed the Demy myth into an object of consumption, which was extended in the proliferation of publications that accompanied the exhibition – including the lavish catalogue that sold for 45 Euros and shiny flyers publicising a weekend in Nantes during which tourists could walk in the director's footsteps and visit the key locations of his cinema. Given Demy's concerns for his films to achieve posthumous recognition, we can assume that he would have been very flattered by such a celebration of his work, although the merchandising *in his name* and the hermetic projection of his legacy may have made him uneasy.

References

Ahmed, Sara (2006) *Queer Phenomenology: Orientation, Objects, Others,* Durham, NC, Duke University Press.

Altman, Rick (1987) The American Film Musical, Bloomington, IN, Indiana University Press.

Barnett, Emily (2013) 'Richard Berry: le prolo incandescent', interview, in *Jacques Demy: L'Enchanteur, les inrockuptibles – hors série*: 56.

Baron, Jérôme (2011) 'Pas de deux', *Jacques Demy*, in Jérôme Baron (ed.), *Jacques Demy, 303: arts, recherches, créations* (115/11): 34–7.

Barthes, Roland (1957) *Mythologies*, Paris, Seuil, transl. Annette Lavers, New York, The Noonday Press, 1991.

—— (1973) *Le Plaisir du texte*, Paris, Seuil, transl. Richard Miller, *The Pleasure of the Text*, New York, Hill and Wang, 1980.

Blondeau, Romain (2013) 'Marc Michel: l'amoureux amer', interview, in *Jacques Demy: L'Enchanteur, les inrockuptibles – hors série*: 57.

Clech, Thierry, Strauss, Frédéric and Toubiana, Serge (1988) 'D'un port à l'autre: Entretien avec Jacques Demy', *Cahiers du Cinéma*, 414, December: 10–11, 57–62.

Danks, Adrian (2010) 'Living Cinema: the "Demy Films" of Agnès Varda', *Studies in Documentary Film*, 4 (2) 159–72.

Katsahnias, Iannis (1988) 'Une Histoire', *Cahiers du Cinéma*, 414, December: 60.

Lalanne, Jean-Marc (1995) 'Le Demy monde', *Cahiers du Cinéma*, 495, October: 6.

—— (2013) 'Catherine Deneuve: la révélation', interview, in *Jacques Demy: L'Enchanteur, les inrockuptibles – hors série*: 52–5.

Lavers, Annette transl. (1991) *Mythologies*, New York, The Noonday Press,.

McKim, Kristi (2008) 'Time, scale and cinephilia in the cinematic elegy: Agnès Varda's *Jacquot de Nantes*', *Studies in French Cinema*, 8 (3): 211–27.

Miller, Richard transl. *The Pleasure of the Text*, New York, Hill and Wang, 1980.

Orléan, Mathieu (2013) '"Aller à l'usine" pour "aller au cinéma"', interview with Bernard Toublanc-Michel, in *Le Monde enchanté de Jacques Demy*, Paris, Skira-Flammarion, La Cinémathèque Française and Ciné-Tamaris: 40–1.

Rabourdin, Dominique (2010a) 'Rosalie Varda: "Il avait choisi de m'aimer"', *Place Publique*, 33: 68–71.

—— (2010b) 'Mathieu Demy: "La petite musique de mon père', *Place Publique*, 33: 72–5.

—— (2010c) 'Entretien avec Agnès Varda: *Jacquot de Nantes* ou l'intelligence du coeur', *Place Publique*, 33: 59–65.

Sobchack, Vivian (1999) 'Towards a Phenomenology of Nonfictional Film Experience', in J.M. Gaines and M. Renov (eds), *Collecting Visible Evidence*, vol. 6, Minneapolis, University of Minnesota Press: 241–54.

Concluding remarks

In his definition of the phenomenon, at the beginning of *L'Etre et le néant*, Sartre argues that the material object is nothing more than its appearance in the now of my encountering it. There is, according to Sartre, no underlying interior, nor is there an exterior distinct from and thus dissimulating an internal core. And yet, Sartre also affirms, the appearance of the object 'exige en même temps, pour être saisie comme apparition-de-ce-qui-apparaît, d'être dépassée vers l'infini' (1943: 13) ('in order to be grasped as an appearance-of-that-which-appears, it requires that it be surpassed toward infinity') (Barnes, 1993: xxiii). For Sartre, 'ce qui apparaît, en effet, c'est seulement un *aspect* de l'objet et l'objet est tout entier *dans* cet aspect et tout entier hors de lui' (1943: 13; emphasis in original) ('what appears in fact is only an *aspect* of the object, and the object is altogether *in* that aspect and altogether outside of it' (Barnes, 1993: xxiii). Such a phenomenological understanding of the object can readily be applied to Demy's cinema as critics and audiences have received it. Often disregarded because of its appearance as superficial, it points, at multiple moments, to a (possibly infinite) series of other meanings, and elicits a (possibly infinite) series of interpretations. As this book and other works on Demy have striven to demonstrate, beneath its apparently sugary coating lie more philosophical reflections on some of the most pressing issues that preoccupy Western societies: happiness, subjectivity, self–other relations, self–world relations, alterity, fate, free will, self-determination, affect, gender, sexuality, consumerism and post-colonialism.

My own encounter with Demy's cinema may be described in terms of a (phenomenological) turn. At first, I apprehended it as uninteresting, alienated by what I saw as an excessive sentimentality in *Les Parapluies de Cherbourg*, and I promptly oriented my attention elsewhere. I later watched *Lola*, which I enjoyed more, but was discouraged by what I hastily saw as amateur, pantomime dramatics and outdated special effects in *Peau d'âne*. It was not until I was interviewing participants for my audience research as part of my doctoral studies that I became aware of Demy's significance for many French spectators. Some of my respondents praised *Les Demoiselles de Rochefort* and *Peau d'âne* in their responses to films such as *Jeanne…* and *Drôle de Félix*. I soon watched *Les Demoiselles de Rochefort*, which I thoroughly enjoyed because it appealed to my love of camp and queer frivolity. Uplifted, I returned to *Les Parapluies de Cherbourg*, but I only truly understood its qualities when studying it for this book. Hence, my decision to write this monograph comes not from an established interest in and admiration for Demy, but from a desire to understand why the director means so much for so many of the French people I knew or with whom I had come into contact. Demy's audience, then, directed me to him.

Within a very short period of time after starting the research for this book, I was hooked, predisposed, it seemed, to enjoying and comprehending Demy's films because of my respondents' enthusiasm and the knowledge I had accrued as a university lecturer. I discovered another world, the *Demy-monde*, which satisfied my attraction for revisiting cultural products I had previously discarded. I have often been enthralled during the process of writing this book. At times, I have experienced the films like some sort of therapy. Such an experience is probably common among researchers who work on single authors and who become cast in their spell, undergoing a kind of 'enamoration' with them. Whatever the reason, I found myself subscribing to the Demy myth, believing the discourse, originating in many of the interviews with the director I had read and books and articles on his work I had consulted, that his talents and foresights had been reductively dismissed and/or overlooked by both producers and critics.

That Demy's characters and narratives are often interlinked, that his heroes' and heroines' experiences are similar, and that we later learn that their happiness is short-lived no doubt render his films likely objects of poignant appreciation. Moreover, that his protagonists surmount the challenges they face facilitates their capacity to stay in the minds of the audience; *Model Shop* is a particularly apposite example. Whichever way it is interpreted, the *Demy-monde* is one in which instinct, intuition, embodiment and fidelity take precedence, thus furnishing a worldview that may well be welcoming for modern spectators. Although dismissed as nostalgic by some commentators, Demy's films can be seen as demonstrating foresight, as early commentaries on the nefarious effects of modernity and capitalism for affect and community. Many seem relevant decades after their production, when town centres have been irrevocably transformed and new media and technologies have immutably impacted on social relations.

Where modernity may be said to encourage rationality over instinct, individualism over altruism, in Demy's world, cogitation and vanity alienate people from their environment. Moreover, Demy's cinema plays out the tensions between predestiny and freedom of choice. As such they lend themselves well to readings informed by phenomenology. Through his manipulation of time and space, his characters are forced to adopt strategies to cope with their environment, including perceiving the real, material world through a knowing, theatrical and/or fantastical lens. Liberty, like happiness, for Demy, is neither free nor guaranteed, but those who manage to affirm their agency and achieve mastery over their lives avoid the existential *ennui* that hinders their peers. Though melancholy, Demy's cinema offers his audience a temporary respite from the exigencies of their homogenised existences, and alludes to realms in which alterity, rather than assimilation, agency instead of compliance, can be celebrated and encouraged. It is for these reasons, in addition to its potential to entertain and divert, that many of Demy's films have enjoyed longevity within the popular imaginary, and that his significance as a filmmaker for French cinema and audiences is being both cumulatively appreciated and repeatedly recalled by his many admirers. The film-poet's resonance has transcended the decades after his material death, and, it seems, will continue to do so.

References

Barnes, Hazel E., transl. (1993) *Being and Nothingness: an Essay on Phenomenological Ontology by Jean-Paul Sartre*, London and New York, Routledge.
Sartre, Jean-Paul (1943) *L'Être et le néant*, Paris, Gallimard, transl. Hazel E. Barnes, *Being and Nothingness: an Essay on Phenomenological Ontology by Jean-Paul Sartre*, London and New York, Routledge, 1993.

Filmography

Le Sabotier du Val de Loire (1955) 26 mins, b/w

Production company: La Société Nouvelle Pathé-Cinéma and Les
   Films Georges Rouquier
Screenplay: Jacques Demy
Photography: Henri-Georges Lendi
Sound: Francis Rémoué and Jean-Claude Marchetti
Music: Elsa Barraine
Editing: Anne-Marie Cotret
Actors: Yves Demy (le commis à Victorien)

Le Bel Indifférent (1957) 29 mins, col.

Production company: La Société Nouvelle Pathé-Cinéma
Adaptation: Jacques Demy from a play by Jean Cocteau
Photography: Marcel Fradetal
Sound: Jean-Claude Marchetti
Music: Maurice Jarre
Decors: Bernard Evein
Editing: Denise de Casabianca
Actors: Jeanne Allard (C), Angelo Bellini (Emile)

Musée Grévin (1958) 21 mins, col.

Production company: Compagnie Française de Films
Screenplay: Jean Masson
Photography: Marcel Fradetal
Music: Jean Françaix
Editing: Guy Michel-Ange
Framing: Jacques Duhamel

Assistant director: Charles Nughe
Actors: Michel Serrault (visitor), Bernard Thomas (a young Mozart), Ludmilla Tcherina, Jean Cocteau, Jean-Louis Barrault, Louise Bobet (as waxwork models of themselves)

La Mère et l'enfant (1959) 22 mins, b/w

Production company: Compagnie Française de Films
Screenplay and commentary: Jean Masson and Jacques Demy
Photography: Serge Rapoutet
Editing: Guy Michel-Ange

Ars (1959) 18 mins, b/w

Production company: Les Productions du Parvis
Screenplay: Jacques Demy based on texts written by the Pastor of Ars
Photography: Lucien Joulin
Sound: René Louze
Music: Elsa Barraine
Editing: Anne-Marie Cotret
Actors: Bernard Toublanc-Michel (the bad christian)

Lola (1960) 85 mins, b/w

Production company: Carlo Ponti and Georges de Beauregard for Rome-Paris Films
Screenplay: Jacques Demy
Dialogues: Jacques Demy
Photography: Raoul Coutard
Music: Michel Legrand
Decors: Bernard Evein
Editing: Anne-Marie Cotret
Actors: Anouk Aimée (Lola), Marc Michel (Roland Cassard), Jacques Harden (Michel), Alan Scott (Frankie), Elina Labourdette (Madame Desnoyers), Annie Dupéroux (Cécile Desnoyers), Margo Lion (Jeanne), Catherine Lutz (Claire), Corinne Marchand (Daisy)

La Luxure (1961) 14 mins, b/w

Production company: Gibé (Joseph Bercholz), Franco-London-Film (Paris)/Titanus (Rome)
Screenplay: Jacques Demy
Dialogues: Jacques Demy
Photography: Henri Decae

Sound: Antoine Archimbault
Music: Michel Legrand
Decors: Bernard Evein
Editing: Jean Feyte
Actors: Laurent Terzieff (Jacques), Jean-Louis Trintignant (Bernard), Jean Desailly (the father), Micheline Presle (the mother), Corinne Marchand (the passer-by in the street), Bernard Evein and Geneviève Thénier (the lovers in the café)

La Baie des Anges (1962) (*Bay of Angels*) 82 mins, b/w

Production company: Sud-Pacifique Films
Screenplay: Jacques Demy
Dialogues: Jacques Demy
Photography: Jean Rabier
Sound: André Hervée
Music: Michel Legrand
Decors: Bernard Evein
Editing: Anne-Marie Cotret
Actors: Jeanne Moreau (Jacqueline Demaistre), Claude Mann (Jean Fournier), Paul Guers (Caron), Henri Nasset (M. Fournier)

Les Parapluies de Cherbourg (1963) (*The Umbrellas of Cherbourg*) 91 mins, col.

Production company: Parc-Film – Madeleine Film (Paris)/Beta-Film (Munich)
Screenplay: Jacques Demy
Sung dialogues: Jacques Demy
Photography: Jean Rabier
Music: Michel Legrand
Decors: Bernard Evein
Costumes: Jacqueline Moreau
Editing: Anne-Marie Cotret
Actors: Catherine Deneuve (Geneviève Emery), Nino Castelnuovo (Guy Foucher), Anne Vernon (Mme Emery), Marc Michel (Roland Cassard), Ellen Farmer (Madeleine), Mireille Perrey (tante Elise), Harald Wolff (M. Dubourg)
Voices: Danielle Licari (Geneviève), José Bartel (Guy), Christiane Legrand (Mme Emery), Georges Blanès (Roland Cassard), Claudine Meunier (Madeleine), Claire Leclerc (tante Elise)

Les Demoiselles de Rochefort (1966) (*The Young Girls of Rochefort*)
120 mins, col.

Production company: Parc Film – Madeleine Film, Paris
Screenplay: Jacques Demy
Dialogues and lyrics: Jacques Demy
Photography: Ghislain Cloquet
Sound: Jacques Maumont
Music: Michel Legrand
Decors: Bernard Evein
Costumes: Jacqueline Moreau
Editing: Jean Hamon
Choreography: Norman Maen
Actors: Catherine Deneuve (Delphine Garnier), Françoise Dorléac
   (Solange Garnier), Danielle Darrieux (Yvonne Garnier), Michel
   Piccoli (Simon Dame), Jacques Perrin (Maxence), Gene Kelly (Andy
   Miller), Grover Dale (Bill), George Chakiris (Etienne), Jacques
   Riberolles (Guillaume Lancien), Geneviève Thénier (Josette),
   Henri Crémieux (Subtil Dutrouz), Patrick Jeantet (Boubou), René
   Bazart (Pépé)
Voices: Anne Germain (Delphine Garnier), Claude Parent (Solange
   Garnier), Danielle Darrieux (Yvonne Garnier), Georges Blanès
   (Simon Dame), Jacques Revaux (Maxence), Donald Burke (Andy
   Miller), José Bartel (Bill), Romuald (Etienne), Jean Stout (Guillaume
   Lancien), Alice Herald (Josette), Olivier Bonnet (Boubou)

Model Shop (1968) 92 mins, col.

Production company: Columbia Pictures Corporation
Screenplay: Jacques Demy
Dialogues: Jacques Demy with Adrien Joyce and Gerry Ayres
Photography: Michel Hugo
Sound: Les Fresholtz, Arthur Piantadosi
Music: The Spirit
Editing: Walter Thompson
Actors: Anouk Aimée (Lola/Cécile), Gary Lockwood (George Matthews),
   Alexandra Hay (Gloria), Carole Cole (Barbara), Tom Fielding (Jerry)

Peau d'âne (1970) (*Donkey Skin*) 89 mins, col.

Production company: Parc Film – Marianne Productions (Paris)
Screenplay: Jacques Demy based on Charles Perrault's version of the
   ancient tale

Dialogues and lyrics: Jacques Demy
Photography: Ghislain Cloquet
Sound: André Hervée
Music: Michel Legrand
Decors: Jim Leon and assembled by Jacques Dugied
Editing: Anne-Marie Cotret
Actors: Catherine Deneuve (Peau d'âne / the first Queen of the Blue
    Kingdom), Jean Marais (the Blue King), Jacques Perrin (Prince
    Charming), Micheline Presle (the Red Queen), Delphine Seyrig
    (the Lilac Fairy), Fernand Ledoux (the Red King)

The Pied Piper (1971) 90 mins, col.

Production company: Goodtimes Enterprises
Screenplay: Jacques Demy, Andrew Birkin, Mark Peploe
Photography: Peter Suschitzky
Sound: Tony Jackson
Music: Donovan and Kenneth Clayton
Decors: George Djurkovic
Editing: John Trumper
Actors: Donovan (the Pied Piper), Jack Wild (Gavin), Donald Pleasence
    (the baron), John Hurt (Frantz), Michael Hordern (Melius), Roy
    Kinnear (Burgermaster Poppendick), Peter Vaughan (archbishop),
    Cathryn Harrison (Lisa), Keith Buckley (Mattio)

***L'Evénement le plus important depuis que l'homme a marché sur
la lune*** (1973) (*Slightly Pregnant Man*) 94 mins, col.

Production company: Lira Films (Paris)/Roas Produzioni (Rome)
Screenplay: Jacques Demy
Dialogues and lyrics: Jacques Demy
Photography: Andreas Winding
Sound: Louis Hochet
Music: Michel Legrand
Decors: Bernard Evein
Editing: Anne-Marie Cotret
Actors: Catherine Deneuve (Irène de Fontenoy), Marcello Mastroi-
    anni (Marco Mazetti), Micheline Presle (Dr Delavigne), Raymond
    Gérôme (Prof Gérard Chaumont de Latour), Claude Melki (Lucien
    Soumain), Alice Sapritch (Ramona Martinez), André Falcon
    (Scipion Lemeu), Madeleine Barbulée (Mlle Janvier), Micheline
    Dax (Mme Corfa), Benjamin Legrand (Lucas)

Lady Oscar (1978) 124 mins, col.

Production company: Kitty Music Corporation with Shiseido Co Ltd. Nippon Television Network Corporation and Toho Co Ltd.
Screenplay: Patricia Louisiana Knop adapted from Riyoko Ikeda's novel *Rose of Versailles*
Photography: Jean Penzer
Sound: Anthony Jackson
Music: Michel Legrand
Decors: Bernard Evein
Editing: Paul Davies
Actors: Catriona MacColl (Oscar-François de Jarjayes), Barry Stokes (André Grandier), Christine Böhm (Marie Antoinette), Jonas Bergström (Hans Axel von Fersen), Terence Budd (Louis XVI), Constance Chapman (nanny), Rosemary Dunham (marquise de Boulainvilliers), Gregory Floy (Cardinal de Rohan), Anouska Hempel (Jeanne de La Motte), Mark Kingston (Général de Jarjayes), Sue Lloyd (comtesse Gabrielle de Polignac), Shelagh McLeod (Rosalie), Martin Potter (comte de Girodet), Mike Marshall (Nicolas de La Motte)

La Naissance du jour (1980) (*Break of Day*) 90 mins, col.

Production company: France 3 and Technisonor
Screenplay: Jacques Demy based on Colette's novel (1928)
Photography: Jean Penzer
Sound: Auguste Galli
Decors: Hubert Monloup
Editing: Anne-Marie Cotret
Actors: Danièle Delorme (Colette), Dominique Sanda (Hélène Clément), Jean Sorel (Vial), Orane Demazis (Sido)

Une chambre en ville (1982) (*A Room in Town*) 92 mins, col.

Production company: Progéfi – TF1 Films Productions – UGC
Screenplay: Jacques Demy
Lyrics: Jacques Demy
Photography: Jean Penzer
Sound: André Hervée
Music: Michel Colombier
Decors: Bernard Evein
Editing: Sabine Mamou

Actors: Dominique Sanda (Edith Leroyer), Richard Berry (François Guilbaud), Danille Darrieux (Margot Langlois), Michel Piccoli (Edmond Leroyer), Fabienne Guyon (Violette Pelletier), Jean-François Stévenin (Dambiel)

Voices: Danielle Darrieux (Margot Langlois), Fabienne Guyon (Violette), Florence Davis (Edith), Jacques Revaux (François), Aldo Franck (Dambiel), Georges Blaness (Edmond)

Parking (1985) 95 mins, col.

Production company: Dominique Vignet for Garance/France 3 Productions
Screenplay: Jacques Demy
Dialogues and lyrics: Jacques Demy
Photography: Jean-François Robin
Sound: Bernard Ortion
Music: Michel Legrand
Decors: Patrice Mercier
Costumes: Rosalie Varda
Editing: Sabine Mamou
Actors: Francis Huster (Orphée), Laurent Malet (Calaïs), Keïko Itô (Eurydice), Gérard Klein (Aristée), Marie-France Pisier (Claude Perséphone), Jean Marais (Hadès), Eva Darlan (Dominique Daniel), Caron (Hugues Quester)

Trois places pour le 26 (1988) (*Three Seats for the 26th*) 106 mins, col.

Production company: Claude Berri for Renn Productions
Screenplay: Jacques Demy
Dialogues and lyrics: Jacques Demy
Photography: Jean Penzer
Sound: André Hervée
Music: Michel Legrand
Decors: Bernard Evein
Editing: Sabine Mamou
Actors: Yves Montand (himself), Mathilda May (Marion), Françoise Fabian (Mylène de Lambert), Patrick Fierry (Toni Fontaine), Catriona MacColl (Betty Miller), Paul Guers (Max Lheeman)

Select bibliography

Books

Anon. (eds) (2013) *Le Monde enchanté de Jacques Demy*, Paris, Skira Flammarion, La Cinémathèque Française and Ciné-Tamaris. A beautifully illustrated hardback published to accompany the exhibition at the *Cinémathèque* in the summer of 2013. The book is structured into chapters that reflect the six sections of the exhbition. It contains many illuminating articles and interviews that shed light on such aspects as Demy's collaborations with Jean Cocteau and Agostino Pace and his time in the USA.

Baron, Jérôme (ed.) (2011) *Jacques Demy, 303: arts, recherches, créations* (115). Insightful special issue devoted to Demy of the Nantes-based arts review, which includes articles on a range of issues, such as the city locations that were significant in the director's life and a study of his short films, as well as reviews of *Les Parapluies de Cherbourg* and *Les Demoiselles de Rochefort*.

Berthomé, Jean-Pierre (1996) *Jacques Demy et les racines du rêve*, 2nd edition, Nantes, L'Atalante. An essential text devoted to Demy and his cinema in the French language. Each film is analysed separately and each discussion includes a review of the contexts surrounding the film's production, release and reception. The author benefitted from having direct access to Demy, and the detail of knowledge displayed is extremely impressive.

Casas, Quim and Iriarte, Ana Cristina (eds) (2011) *Jacques Demy*, Donostia-San Sebastián, Festival de San Sebastián S.A./Filmoteca Española/ICAA/Ministerio de Cultura, and Ciné-Tamaris. An illustrated collection of essays exploring various aspects of Demy's work and life, including the links between his films and American cinema and his use of animation, sets and stars. Written in Castillian Spanish with English translations.

Jullier, Laurent (2007) *Abécédaire des* Parapluies de Cherbourg, Paris, Broché. Very useful, detailed and original study of *Les Parapluies de Cherbourg*, structured alphabetically according to key features and associations.

Lefèvre, Raphaël (2013) *Une chambre en ville*, Crisnée, Belgium, Editions Yellow Now. Particularly insightful, precise and comprehensive study of *Une chambre en ville*. This book includes illuminating analyses of the musical score, the setting of the words to instrumental arrangements and the comparison between the film and musicals more broadly.

Père, Olivier and Colmant, Marie (2010) *Jacques Demy*, Paris, Éditions de la Martinière. A beautifully illustrated volume. Each film is treated separately in chronological order and each section includes a short plot synopsis and analysis. A brief spotlight is shone on specific aspects of Demy's cinema, including his use of fairytales and representations of class struggle and gender.

Taboulay, Camille (1996) *Le Cinéma enchanté de Jacques Demy*, Paris, *Cahiers du Cinéma*. Detailed and poetic examination of Demy's cinema and his life by a seasoned and knowledgeable fan who has become a film critic and commentator. Sharp analyses are organised originally according to different interests of the director. The illustrations include rare items such as sketches of costumes and decors, drafts of scripts and music score sheets for songs.

Articles

Clech, Thierry, Strauss, Frédéric and Toubiana, Serge (1988) 'D'un port à l'autre: Entretien avec Jacques Demy', *Cahiers du Cinéma*, 414, December: 10–11, 57–62.

Colomb, Philippe (1998) 'L'Étrange Demy-monde', in Marie-Hélène Bourcier (ed.) *Q comme Queer*, Paris: Cahiers Gay, Kitsch, Camp: 39–47.

Daney, Serge, Narboni, Jean and Toubiana, Serge (1982) 'Le Retour au pays des rêves: Entretien avec Jacques Demy', *Cahiers du Cinéma*, 341: 6–13, 56–66.

Herzog, Amy (2010) 'En Chanté: Music, Memory and Perversity in the Films of Jacques Demy', in *Dreams of Difference, Songs of the Same*, Minneapolis and London, University of Minnesota Press: 115–53.

Hill, Rodney (2008) (2008) 'Demy-Monde: the New Wave Films of Jacques Demy', *Quarterly Review of Film and Video*, 25 (5): 382–94.

—— 'The New Wave Meets the Tradition of Quality: Jacques Demy's *The Umbrella's of Cherbourg*', *Cinema Journal*, 48 (1): 27–50.

Lazen, Matthew (2004) '"En perme à Nantes": Jacques Demy and New Wave Place', *Studies in French Cinema*, 4 (3): 187–96.

Marshall, Bill and Lindeperg, Sylvie (2000) 'Time, History and Memory in *Les Parapluies de Cherbourg*', in Bill Marshall and Robynn Stilwell (eds) *Musicals: Hollywood and Beyond*, Chicago, University of Chicago Press: 98–106.

Rabourdin, Dominique (2010) 'Rosalie Varda: "Il avait choisi de m'aimer"', *Place Publique*, 33: 68–71.

—— (2010) 'Mathieu Demy: "La petite musique de mon père"', *Place Publique*, 33: 72–5.

—— (2010) 'Entretien avec Agnès Varda: *Jacquot de Nantes* ou l'intelligence du coeur', *Place Publique*, 33: 59–65.

Roud, Richard (1964) 'Rondo Galant: the World of Jacques Demy', *Sight and Sound*, Summer: 136–9.

Index

EU authorised representative for GPSR:
Easy Access System Europe, Mustamäe tee 50,
10621 Tallinn, Estonia
gpsr.requests@easproject.com

www.ingramcontent.com/pod-product-compliance
Ingram Content Group UK Ltd.
Pitfield, Milton Keynes, MK11 3LW, UK
UKHW021908060726
6981IPUK00003B/31